Tourism Development

ASPECTS OF TOURISM
Series Editors: Professor Chris Cooper, *University of Queensland, Australia*
Dr C. Michael Hall, *University of Otago, Dunedin, New Zealand*
Dr Dallen Timothy, *Arizona State University, Tempe, USA*

Aspects of Tourism is an innovative, multifaceted series which will comprise authoritative reference handbooks on global tourism regions, research volumes, texts and monographs. It is designed to provide readers with the latest thinking on tourism world-wide and in so doing will push back the frontiers of tourism knowledge. The series will also introduce a new generation of international tourism authors, writing on leading edge topics. The volumes will be readable and user- friendly, providing accessible sources for further research. The list will be underpinned by an annual authoritative tourism research volume. Books in the series will be commissioned that probe the relationship between tourism and cognate subject areas such as strategy, development, retailing, sport and environmental studies. The publisher and series editors welcome proposals from writers with projects on these topics.

Other Books in the Series
Tourism Employment: Analysis and Planning
  Michael Riley, Adele Ladkin and Edith Szivas
Marine Ecotourism: Issues and Experiences
  Brian Garrod and Julie C. Wilson (eds)
Classic Reviews in Tourism
  Chris Cooper (ed.)
Progressing Tourism Research
  Bill Faulkner, edited by Liz Fredline, Leo Jago and Chris Cooper
Managing Educational Tourism
  Brent W. Ritchie
Recreational Tourism: Demand and Impacts
  Chris Ryan
Coastal Mass Tourism: Diversification and Sustainable Development in Southern Europe
  Bill Bramwell (ed.)
Sport Tourism Development
  Thomas Hinch and James Higham
Sport Tourism: Interrelationships, Impact and Issues
  Brent Ritchie and Daryl Adair (eds)
Tourism, Mobility and Second Homes
  C. Michael Hall and Dieter Müller
Strategic Management for Tourism Communities: Bridging the Gaps
  Peter E. Murphy and Ann E. Murphy
Oceania: A Tourism Handbook
  Chris Cooper and C. Michael Hall (eds)
Tourism Marketing: A Collaborative Approach
  Alan Fyall and Brian Garrod
Music and Tourism: On the Road Again
  Chris Gibson and John Connell

For more details of these or any other of our publications, please contact:
Channel View Publications, Frankfurt Lodge, Clevedon Hall,
Victoria Road, Clevedon, BS21 7HH, England
http://www.channelviewpublications.com

ASPECTS OF TOURISM 20
Series Editors: Chris Cooper (*University of Queensland, Australia*),
C. Michael Hall (*University of Otago, New Zealand*)
and Dallen Timothy (*Arizona State University, USA*)

Tourism Development
Issues for a Vulnerable Industry

Edited by
Julio Aramberri and Richard Butler

CHANNEL VIEW PUBLICATIONS
Clevedon • Buffalo • Toronto

Library of Congress Cataloging in Publication Data
Tourism Development: Issues for a Vulnerable Industry/Edited by Julio Aramberri and Richard Butler.
Aspects of Tourism: 20
Includes bibliographical references and index.
1. Tourism. 2. Tourism–Research. I. Aramberri, Julio. II. Butler, Richard. III. Series.
G155.A1T59135 2004
338.4'791–dc22   2004014457

British Library Cataloguing in Publication Data
A catalogue entry for this book is available from the British Library.

ISBN 1-873150-96-2 (hbk)

Channel View Publications
An imprint of Multilingual Matters Ltd

UK: Frankfurt Lodge, Clevedon Hall, Victoria Road, Clevedon BS21 7HH.
USA: 2250 Military Road, Tonawanda, NY 14150, USA.
Canada: 5201 Dufferin Street, North York, Ontario, Canada M3H 5T8.

Typeset by Florence Production Ltd.
Printed and bound in Great Britain by the Cromwell Press.

Contents

Contributors

David Airey is Professor of Tourism Management at the School of Management Studies for the Service Sector, University of Surrey, Guildford, UK.

Julio Aramberri is Professor of Tourism at Drexel University, Philadelphia, US.

Richard Butler is Professor of Tourism at the School of Management Studies for the Service Sector, University of Surrey, Guildford, UK.

Nevenka Čavlek is Associate Professor at the Graduate School of Economics and Business, University of Zagreb, Croatia.

Geoffrey I. Crouch, Ph.D., is Professor and Chair of Marketing at La Trobe University, Bundoora, Melbourne, Australia.

Graham M.S. Dann is Professor at the International Tourism Research Centre, University of Luton, UK.

William C. Gartner was President of the International Academy for the Study of Tourism (1999–2003) and is Professor of Applied Economics at the University of Minnesota, US.

Anton Gosar is Professor at the University of Lubljiana, Eslovenia.

Myriam Jansen-Verbeke is Professor at the Catholic University, Leuven, Belgium.

Kelly J. MacKay is Associate Professor at the University of Manitoba, Canada.

Peter Murphy, PhD., is Foundation Professor and Head of the School of Tourism and Hospitality at La Trobe University, Bundoora, Melbourne, Australia.

Roslyn Russell, Ph.D., is Senior Research Fellow at the Research Development Unit, RMIT Business, Melbourne, Australia.

Stephen L.J. Smith is Professor in the Department of Recreation and Leisure Studies, University of Waterloo, Ontario, Canada.

Valene S. Smith is Research Professor at the California State University, Chico, California, US.

Stephen Wanhill is Professor of Tourism at the School of Service Industries, Bournemouth University, UK, and Head of Tourism Research at the Centre for Regional and Tourism Research, Bornholm, Denmark.

Abbreviations

ATSA	Aviation and Transportation Security Act
ATSSSA	Air Transportation Safety and System Stabilization Act
BTA	British Tourist Authority
CCRA	Canada Customs and Revenue Agency
CSQ	commitment to the status quo
DEFRA	Department for Environment, Food and Rural Affairs
EAP	East Asia and the Pacific
ETC	English Tourism Council
EU	European Union
FMD	foot-and-mouth disease
GDP	gross domestic product
GNP	gross national product
GPS	Global Positioning System
ISS	International Space Station
MAFF	Ministry of Agriculture, Fisheries and Food
MDS	multidimensional scaling
NASA	National Aeronautics and Space Administration
NHS	National Historic Site (Canada)
NMGW	National Museums and Galleries of Wales
OE	Other Exports
OI	Other Imports
PFI	Private Finance Initiative
PPP	purchasing power parity
RMNP	Riding Mountain National Park (Canada)
SARS	Severe Acute Respiratory Syndrome
SIC	Standard Industrial Classification
SMEs	small and medium-sized enterprises
STA	Space Transportation Association
T&T	Travel and Tourism

T&TE	Travel and Tourism Economy
TE	Total Exports
TI	Total Imports
TIA	Travel Industry of America
TIS	Tourism Information System
TSA	Tourism Satellite Accounts
UN	United Nations
VE	Visitor Exports
VEP	visitor-employed photography
VI	Visitor Imports
WTO	World Tourism Organization
WTTC	World Travel and Tourism Council

Part 1: General Introduction

Chapter 1

A Synthesis of Tourism Trends

WILLIAM C. GARTNER

Introduction

The collection of chapters in this book is varied both in subject matter and in length. Yet within this seemingly disparate compilation certain trends can be identified. Each one of the chapters contains information regarding one or more tourism trends that have been in place for years. It is my job to try and relate what is contained in each chapter to a specific trend affecting how we travel and what we do while away from home. However, before diving deep into that task it is important to discuss what a tourism trend is and what is not.

Trends are not predictions but rather traceable changes in how people react, how businesses operate or how systems evolve in response to some long-term influence. For example, population growth is a mega-trend with a sixfold increase recorded in the number of people on earth from 1900 to 2000 (1 billion to 6 billion). This mega-trend, together with other changes usually spawned by it, is responsible for how we live, work and play today. For example, urbanization is a result of increased population growth, industrialized societies and declining rural-based economic opportunities. Today there are at least 14 cities with over 10 million inhabitants, whereas in 1900 there were none (Brown & Flavin, 1999). On the other hand worldwide terrorism is not yet a trend but an exogenous influence that can seriously disrupt traditional travel patterns. Whether the new travel patterns that emerged in the wake of September 11, 2001, which were later reinforced by additional terrorist attacks such as occurred in Bali, are trends or short-term changes is not yet known. Images of a place may change due to a worldwide event (Gartner & Shen, 1992) but they just as readily return to pre-event levels in the absence of reinforcing information that supports the image change (Gartner, 1993). Terrorist attacks have resulted in reduced air travel

3

globally but analysis shows that, in the developed world, short-haul air travel seems to be down more than long-haul, with increased use of the private motor vehicle or other forms of public transport (e.g. train). Attacks have also led to a search for safe havens, such as Vietnam for Southeast Asia or maybe Finland for Europe (Figure 1.1).

In this book you will encounter a chapter (11) by Geoffrey I. Crouch on space tourism. The adventure spirit, manifest by the search for the exotic, has been noted in works by Van Den Berghe (1994), Plog (1974), and Monteiro and Rowenczyk (1992, from Teigland, 2000). "Space, the final frontier", a phrase coined by Gene Roddenberry, the creator of the television series *Star Trek*, exemplifies what tourism means to the human spirit. A $20 million price tag for the trip taken by Dennis Tito into space ushered in a new age of adventure travel. Yet, as Crouch points out throughout his chapter, "terrestrial" space tourism has been around for almost as long as we have been putting people into space. Seeking adventure through travel is not new, nor is it a trend, but it is now possible to be more "adventurous" as new technology allows people to fulfill long held wishes. Even in the wake of the destruction of the space shuttle Columbia and all its astronauts, seeking excitement from travel where few have gone before remains a strong motivator governing human decisions about what to do. The trend that empowers these "new-age adventure seekers" has more to do with technological advances in science rather than some fundamental change in human behavior.

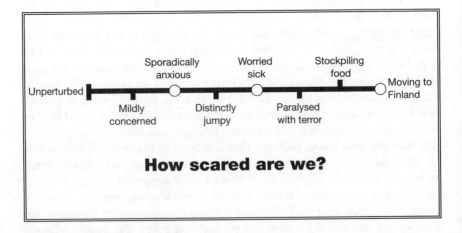

Figure 1.1 The fear gradient

What is affecting how we behave and travel? This is a large question with a multitude of answers. Some of those answers are found in the chapters in this book. As you read through it, links to the trends examined below should become apparent.

There are five trends that will be examined in this chapter and that also appear in at least one other chapter in this book. The trends discussed are: consolidation, consumption center development, devolution, public involvement, and research coming of age.

Trends

Consolidation

The trend of consolidation for tourism dependent businesses is something that has been around for a long time. It is not unique to tourism and it is not widespread for tourism-dependent businesses over all parts of the globe. However, owing to the structural nature of the tourism distribution system, the trend does pose certain challenges for managing a destination-based tourism business.

A tourism distribution system has many parts. Dann (1977) argues that people move out of their home environment because of either a push or pull influence. A push influence can be something as simple as the realization of the need to temporarily remove oneself from the home environment. A pull influence works against the forces that keep one rooted in the home environment. Special air fares, a new attraction, or an invitation to visit with someone are all pull forces trying to draw someone away from home. Often pull and push forces have an information component that in tourism is akin to image development. Images of "the other" work to reinforce felt needs to leave home and begin a tourist journey. How images are formed and the influence and market reach those images command have been discussed by Gartner (1993, 1996). Regardless of whether the influence is a push or pull factor, a decision to leave home puts someone into the tourism distribution channel. Even the information flow to a potential tourist works to support some forms of distribution over others. For example, a tour operator obviously has a vested interest in becoming the business that takes care of your travel needs. Cohen (1972) describes a tour operator as being part of the institutionalized part of the distribution channel. Those businesses that facilitate travel are all engaged in activities to become the preferred provider of some or all of an individual's tourist needs.

The physical act of travel is necessary for someone to become a tourist, but whether a distance requirement is necessary for someone to actually enter into touristhood has been addressed by Jafari (1987). Regardless of when someone actually "becomes" a tourist in a spatial or cultural sense is irrelevant to how the distribution channel functions. How people choose to travel is relevant. At some point an individual will make a decision about how to travel. Using a plane, taking a train, or driving a motor vehicle are all popular ways to travel. Which travel option one chooses will determine how much the travel will be affected by the trend of consolidation. Nevenka Čavlek (Chapter 8) points out that, within Europe, a wave of consolidation has swept through the ranks of tour operators. This consolidation has been made easier by the formation of the European Union (EU), which created a free trade zone rivalling that which has existed for centuries in the United States. Prior to the formation of the EU tour operators were subject to the laws of their own nation, which included prohibitions against purchasing firms operating in other countries.

According to Čavlek the business of tour operators was created and developed in Europe (i.e. Thomas Cook). Since many European countries are relatively small and a common language is not spoken, tour operators were able to overcome language and cultural barriers through the packaging of tour products and services. Čavlek cites the World Tourism Organization claim that as much as 25% of all international tourism travel is accounted for by tour operators, with 50% of that total shared by European tour operators. Recently, as the EU has grown and developed, there has been a wave of consolidation taking place within the ranks of European tour operators. Čavlek claims that as few as four major tour operators today control over 70% of all European package holiday travel. How will this form of consolidation affect the tourism distribution channel?

Stephen Smith (Chapter 7) presents a thorough analysis of the size of tourism businesses vis-à-vis other industrial sectors using Canada as an example. His analysis convincingly shows that the supply side of tourism is indeed dominated by small and medium-sized enterprises (SMEs) as others have argued, but that surprisingly when compared to other industrial sectors there is no discernible pattern. In other words almost all industrial sectors are dominated by SMEs. Tourism-dependent businesses are no more likely to be heavily concentrated in SMEs than in non-tourism sectors. In fact for the smallest-sized businesses Smith found that non-tourism sectors have a higher percentage of this type of establishment than is associated with tourism sectors. Although

Smith's analysis is specific to Canada, there are strong similarities throughout the developed world to the economic system operating in Canada. Smith's analysis also shows that the concentration of SMEs is not the same across the industrial sectors that comprise tourism. Transportation firms have a higher level of small enterprises than any other tourism sector. Smith attributes this finding to the high number of small taxi companies operating in Canada. However, when air and rail transport firms are compared to other businesses in the transportation sector, it is clear a few large firms dominate. Within the travel trade sector tour operators were over-represented in the $1million+ revenue categories. Smith also reveals that the provinces of Canada with the least economic development (i.e. poorest provinces) will have a higher percentage of micro-level (< 5 employees) firms.

Returning to the trend of consolidation and implications for tourism we again look at the distribution channel. Assuming, as Smith has shown, that SMEs dominate at the destination (e.g. restaurants, hotels, attractions) but larger firms are becoming the norm during the travel to and from destination stage, then significant implications are noted. Tighter control over the movement of people into a destination puts enormous market control into those firms that control the flow. Čavlek discusses this outcome with respect to destinations in Europe that find they are no longer in control over the sale of their products. This same situation was recorded by this author while on a consulting assignment in Puno, Peru. Figure 1.2 shows the distribution channel for international tourists to Puno. There are at least four firms controlling parts of the distribution channel with the most powerful being located in Lima. People do find ways around dealing with some of the firms in the distribution channel by using informal networks, but this brings with it risks that many tourists are unwilling to accept. Even though web-based technology allows even the smallest firm to reach out independently to the market (Buhalis, 2000) the reality is that there is too much dependency on those who currently control the flow of visitors to a destination to reject them and rely on a web-based system. There is some evidence to suggest that consumers do not want to peruse numerous home pages to find the destination products they want but rather would prefer a central clearing house to perform this service (Gartner et al., 2002).

Stephen Wanhill (Chapter 5) discusses the ownership of attractions and the implications of different forms of ownership. Although this chapter may not seem directly related to the consolidation trend, it does reveal what effect consolidation may have on attraction ownership. For example, Wanhill argues that public ownership of attractions does not

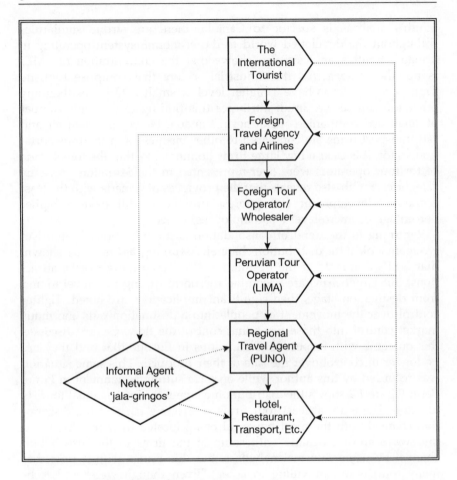

Figure 1.2 Distribution channel for Puno, Peru

leave much opportunity for development since they essentially have no assets that can be used to leverage development funds. Public owner-ship means the product cannot be easily changed or the physical structure altered in such a way that the significance of the public attraction changes. Revenues for development must be obtained from gifts, grants, or by petition to the government. Because of the reliance on non-market revenue streams, public attractions may actually be better off than their private sector counterparts from the effects of consolidation. Private attractions, on the other hand, must continually change their product offering to maintain market share. This is especially true for businesses such as theme parks, which base forecasted attendance on 80–85% of the year in which the theme park is launched. Helping to maintain that market share is a continual revamping of offerings, including the introduction of a new product every few years. The highly competitive environment private attractions find themselves in plus the need for a reliable stream of cash flow to maintain and upgrade puts private sector attractions at the mercy of firms that control the distribution channel. If some firms heavily control the distribution channel then it is highly unlikely that private sector firms at the destination will be able to do much about downward pressure on revenues exerted by the controlling firms.

Wanhill also discusses the classification of goods and services with respect to whether they are considered publicly or privately owned attractions. He argues that there is no clear-cut delineation between the two sectors for most of the attractions and it is up to the public to decide through the political process. Expect to see more of this debate in the coming years, especially if consolidation trends put revenue-generation pressure on these mixed types of attractions. If history is any indicator more of the quasi-private sector attractions and some privately owned attractions will eventually become much more state-owned, managed, and controlled should the distribution channel squeeze expected from consolidation pressures reduce the revenue-generating power of these attractions.

The eventual outcome of the consolidation trend for tourism, especially when so many different industrial sectors are involved and the degree of firm size is unevenly distributed between them, is more power being vested in fewer firms. Many researchers, including this author, have argued through the years about the importance of image development for destinations. It must be recognized that image formation takes place throughout the distribution channel and destinations may not be in control over the messages sent to the market. Gartner (1993) terms the type of image formation practiced by tour operators and wholesalers "Overt Induced II", meaning that the normal channels for image formation through commercial media are being used but with limited input provided by the destinations whose image(s) are being promoted. The opportunity to achieve sustainable destination image development when control over images projected and the flow of visitors is being increasingly concentrated in fewer companies is questionable at best.

Consumption center development

The second trend to be examined in this chapter is consumption center development. Its relationship to the consolidation trend is direct. The more a place develops as a consumption center for mass tourism the better it becomes at controlling the images projected of the destination and the more market power it acquires, allowing the destination to overcome some of the distribution channel consolidation trends noted above. Gartner and Lime (2000) discuss in some detail the formation of modern-day consumption centers and the rejuvenation of older industrial cities into new-look consumption centers for tourism purposes. Myriam Jansen-Verbeke (Chapter 12) takes this discussion further by noting that cities all over the world are now engaged in developing their cultural resources into tourist attractions. Richards (2000) argues that claims of a "new wave" of culture seeking tourists may be due more to definitional expansion of what constitutes a cultural attraction than to a new-found interest in culture. Richards also argues that an expanded definition for cultural attractions has led to an oversupply of this commodity. Jansen-Verbeke claims that to successfully make the transition into a viable cultural urban environment for tourism will require significant changes in governmental organization and planning. This is especially true when tourism development issues are being integrated into government development policies rather than being treated as an afterthought or, in the case of the world's premier consumption centers (e.g. Las Vegas, Nevada, or Orlando, Florida), as the main means for development.

Jansen-Verbeke in her chapter discusses some of the issues concerning urban development when cultural tourism events become part of the urban attraction package. Will success be measured as it usually is (i.e. revenues, additional bed nights) or is there a better way to examine "success". What appears to concern Jansen-Verbeke is the propensity of cultural events to induce "mutations" into city life and hasten the process of "tourismification". This process may be evident by the construction of new conference centers, hotels, museums, and other tourist products that had as their impetus short-term events which were deemed economically successful. Whether they are socio-culturally acceptable is usually never an issue.

Consumption center development is being increasingly viewed as a way to overcome some of the barriers imposed by distribution channels. The more tourist traffic a consumption center can generate, the more competition there is between businesses engaged in moving tourists into the destination and the less control a single transport company can exert. Large consumption centers are also able to control the formation of most tourist images. Sustainable development with respect to socio-cultural issues is for the most part not a concern. Consumption centers are, after all, for the purpose of tourist consumption and the people that eventually come to live there are enticed by the economic opportunities. One can examine the development of Cancun, Mexico, and see that, before tourism, there were very few people living in the area primarily because the shallow limestone soil was not suitable for agriculture. Similarly, Las Vegas, a desert community, was developed as a gaming center and redeveloped as a tourist center, with gaming at is core, in the 1900s. Orlando, Florida, was not much more than orange and grapefruit groves when Disney Corporation began its land purchases and eventually built one of the largest consumption centers in the world anchored by Disneyland.

The situation is different, as pointed out by Jansen-Verbeke, when tourism is not the main reason for city development but the influence of tourism begins to transform the city. In this situation a whole host of sustainable development issues result and new paradigms are needed to deal with the trend to consumption center development. The consumption center trend is not temporary. There are too many economic efficiencies associated with consumption center development for it to be a passing trend. What that means, as argued by Jansen-Verbeke, is new ways of dealing with the problems associated with this trend when it takes place in a destination not originally conceived as a tourist consumption center.

Devolution

Diamond (1999), in his Pulitzer winning book *Guns, Germs and Steel*, describes how the fate of human societies is due more to geography than innate intelligence on the part of any one group of people in the world. The transfer of knowledge and the resulting development that comes from the synergy of knowledge combining with knowledge argues for open societies and the sharing of information. During the 20th century many nation states were formed out of large tracts of land controlled by families or tribes. Many of the new nation states formed during this period, especially in Africa, have fared poorly in spite of abundant natural wealth. Teigland (2000) argues that democratization and market system ideology are the primary reasons for tourism growth. Teigland's conclusions are warranted if only developed nations are examined. Yet, as Anton Gosar (Chapter 9) points out, it was during the period of Tito that the Istrian coast (Istria is a peninsula in old Yugoslavia that is now shared by Croatia and Slovenia) achieved its highest level of visitors and tourism development.

The trend during the early 20th century may be termed the evolution of nation states. However, during the last part of the 20th century and continuing into the 21st century the trend is one of devolution into smaller nation states. The disintegration of the Soviet Union resulted in the formation of many new nations, although some, such as Poland or Romania, were not new at all, but were instead occupied by the Soviets. A better term might be "newly freed states". In the wake of the Soviet implosion, the United States reigns as the only superpower trying with military coercion, personal persuasion and economic incentives to spread its concepts of democracy and market systems.

One might argue that we are not discussing devolution at all but instead just another step on the evolutionary path of nation-building. Surely many people such as those who lived under Soviet rule in East Germany are better off now, in at least a human rights sense, after reunification with Germany. In a similar way, the Stalinist regimes in Albania and Romania are gone, leaving the people who suffered under the oppressive cloak of tyranny to forge their own path in life. Yet, if we accept a dictionary definition of devolution as passing down authority from a central government to a local one, then devolution is the right term to describe a trend that appeared in the late 20th century.

How then does this trend of devolution impact tourism? Two chapters in this book (13 and 9) have different perspectives to share on the subject. Valene Smith (Chapter 13) discusses the seeds and history of decisions taken to "evolve" the Middle East into nation states upon the disintegration of the Ottoman empire after World War I and the resulting control of those lands by European powers. The seeds of conflict leading to modern-day terrorism attacks can be traced to European and American policies that sponsored nation states without the democratic institutions and market ideology present to lead to peaceful, locally based solutions to problems. This devolution of authority to families and thugs to run strategically important nations is part of the terrorism problem faced today.

Smith argues that the new war, which is covert and devoid of heroics, leaves few tourist markers. The exception of course would be memorials erected to those who lost their lives in major terrorist attacks such as at the World Trade Center. Old wars left many tourist markers for consumption by later generations, such as the battlefields of the US Civil War, the graveyards in France, or the concentration camps in Germany.

This new war will be largely fought without the heroics and constant media attention that overt wars receive today. Smith also details some of the costs of the war on terrorism. It is safe to say that, at the time of writing, the costs in lost tourism revenue are significant. While it might be convenient to blame lost tourism revenues on terrorism alone, significant signs of economic weakness were in place before September 11, 2001. Terrorism only exacerbated a worsening condition and with conflict around the globe increasing it stands to prolong an already severe recession. When security and safety concerns are alleviated enough for visitor numbers to increase, the cost of the war on terror may be known by a reduction in competitive airline operations thereby reinforcing the consolidation trend noted above.

Anton Gosar (Chapter 9) examines devolution's impact by comparing tourism to Croatia and Slovenia along the Istrian coast after these newly formed nations fought and gained independence from what used to be known as Yugoslavia. Structural change in both countries was substantial as they began to transform their centrally planned economy to a market-based one. The interdependence that once existed between elements of the tourism sectors disintegrated once the two nations established international borders and laws governing how businesses located in each nation are allowed to operate. Border complexities have made it much more difficult for tourists to easily and without delay move up and down the Istrian coast. Owing to all of the above changes, Gosar claims that tourist arrival numbers recorded in the 1980s to the Istrian coast have not yet been equaled. Forming a country, changing its market ideology, and restructuring tourism sectors are monumental tasks that, as Gosar illustrates, can have serious and long-lasting implications for tourism development.

Public involvement

Teigland's (2000) mega-trend of democratization discussed above has an ancillary trend and that is increased public involvement. Public involvement is a democratic process and as more countries embrace the concept of market-based systems the call for more involvement in all issues that affect one's life increases. Tourism development issues do not escape this trend. For example, in 2001 a lawsuit was filed against the state of Hawaii by some of its citizens belonging to an environmental organization. Their contention was that the amount of money authorized for tourism marketing (approximately $10 million per annum) reflected a decision by state government to expand tourism on the islands.

Hawaii, like many other US states, requires the government to complete an environmental impact statement before development funds can be spent. Those bringing suit argued that state expenditures on tourism marketing were in fact development dollars as more tourists will put greater strain on the islands' delicate ecological balance. It should be noted that Hawaii's environment has been seriously degraded over the years, in part by the movement of people and the things they bring with them to the islands. Therefore, the litigants claim additional inflows of visitors have the potential to further damage an already compromised ecosystem. At the time of writing there has been no decision regarding this lawsuit.

McCool and Patterson (2000) describe the history of public involvement for natural resource management issues in the United States. They argue that the "tame" problems of yesterday have turned into "wicked and messy" problems today. A large part of that change can be attributed to fewer people believing in the infallibility of natural resource managers. That belief has led to the formation of interest groups that possess greater information about environmental change from development activities and a stronger base of funding support from membership and other partners.

Propst *et al.* (2000) argue that there is a growing schism between rural-based residents of the United States and those living in urban areas. As urbanization continues to increase (a consequence of the mega-trend, population growth) friction between the two groups over how natural resources are to be managed will surely increase. This supports McCool and Patterson's argument that the problems of tomorrow will be more "wicked and messy" and hence more difficult to manage. New methods and paradigms will be needed for tomorrow's professionals to deal with the problems that are being created today.

Jafari (1988) has studied the evolution of tourism research using journal articles as his source. He concluded that, when the first spate of academic treatments of tourism were published, the authors were overwhelmingly supportive of tourism development as a means to increase economic benefits without all the negatives (e.g. pollution) associated with other forms of industrial development. Jafari termed this early work the "Advocacy Platform". Support for tourism as a "clean" form of development faded during the 1980s as some of the negative influences of the phenomenon became better understood. Almost all the positive benefits from tourism development noted in the Advocacy Platform were countered by examples of negative externalities discussed by what Jafari termed members of the "Cautionary Platform". Jafari went on to conclude that we are now in the "Knowledge-based Platform" as current research searches more for fundamental knowledge that can be used to develop theories that ostensibly can be utilized to deal with some of the problems identified with tourism development.

Roslyn Russell and Peter Murphy (Chapter 4) acknowledge the work of Jafari and suggest that we should be entering into a period of how to cope with uncertainty. Leadership qualities such as adaptability, risk-taking, and creativity will be needed by those making tomorrow's decisions. They argue that educational systems need to accept this era of uncertainty and include ways to cope with it through their curriculum. In a similar manner continuing education programs for leaders should emphasize entrepreneurial training. Given what some of the authors cited above argue regarding problems leaders are now facing or will have to deal with in the future, regardless of whether they are in natural resource management or tourism development, Russell and Murphy are on the right track. Decisions over how resources are to be used are surely to be met with more opposition than ever before. The training of yesterday is inadequate to deal with the new management challenges of today. If Teigland's characterization of the "wave of democratization" continues to take hold one of the certain outcomes is less certainty in dealing with issues that affect how public goods are managed.

Research coming of age

Knowledge builds on knowledge, so one may argue that research coming of age is not a trend but a foregone conclusion. However, tourism is a relatively new field of study and, as was pointed out in the previous section, early tourism research (i.e. in the 1970s and 1980s) appeared to be self-serving. First, there was the group of researchers supporting tourism development as a beneficial form (i.e. Advocacy Platform) of development. This was quickly followed by a decade-long review of tourism's not so beneficial impacts. The next era of research looked at alternative ways to develop tourism (e.g. eco-tourism) with the last era focused on developing theories to guide research and ultimately tourism development decisions (Jafari, 1988).

Image research is arguably one of the most prolific areas of study in the field of tourism. The roots of image research can be traced to Boulding (1956) when he introduced the concepts of cognitive, affective, and cona-tive image evaluation. However, the leap into tourism occurred in 1971 with Hunt's original study that focused on four western states. That was soon followed by Gunn's (1972) discussion of induced and organic image formation agents and Mayo's (1973) look at regional differences of image perception. Shortly after Boulding's (1956) book on image, Howard (1963) introduced the concept of the evoked set. A few years later Campbell (1969) established the size of the evoked set with relationship to the amount of product knowledge held by a decision maker. Finally, Woodside and Sherrell (1977) were among the first to bring the concept of the evoked set into the tourism realm and link it with image.

Methods to measure held images were, for a number of years, similar to Hunt's approach, which was to use bipolar adjectives anchoring Likert-type, semantic differential scales. The use of these scales effectively converted nominal-level data into interval-level data, allowing sophisticated analysis such as multi-dimensional scaling (Goodrich, 1978; Gartner, 1989), correspondence analysis (Calantone *et al.*, 1989), and factor analysis (Uddin, 1988).

Echtner and Ritchie (1993) explored a new method of measuring tourist destination image by introducing the concept of self-assessment – free elicitation. The work to find different ways of measuring tourists' perception of place continues today and there are two chapters in this book that deal with image measurement. Kelly J. MacKay (Chapter 3) lets tourists record their own images of place by giving them cameras and asking them to take pictures of whatever strikes their fancy. This is a more time-consuming process as, after pictures are taken, study subjects submit to a debriefing where the images recorded can be analyzed with respect to their individual meaning. One of the advantages of this approach, however, is the high rate of cooperation from those tourists taking pictures. Another, albeit hidden, advantage is that images are being recorded by tourists during the act of touristhood, which Jafari (1987) argues puts the survey subject into a different cultural mode. Further analysis using MacKay's method when compared to traditional image study methods that usually ask for image(s) of place while the subject is in a different place than their home may reveal to what extent image impressions are affected by the act of becoming a tourist. MacKay's work opens up a new frontier in the study of tourist images.

A second contribution dealing with tourist images is presented by Graham M.S. Dann (Chapter 2). In his chapter, Dann suggests destination images can be better studied by structured content analysis. Instead of asking how people perceive a place, he looks at how places present themselves. Using content/semiotic analysis as a history of destination images, as they have been presented through human communication, trends can be unearthed, ideology and motivation ascertained, typologies classified, perennial themes identified, and areas of under-representation or significant omission determined. Using content/semiotic analysis, a destination area can undertake its own analysis of what it has been projecting through the years and determine, in part, if these images match what identified target markets perceive. Held images are resistant to change and when they do change it happens slowly in the absence of any overwhelming new information (Gartner, 1993). Dann suggests content/semiotic image analysis is rich with data that could help destinations understand their position within specific markets.

Although the two chapters discussed above lend credence to the argument that research in tourism is maturing, many gaps remain. Richard Butler and Airey (Chapter 10) discuss a relatively minor health issue but one of enormous consequence for regional tourism. Foot-and-mouth is a viral disease that affects numerous species of farm and some wild animals but is of relatively minor importance to the long-term health of affected animals and poses no known risks to humans. Yet, when it appears, as it did in the English countryside in 2001 (this is only the most recent outbreak as other outbreaks can be traced back to 1922) authorities react by quarantining areas where affected animals are found and by killing off any animal suspected of carrying the virus. While these actions may have been economically troublesome for herd keepers in the 1920s through the 1960s, the relative economic significance of tourism vis-à-vis farming has changed the rural economic picture over the years.

Butler and Airey point out that impacts on tourism are not even discussed when quarantine decisions are taken and, based on image research (cited above), continual news stories, and other markers of the disease (e.g. international travelers having to disinfect their shoes upon departure from the UK or arrival home), there may be long-term economic consequences for areas where foot-and-mouth is identified. Although we may know a lot about how tourism operates and the impacts it produces, we know very little about the long-term consequences of exogenous forces (impacts) on tourism. This is both a major gap in knowledge and a concern regarding the importance of tourism to a regional economy. Governments often do not have a crisis plan in place for dealing with exogenous shocks to the tourism system.

Julio Aramberri (Chapter 6) also addresses the gaps in tourism knowledge by examining some of the world's tourism statistics in ways that have not been addressed before. By doing so he calls into question some of the "accepted" knowledge regarding tourism's impacts. For example, he questions the overwhelming research focus on international tourism when his analysis, and that of others, show that international tourism is only a fraction of domestic or national tourism. Aramberri also takes on the myth of neocolonization, through tourism dependency, of the north over the south by close scrutiny of international travel flows. His analysis shows that tourism is not as widespread across the globe as some argue, but instead is concentrated in less than a tenth of the planet's recognized states and territories. Even more damaging to long-held beliefs is his statistically convincing argument that tourism economic leakages affect industrialized, larger northern economies much more so than the less developed southern countries.

Aramberri's work can be summed up by stating that "the more we think we know the less we really do know". Research coming of age does not just mean accepting as truth that which has come before. A fresh look at accepted wisdom can reveal myths disguised as facts. Tourism, as a multidisciplinary field with a limited history of scientific inquiry, is a fertile area for the creation of new knowledge and the revision of long-held beliefs. The rapid increase in the number of scientific journals devoted to tourism may be viewed by some as dilution of scientific thought, but, as shown in the few chapters addressing the trend of "research coming of age" in this book, there is much left to be discovered and rethought. There is room for much more extensive and intensive research concerning tourism.

Conclusions

A number of tourism trends addressed in this book were examined in this chapter. It was argued that terrorism is not really a trend but an exogenous shock to the world's economic system that includes tourism. It was frequently heard after September 11, 2001 that nothing is the same and everything has changed. What this chapter attempts to show is that nothing was ever the same or should be expected to remain the same. A few trends underscoring some of the changes we observe formed the basis for this chapter.

Consolidation is a trend that has been affecting businesses in many industrial sectors for as long as there have been businesses to acquire. However, there are periods when it picks up more steam and this has been occurring in the last 20 years. Why it has occurred is related to political change and new regulations that reinforce market ideology.

Consumption center development is a trend that has its roots in the mega-trends of population growth and technological change. Increasingly mobile tourists with more disposable income than ever before and the concentration of people in urban environments have made consumption center development possible. Utilizing distribution channel efficiencies destinations are now able to concentrate tourism products in relatively small geographical areas, enabling access costs to decrease and total product offering to increase.

Public involvement in all issues has been on the increase in recent years. The magnitude of demonstrations against organizations such as the World Trade Organization has been telling not only in the degree of opposition they show but the ability of opposition groups to use all technological means for organization. The ease of information exchange makes organizing much easier. This, coupled with a more informed and activist population, means that development decisions including those that are tourism-related are more likely than ever to be challenged in public forums or courts of law. The time and cost of development decisions should increase as a result of this trend.

Devolution is the opposite of consolidation. However, the consolidation trend is primarily concerned with operational issues, whereas the devolution trend affects political systems. The political forces of devolution initiated during the Soviet break-up of the late 1980s have been changing the face of tourism development in many newly created nations. However, early devolutionary forces provided a fertile breeding ground for the terrorist threat that has hit tourism in recent years. What is clear from witnessing what has been happening is that the devolution trend offers new opportunities for tourism development even if the only thing to change is the name for the region where tourism has been taking place for many years. Countering the positives of a newly named tourism region are barriers, such as increased time at border crossings, that devolution brings.

Finally, the last trend to be discussed concerns research and its "coming of age". Tourism research, like other research, builds on its knowledge base. We are now at a time where theories from other disciplines have been successfully imported to the study of tourism and tourism researchers are now developing their own theoretical constructs. The proliferation of tourism journals, books, and conferences is an indication that we have reached critical research mass, allowing the academic community to accept tourism as a legitimate field of study. Yet, significant gaps in knowledge remain and old knowledge should be closely scrutinized and not simply accepted as truth because a number of writings contain this "knowledge". The two chapters in this book related to image and tourism (Chapters 2 and 3), a frequent line of inquiry, lend credence to the trend "research coming of age" as do the two chapters that point out there is much we do not yet know or think we know but in reality do not.

Of course there are other trends not mentioned in this chapter that also relate to tourism. Some of those may counter the forces of the trends discussed here. What should be apparent to those who study the tourism phenomenon is that it is a vital force in our life and there are other forces that interact and act upon it. The chapters in this book shed light on some of those forces and lend further support to the statement "nothing was ever the same or will ever be the same".

Postscript

It was my pleasure to provide a synthesis of the chapters in this book. The editors of this book, Julio Aramberri and Richard Butler, were kind enough to let me develop this chapter any way I wanted. In writing it I had to thoroughly read each one of the chapters. That was the fun part. As you read through this book you will find out what I mean. The authors have been contributing to the literature for a number of years. Most are senior academics and members of the International Academy for the Study of Tourism. Some are "younger" academics who were invited to present their research and have their work included in this book. As I survey the field of "young researchers" it is apparent that their work is so much more advanced than that of the senior researchers at a comparable point in time. Truly the axiom that knowledge builds on knowledge is true at least in the case of tourism research. Speaking for the Academy it is my wish that you will find some grains of knowledge from the information contained in this book. If that happens then the Academy is indeed achieving its mission. Use what you find useful herein, refute what you disagree with, but in doing either write about what you learn and help all of us do a better job.

References

Boulding, K. (1956) *The Image: Knowledge in Life and Society*, Ann Arbor, MI: University of Michigan Press.

Brown, L. and Flavin, C. (1999) A new economy for a new century. In L. Brown and C. Flavin *State of the World*. New York: W.W. Norton and Company.

Buhalis, D. (2000) Trends in information technology and tourism. In W.C. Gartner and D.W. Lime (eds) *Trends in Outdoor Recreation, Leisure and Tourism*. Wallingford: CABI.

Calantone, R., die Benedetto, C., Hakam, A. and Bojanic, D. (1987) Multiple multinational tourism positioning using correspndence analysis. *Journal of Travel Research* 28 (2): 25–32.

Campbell, B. (1969) The existence of evoked set and determinants of its magnitude in brand choice behavior. Unpublished doctoral dissertation. New York: Columbia University.

Cohen, E. (1972) Toward a sociology of international tourism. *Social Research* 39, 164–118.

Dann, G. (1977) Anomie, ego enhancement and tourism. *Annals of Tourism Research* 4, 184–194.

Diamond, J. (1999) *Guns, Germs, and Steel.* New York: Norton.

Echtner, C. and Ritchie, J. (1993) The measurement of destination image: An empirical assessment. *Journal of Travel Research* 31, 3–13.

Gartner, W.C. (1989) Tourism image: Attribute measurement of state tourism products using multidimensional scaling techniques. *Journal of Travel Research* 28 (2), 16–20.

Gartner, W.C. (1993) Image formation process. *Journal of Travel and Tourism Marketing* 2 (3), 191–212.

Gartner, W.C. (1996) *Tourism Development: Principles, Processes and Policies.* New York: John Wiley.

Gartner, W.C. and Lime, D.W. (eds) (2000) *Trends in Outdoor Recreation, Leisure and Tourism,* Wallingford: CABI.

Gartner, W.C. and Shen, J. (1992) The impact of Tiananmen Square on China's tourism image. *Journal of Travel Research* 30 (4), 47–52.

Gartner, W.C., Love, L. and Erkkila, D. (2002) *Profile of Visitors to Five Minnesota Communities.* St Paul, MN: Tourism Center, University of Minnesota (www.tourism.umn.edu).

Goodrich, J. (1978) A new approach to image analysis through multi-dimensional scaling. *Journal of Travel Research* 16, 10–13.

Gunn, C. (1972) *Vactionscape: Designing Tourist Regions,* Austin, TX: Bureau of Business Research, University of Texas.

Howard, J. (1963) *Marketing Management.* Homewood, IL: Irwin Publishing Company.

Hunt, J. (1971) Image: A factor in tourism. Unpublished doctoral dissertation, Colorado State University, Fort Collins, Colorado.

Jafari, J. (1987) Tourism models: The sociocultural aspects. *Tourism Management* 8 (2), 151–159.

Jafari, J. (1988) Retrospective and prospective views on tourism as field of study. Paper presented at the 1988 meeting of the Academy of Leisure Sciences, Indianapolis, Indiana.

Mayo, E. (1973) Regional images and regional travel behavior. In *Proceedings of the Fourth Annual Travel Research Association Conference* (pp. 211–217). Salt Lake City, UT: Travel Research Association.

McCool, S. and Patterson, M. (2000) Trends in recreation, tourism and protected area planning. In W.C. Gartner and D.W. Lime (eds) *Trends in Outdoor Recreation, Leisure and Tourism.* Wallingford: CABI.

Monteiro, S. and Rowenczyk, C. (1992) Les vacances des Français: Tendances économiques et resultats, Institut National de la Statistique et des Etudes Economiques (INSEE), Paris, from Teigland, J. (2000) The effects on travel and tourism demand from three mega-trends: Democratization, market ideology and post-materialism as cultural wave. In W.C. Gartner and D.W. Lime (eds) *Trends in Outdoor Recreation, Leisure and Tourism.* Wallingford: CABI.

Plog, S. (1974) Why destination areas rise and fall in popularity. *Cornell Hotel and Restaurant Administration Quarterly* 14 (4), 55–58.

Propst, D., Wellman, D., Campa III, H. and McDonough, M. (2000) Citizen partic-
    ipation trends and their educational implications for natural resource
    professionals. In W.C. Gartner and D.W. Lime (eds) *Trends in Outdoor
    Recreation, Leisure and Tourism*. Wallingford: CABI.

Richards, G. (2000) Cultural tourism: Challenges for marketing and manage-
    ment. In W.C. Gartner and D.W. Lime (eds) *Trends in Outdoor Recreation, Leisure
    and Tourism*. Wallingford: CABI.

Teigland, J. (2000) The effects on travel and tourism demand from three mega-
    trends: Democratization, market ideology and post-materialism as cultural
    wave. In W.C. Gartner and D.W. Lime (eds) *Trends in Outdoor Recreation, Leisure
    and Tourism*. Wallingford: CABI.

Uddin, Z. (1988) Determinants of the components of a state's tourist image and
    their marketing implications. Unpublished doctoral dissertation, Utah State
    University, Logan, Utah.

Van Den Berghe, P. (1994) *The Quest for the Other*. Seattle, WA: University of
    Washington Press.

Woodside, A. and Sherrell, D. (1977) Traveler evoked set, inept set and inert
    sets of vacation destinations. *Journal of Travel Research* 16 (1), 14–18.

Part 2: The Toolbox: Methodological Approaches

The Toolbox: Methodological Approaches

This first section deals with some theoretical issues. In a Kuhnian perspective, theoretical probes can either be paradigm-confirming or paradigm-questioning. Graham Dann's contribution (Chapter 2) falls in the latter category. In his view, both in and outside the tourism field, researchers in the social sciences exude excessive confidence in surveys and other quantitative methods that prize reliability and validity. But there are other affordable and effective ways to scrutinize social communication in different settings. Content analysis coupled with semiotics is one of them, even though it has been overlooked for a long time. Dann offers a state-of-the-art review of its potential to improve tourism research from different angles – revealing latent ideology and motivation in tourist behaviour; generating tourist typologies; providing multimedia treatments of promotional materials; exploring perennial themes, such as "the sacred" and "authenticity"; and pointing to areas of significant omission in marketing techniques. The chapter refers to a vast range of research projects that have geared content/semiotic analysis to successful fruition and includes a long reference list that will help practitioners to draw on this methodological tool.

The rest of the chapters adhere to a more paradigm-confirming frame of reference. Kelly McKay (Chapter 3) examines the oft-quoted aphorism that an image is worth a thousand words, while emphasizing that the connection between the mental construct held by tourists and the pictorial representations supplied by destination marketers tends to be ambiguous. This ambiguity stems from the use of the term "image" both as an advertising/promotional tool for a product or destination, and as the collection of beliefs and expectations about it held by actual or potential consumers. Based on four different experiments probing into this relation, McKay confirms that pictorials often are a source of dissonance and concludes that new methodological approaches are needed to fill the gap and to better integrate visuals into conceptual models of destination image formation.

Roslyn Russell and Peter Murphy (Chapter 4) address the issue of effective leadership. In times of uncertainty as at present leadership is the most sought after entrepreneurial attribute. How can researchers and educators contribute to breed effective leaders set to respond to rapidly changing environments? For the authors, the best way lies in the study of exemplary cases, both at the international (Thomas Cook and Walt Disney) and at other, lesser known regional success stories (Paul Miller and the Victoria Harbor Ferry in Canada and Tom O'Toole of the Beechworth Bakery in Australia). In those cases, and in many others, it is possible to single out a number of features (risk-taking, creativity, following good business practices) that can stimulate the imagination of students. However, an educational environment that encourages and rewards them for developing "attributes" rather than just knowledge is also needed to teach potentially effective leaders ready to cope with today's shifting political and economic environment.

Steven Wanhill (Chapter 5) debates the thorny issue of how to classify the vast array of tourist attractions, and how to measure their success, with special attention to those owned by the not-for-profit sector where commercial goals should not play a prominent role. However, once attractions in the not-for-profit sector have been adapted for visitors, there is increasing pressure to interpret success in terms of the quality of the experience, visitor numbers and, where admission is charged, some level of financial viability, which brings this sector closer to the workings of commercial operators. For Wanhill such limited criteria are flawed. It is also important to balance the outcomes of publicly owned attractions against the priorities assigned to other objectives. In fact, the profit goal may not always be the only measure for success, as is the case in many avant-garde or anticipatory imagescapes that have a high probability of economic failure, both commercially and also in the wider sense of attracting visitor expenditure to an area. However, they may be judged to involve significant cultural values. This logic implies that non-market models of resource allocation are needed to understand how publicly owned attractions operate. The case of the Millennium Dome in Greenwich, UK, is examined under this light.

Chapter 2
Content/Semiotic Analysis: Applications for Tourism Research

GRAHAM M.S. DANN

Introduction

Without wishing to enter any of the controversy surrounding content analysis (Markoff *et al.*, 1974), this social scientific technique is defined here as an unobtrusive measure (Webb *et al.*, 1966) for systematically classifying and making inferences (Holsti, 1969) from the manifest, realist, denotative or literal content of any type of human communication (Abrahamson, 1983), according to the classical questions of "who says what, to whom, how, why and with what effect?" (Babbie, 1995: 306–307). While content analysis as a type of coding (Moser & Kalton, 1986: 414) can be quantitative (Berelson, 1952), qualitative (Sellitz *et al.*, 1959) or a mixture of the two approaches (Smith, 1975), depending on the nature of the data, the criteria for selecting categories (Berg, 1989: 106) must be conceptually framed (Babbie, 1995: 311). That is to say, they should be theoretically driven by the research problem, where such hypothesising operates in the deductive (coding down), inductive (coding up), or a combination of both modes (Glaser & Strauss, 1967). Semiotic analysis is understood as a continuation of this exercise at the latent or connotative level by supplying a "subversive reading" (Denzin, 1989: 220, 229–230) and thick description of the sign content and underlying meaning structure of verbal and non-verbal messages (Seaton, 2000: 106). Since semiotic analysis is here considered to be a natural, in-depth extension of content analysis, without which the latter is incomplete, the two forms may be regarded as complementary and successive stages of the same research process. For this reason, reference is hereafter made to content/semiotic analysis.

The drawbacks of this binary technique are relatively few. Apart from being limited to recordable, available and received communication and, in some cases, to information that may have been collected for purposes other than the focus of scholarly attention, researchers may not always be sure that they are employing the most valid classification device within an unexamined broader cultural context. Nor, for that matter, are they able to probe or experiment with the data. Hence they cannot necessarily attribute causality to the associations that they discover.

On the other hand, there are numerous merits that well outweigh the foregoing disadvantages (Babbie, 1995: 320–321). Perhaps the most important positive consideration is the economy of content/semiotic analysis in terms of time and money. The technique is extremely low budget, does not require a large research staff or expensive equipment, and the data, if not totally free of cost, can usually be obtained with minimum financial outlay. If the preliminary analysis is faulty (unlike ethnography or survey work), it can be gone over again without re-entering the field, and reliability may be enhanced by recoding. It is a non-reactive procedure and (unlike many other social science methods) does not affect the attitudes, behaviour or responses of subjects. Content/ semiotic analysis can also be conducted longitudinally over substantial periods of time and, as such, is an excellent monitor of social change within a given domain.

For the last 40 or so years much of the drudgery of carrying out content/semiotic analysis by hand has been reduced by the introduction of computer software (Gerbner *et al.*, 1969; Sebeok & Zeps, 1958; Stone *et al.*, 1966). Indeed, more recent programs (Nissan & Schmidt, 1994; Popping, 2000; Weitzman & Miles, 1995; West, 2000a, 2000b), complete with dictionaries for assigning items to synonymous meaning clusters, constitute evidence of the related progress made. An evaluation and application of one such program – Atlas/ti – has recently been undertaken by Mehmetoglu and Dann (2003).

This chapter seeks to highlight the potential, richness and extraordinary versatility of content/semiotic analysis as an unobtrusive measure (Pizam, 1993) that combines quantitative and qualitative approaches (Walle, 1997) in tourism research by focusing on its ability to:

(1) unearth trends;
(2) reveal latent ideology and motivation;
(3) generate typologies;
(4) provide multimedia treatments;
(5) explore perennial themes; and
(6) point to areas of significant omission.

Since the literature review and list of references are fairly extensive, this chapter may also be considered as a state-of-the-art exercise.

Unearthing Trends

According to Krippendorff (1980: 13), the first application of content/semiotic analysis was textual in nature. Its roots strangely originated from an examination of the heretical content of the *Songs of Zion*, which first appeared in 18th-century Sweden and which were hymns that threatened to undermine the orthodoxy of the State church (Døvring, 1954–1955: 13). About a hundred years later, attention turned to the content of newspapers, as to whether in fact they merited their designation as bearers of significant national tidings or if they had simply become trivial vehicles of gossip and rumour. To this end, several longitudinal studies were conducted that counted the column inches devoted to such serious matters as science and religion and contrasted them with the measurable amounts of newsprint dedicated to sport and scandal (Mathews, 1910; Speed, 1893; Street, 1909; Willey, 1926, in Krippendorff, 1980: 14). Analysis of the written word was subsequently extended to the content of history texts (Walworth, 1938), children's books (Martin, 1936) and scholarly publications (Becker, 1930, 1932, in Krippendorff, 1980: 15–16).

Although there has been an interesting investigation of the social impact of tourism on developing regions via an examination of newspaper articles over time (Crandall, 1987), tourism research has tended to concentrate more on state-of-the-art appraisals of the emerging field based on the content of academic journals (Sheldon, 1991; van Doren *et al.*, 1994). One of the earliest of these textual studies was van Doren and Heit's (1973) evaluation of the *Journal of Leisure Research*. Dann *et al.* (1988: 6–10) subsequently presented a meta-analysis of that journal from 1976 to 1985 and compared it with developments in *Annals of Tourism Research* from 1974 to 1986. Here they examined the predominant style of the articles, the disciplinary backgrounds of the authors and the ways in which they treated their data. In the same paper, they outlined a model for gauging theoretical awareness and methodological sophistication, one which Dann (1988b) later applied to a detailed analysis of trends in Caribbean tourism research. Here he was additionally able to divide up the literature into three time periods (corresponding with the stages of tourism evolution in that region), country focus, disciplinary emphasis and native versus foreign authorship. By cross-tabulating the data he could point to steady increases in the indigenisation of research, territorial specificity, social scientific orientation and quality of analysis.

Revealing Latent Ideology and Motivation

According to Krippendorff (1980: 16–17), just before the outbreak of the Second World War, practitioners of content/semiotic analysis became highly attracted to the study of propaganda, so much so that a dedicated Institute for Propaganda Analysis (1937) was established precisely for that purpose. During the 1940s two more centres in the US came into being under the eminent directorships of Harold Lasswell and Hans Speier. However, it was not until the war was well over that their respective findings became known (George, 1959; Lasswell *et al.*, 1965). Immediately prior to this period, a number of psychologists were beginning to display an interest in studies of attitude valence, stereotypes and the ways in which minorities were textually portrayed (Lippmann, 1922; Simpson, 1934). A parallel development was the use of verbal records and projective tests by members of that discipline in order to explore the motivational and personality characteristics of subjects (Allport, 1942, in Krippendorff, 1980: 18). These two strands of research complemented each other, to the extent that, while the former concentrated on the ideology of the senders, the latter dwelt on the receivers of messages.

In tourism content/semiotic analysis, although there has been a steady growth in the number of works dealing with imagery, only recently has attention turned respectively to its ideological and motivational infrastructure. As regards ideology, one of the best examples of this type of research is that of Morgan and Pritchard (1998) with its concentration on the power of tourism image makers, especially regarding the hegemony of "othering" and "gendering" in the promotional process (Morgan & Pritchard, 1998). Another recent instance of the genre is Echtner's (2000) doctoral dissertation on brochures depicting developing countries and their inhabitants. What is particularly fascinating about Echtner's study is the way that she effects the transition from content to semiotic analysis by detecting ideological structures (that she calls "un-myths") underpinning the word clusters used to portray "unchanged" (Orientalist), "unrestrained" (sun and sea) and "uncivilised" (frontier) destination societies. The point that she makes (and one that has been highlighted by others (Dann, 1996e; Selwyn, 1993)), is that it is only by peeling off the layers of discourse and subjecting them to deeper readings (Denzin, 1989) that such latent structures are exposed.

On the motivational side, Dann (1995), during the course of lengthy in-depth interviews with 535 tourists visiting Barbados, questioned them about their images of that Caribbean territory before they had visited it and now that they were there. Respondents were next shown four pictures with increasing degrees of stranger-hood and asked to say what they meant in the pre- and on-trip stages of their holiday. The first phase of the analysis uncovered a number of interesting sociolinguistic features, with and without pictorial stimuli, including the most frequently occurring words that were employed to describe the island and its people, and how they became more positive and place-specific as a result of the vacation experience. The second phase of the analysis (Dann, 1996a) went on to demonstrate how the interviewees revealed their inner motives in the descriptions they offered, a notoriously difficult area to research by traditional methods, but one considerably facilitated by the use of projective tests. A future phase could usefully explore the degrees of convergence or mismatch between the language of publicity promoting Barbados (supply) and that articulated by those visiting its shores (demand). In terms of motivation, it would then be possible to discover the extent to which there is a goodness of fit or lack of fit between push and pull factors. Further research could also investigate the degree to which ideology impacts on motivation, as shown, for example, in Dann's (2000a; 2000b; 2001b) studies of promotional difference and their appeal to the quest for novelty in the consumer.

Generating Typologies

Just as propaganda analysis was able to identify typical strategies adopted by the disseminators of such messages, so too did studies of political speeches. McDiarmid (1937), for instance, analysed 30 US presidential addresses and pinpointed several frequently used symbols (national identity, historical reference, concepts of government, etc.), while Lasswell (1938) highlighted the symbolic categories encountered in public communications (self, others, indulgence, deprivation, etc; in Krippendorff, 1980: 15)

Tourism research, perhaps taking a cue from Durkheim (1964) that the first stage of understanding a phenomenon is the act of categorisation, produced a number of early typologies of tourists. However, none of these taxonomies, as far as one is aware, used content/semiotic analysis to arrive at its classificatory scheme. Moreover, only Cohen's typologies appeared to be theoretically grounded, derived, as they were, from the writings of Schutz (1944) and Simmel (1950) on stranger-hood.

Yet typologies can also be useful for discovering elements in new forms of tourism, as, for instance, dark tourism, and in its many varieties (Dann, 1998b). They may also be worthwhile pursuing in the more interactive context of host–guest encounters. A related example from this author's own work (Dann, 1996b) shows how a typology emerged from the analysis of 11 UK holiday brochures containing some 5172 photographs. When these pictures were classified according to their "people content", it transpired that 24.3% featured none at all, 60.1% tourists only, 6.7% locals only and 8.9% locals and tourists together. Subsequently, the data were cross-tabulated according to their settings: beaches, transport, hotels and their surroundings, tourist sights, local scenes, entertainment, sport (other than swimming) and animal scenes. As a result, it was then possible to see how the various people categories were spatially distributed. Although there were some territorial over-laps, absence of people was most closely associated with transport, sights, local and animal scenes; tourists only with the beach, sports and hotels; locals only with entertainment, local scenes, transport, sights and animal scenes; and locals and tourists together with hotels, entertainment and local scenes. So far the analysis had been entirely quantitative. Later, however, it became more qualitative in nature with the respective typo-logical designation of these four "people zones" as "paradise contrived", "paradise confined", "paradise confused" and "paradise controlled". At this juncture, the 1470 pages of text were introduced (the anchoring voice of the anonymous sender), thereby permitting the semiotic and qualitative analysis of the advertising strategy and ideology involved. A sub-typology of alterity was finally explored (natives as scenery, as cultural markers, as servants, as entertainers, as vendors, as seducers, as intermediaries, as familiar and even as tourists) in order to high-light the promotional structures of "othering" and the controlling discourse through which it operated. Although Aramberri (2001: 746–747) objects to this type of conclusion, calling instead for an analysis of the social conditions that make such othering possible, he arguably misses the point that the imposition of imagery by the superordinate First World on the subordinate Third World constitutes the asymmetric and selective manipulation of the latter by the former.

Providing Multimedia Treatments

Although there have been some classical studies of publicity (Goffman, 1979; Williamson, 1983), the spatial breadth of content/semiotic analysis allows for the exploration of a variety of media, ranging from written texts and oral replies to open-ended questions to the realms of art, music, small-group behaviour, kinesics and proxemics (Bales, 1950; Denzin, 1989: 227–228; Dooley, 1984: 89). Indeed such analysis has been carried out by this writer in such diverse areas as graveyards, obituary notices, religious graffiti and seating in public places, and there have been others who have even rummaged amongst the content of people's garbage in order to detect social stratification patterns surrounding the consumption of food and drink.

Tourism research, particularly with the recognition of the linguistic qualities of tourism promotion (Dann, 1996d) and the cliché it often contains (Dann, 2001a; Voase, 2000), has also expanded its multimedia, multidisciplinary repertoire to include the content/semiotic analysis (Echtner, 1999) of literary material (Dann, 2002; Gruffudd, 1994; Squire, 1994), travelogues (Dann, 1992, 1996c; Wilson, 1994; Zeppel, 1999), brochures (Dann, 1988a, 2001b; Echtner, 2000; Pritchard & Morgan, 1995, 1996; Selwyn, 1993; Uzzell, 1984; Weightman, 1987), NTO catalogues (Dann, 2000a, 2000b; Thurot, 1981), advertisements (Dann, 1996d, 1997, 1998a; O'Barr, 1994; Thurot & Thurot, 1983), guidebooks (Bhattacharyya, 1997; Gritti, 1967; Lew, 1991), maps (Pearce, 1977; Seaton, 1994), radio publicity (Albig, 1938; Lewis & Chandrasekar, 1982), TV holiday programmes (Dun, 1998; Voase, 2000), videos (Hanefors & Larsson, 1993), popular songs (Powell, 1988), film (Riley, 1994), narratives of tour guides (Dahles, 1996; Fine & Speer, 1985; Katriel, 1994a, 1994b), postcard messages (Albers & James, 1983; Edwards, 1996; Markwick, 2001; Mellinger, 1994) and even the humble notice board (Dann, 2003).

There have also been studies of the receivers and objects of such messages. There has, for instance, been research on children's drawings of tourists (Gamradt, 1995), essays about tourists (Crick, 1989), tourists' accounts of their own experiences (Gottlieb, 1982; Jackson *et al.*, 1996; Pearce, 1991; Pearce & Caltabiano, 1983; Small, 1999), diaries kept by tourists (Laws, 1998; Pearce, 1988; Selwyn, 1996), tourists' conversations (Dann, 2000c; Fjellman, 1992; Ryan, 1995), the photographs that tourists take while on holiday (Chalfen, 1979; Markwell, 1997; O'Barr, 1994) and the complaints that they make about their vacations (Hannigan, 1980; Pearce & Moscardo, 1984).

Exploring Perennial Themes

Content/semiotic analysis has always been useful for identifying recurring themes. The previously mentioned Institute for Propaganda Analysis (1937), for example, pointed to the employment of such rhetorical ploys as "name calling", "glittering generalities", "band wagon" devices and so on, which appeared time and again in communications of this nature (Krippendorff, 1980: 16). Gerbner (1969) even went so far as to identify "cultural indicators" by means of the technique, while anthropologists, utilising it for the analysis of myth and folktales (Armstrong, 1959; Thompson, 1932), often did so by recourse to such hardy disciplinary concepts as kinship and magic (in Krippendorff, 1980: 18).

In tourism research, too, scholars have identified a number of unit ideas that encapsulate the forms underpinning the phenomenon. The notion of the "sacred" is one, "authenticity" is another. However, relatively few academics have content/semiotically analysed publicity media in this fashion. One exception to this observation is research into promotional videos by Hanefors and Larsson (1993). Another is a trilogy of studies (Dann, 1994a, 1994b, 1994c) examining the many facets of the "nostalgia factor", an ubiquitous trope that goes a long way in contributing to an understanding of tourist motivation in societies where the present is regarded as intolerable and the future as an object of dread. Arguably, by focusing on essential elements of this order which, under a Simmelian (1950) perspective, transcend both space and time, one can obtain insights that speak to the general human condition, a distinct advantage over case studies that are limited to the specifics of a given culture.

This last point is particularly reinforced by examining literary accounts of places (Andersen & Robinson, 2002) and how this perennial framing can capture their very nature. An example of content/semiotic analysis in this area is an investigation (Dann, 2002) of the portrayal of Venice (probably the world's most written-about destination) by such classical authors as Byron, Browning, Dickens, Goethe, James, Shelley and Ruskin. The analysis is heightened by allowing three *in vivo* themes to emerge from the data – "dreams", "love" and "death" – and by showing in turn how they feature ubiquitously in the discourse of tourism itself. In such a manner these writers who travel become travel writers, thereby encouraging another generation comprising the likes of Durrell, Morris, Newby and du Maurier to take over in the same tradition, and in quasi-identical language. The process extends into the popular writing of Sunday supplement travelogues and thereafter into "brochurese", with each subsequent offering referring to and feeding off its predecessor as a form of verbal cannibalism – the continuous recycling of the *mot juste*.

Pointing to Areas of Under-representation and Significant Omission

Perhaps the most difficult challenge for content/semiotic analysis is discovering what is not present, or not sufficiently evident, in a given communication, when all reasonable expectations would seem to justify proportional representation. Thus violence, for example, when compared with national crime rates, may be over-represented on television, while particular groups, such as women, children and the aged, may be under-represented in that medium (Gerbner *et al.*, 1979, in Krippendorff, 1980: 18). Another content/semiotic analysis tackling the issue of imbalance in portrayal was a study conducted by Dann and Potter (1990) of the yellow pages of the *Barbados Telephone Directory*. Here it was discovered that, although over 90% of the user population was Afro-Caribbean, almost 100% of the filler messages (promoting the advantages of tele-phone communication) featured Caucasians. Apart from this glaring racial distortion, there were other instances of under-representation with respect to age and gender. Typically, only young persons were depicted and, whereas males were imaged as smart businessmen running their enterprises efficiently by phone, females were often revealed as helpless housewives using the instrument to summon aid for the simplest domestic task, in the absence of their husbands who were presumably away earning money for the nuclear family. However, while these scenarios may have been applicable to the US, they were quite at odds with the demographic and employment profiles for the developing country at which they were targeted.

Tourism research has uncovered similar anomalies. Urry (1990: 142), for instance, though admittedly without the benefit of content/semiotic analysis, has noted the under-representation of single persons, homo-sexual couples, disabled persons and blacks in British holiday catalogues. Dann (1996d) has relatedly commented on the complete absence of chil-dren in some of the publicity promoting all-inclusive resorts. However, it is only recently that he has begun to analyse under-representation and significant omission more systematically and inferentially.

In a study (Dann, 2001b) of six specialist operators' brochures aimed at the UK over-55-year-old market, he has found, for instance, that, of the 1487 photographs analysed, only one indicated partial disability (an ambulant man requiring the use of a walking stick), and only two showed persons of African descent (and these were of a young lifeguard and a similarly aged beachboy, rather than of the elderly clients). There was also significant under-representation of single parents, gay couples and drinking and smoking behaviour, whose low pictorial incidence rates could be quite easily contrasted with the much higher prevalence derived from official statistics for this age group in the population at large. Indeed, the whole analysis demonstrated that, instead of being addressed realistically, British seniors were being treated as a homogeneous mass, undifferentiated from the rest of the tourist market and dominated by a white, heterosexual gaze (Pritchard & Morgan, 2000). When their imputed motives and supervised activities were added to the equation, these retirees were simply being viewed and presented by operator publicity as a heavily organised and surveyed group indistinguishable from any other type of package tourist. In other words, one had reached the semiotic stage of the analysis where an underlying ideology could be investigated (Dann, 2000c).

Conclusion

Content analysis in tourism studies has for too long been a Cinderella. For most of her short life she has been obliged to live in methodological poverty in the company of her two ugly sisters – reliability and validity. Indeed, only recently has she been allowed to live happily ever after in her transformed and extended persona of semiotic analysis, once she has been to the meaningful Ball and been introduced to the Prince Charming of qualitative research. Only when the state-of-the-art clock strikes midnight does she realise that, in countless conferences dedicated to appraisals of the field, content/semiotic analysis receives barely a mention and that few tourism textbooks devoted to research include it in their pages.

It has been the intention of this chapter to put some detail into this metaphorical rags-to-spiritual-riches saga by pointing to the immense possibilities offered by the technique, potential which has been personally actualised through years of experience in carrying out investigations on a shoestring. Upon reflection, one likely reason for the overlooking or avoidance of content/semiotic analysis by some tourism scholars may be because it seems to attract so little income. If that is the case, it would lend support to a hunch that one has harboured for some time, namely that the quality of a given project is inversely related to the quantity of funding generated. However, in order to verify or invalidate this important hypothesis, a topic that is hereby reserved for future agenda, it would be necessary to conduct some much-needed research. What better method than content/semiotic analysis?

References

Abrahamson, M. (1983) *Social Research Methods*. Englewood Cliffs, NJ: Prentice Hall.

Albers, P. and James, W. (1983) Tourism and the changing photographic image of the Great Lakes Indians. *Annals of Tourism Research* 10 (1), 123–148.

Albig, W. (1938) The content of radio programs 1925–1935. *Social Forces* 16, 338–349.

Allport, G. (1942) *The Use of Personal Documents in Psychological Science*. New York: Social Science Research Council.

Andersen, H.-C. and Robinson, M. (eds) (2002) *Literature and Tourism: Reading and Writing Tourism Texts*. London: Continuum.

Aramberri, J. (2001) The host should get lost: Paradigms in tourism theory. *Annals of Tourism Research* 28 (3), 738–761.

Armstrong, R. (1959) Content analysis in folkloristics. In I. de Sola Pool (ed.) *Trends in Content Analysis* (pp. 151–170). Urbana, IL: University of Illinois Press.

Babbie, E. (1995) *The Practice of Social Research* (7th edn). Belmont, CA: Wadsworth.

Bales, R. (1950) *Interaction Process Analysis*. Reading, MA: Addison-Wesley.

Becker, H. (1930) Distribution of space in the American Journal of Sociology 1895–1930. *American Journal of Sociology* 36, 461–466.

Becker, H. (1932) Space apportioned to forty-eight topics in the American Journal of Sociology 1895–1930. *American Journal of Sociology* 38, 71–78.

Berelson, B. (1952) *Content Analysis in Communications Research*. New York: Free Press.

Berg, B. (1989) *Qualitative Research Methods for the Social Sciences*. Boston, MA: Allyn and Bacon.

Bhattacharyya, D. (1997) Mediating India: An analysis of a guidebook. *Annals of Tourism Research* 24 (2), 371–389.

Chalfen, R. (1979) Photography's role in tourism: Some unexplored relationships. *Annals of Tourism Research* 6 (4), 435–447.

Crandall, L. (1987) The social impact of tourism on developing regions and its management. In J. Ritchie and C. Goeldner (eds) *Travel, Tourism and Hospitality Research: A Handbook for Management Researchers* (pp. 373–383). New York: Wiley.

Crick, M. (1989) The hippy in Sri Lanka: A symbolic analysis of the imagery of school children in Kandy. *Criticism, Heresy and Interpretation* 3, 37–54.

Dahles, H. (1996) The social construction of Mokum: Tourism and the quest for local identity in Amsterdam. In J. Boissevain (ed.) *Coping with Tourists: European Reactions to Mass Tourism* (pp. 227–246). Oxford: Berghahn Books.

Dann, G. (1988a) Images of Cyprus projected by tour operators. *Problems of Tourism* XI (3), 43–70.

Dann, G. (1988b) Tourism research on the Caribbean: An evaluation. *Leisure Sciences* 10, 261–280.

Dann, G. (1992) Travelogs and the management of unfamiliarity. *Journal of Travel Research* 30 (4), 59–63.

Dann, G. (1994a) Tourism and nostalgia: Looking forward to going back. *Vrijetijd en Samenleving* 12 (1/2), 75–94.

Dann, G. (1994b) Travel by train: Keeping nostalgia on track. In A. Seaton *et al.* (eds) *Tourism: The State of the Art* (pp. 775–782). Chichester: Wiley.

Dann, G. (1994c) Tourism: The nostalgia industry of the future. In W. Theobald (ed.) *Global Tourism: The Next Decade* (pp. 55–67). Oxford: Butterworth-Heinemann.

Dann, G. (1995) A sociolinguistic approach towards changing tourist imagery. In R. Butler and D. Pearce (eds) *Change in Tourism: People, Places, Processes* (pp. 114–136). London: Routledge.

Dann, G. (1996a) Tourists' images of a destination: An alternative analysis. *Journal of Travel and Tourism Marketing* 5 (1/2), 41–55.

Dann, G. (1996b) The people of tourist brochures. In T. Selwyn (ed.) *The Tourist Image: Myths and Myth Making in Tourism* (pp. 61–81). Chichester: Wiley.

Dann, G. (1996c) Images of destination people in travelogues. In R. Butler and T. Hinch (eds) *Tourism and Indigenous Peoples* (pp. 349–375). London: International Thomson Business Press.

Dann, G. (1996d) *The Language of Tourism: A Sociolinguistic Perspective.* Wallingford: CAB International.

Dann, G. (1996e) Greenspeak: An analysis of the language of eco-tourism. *Progress in Tourism and Hospitality Research* 2 (3/4), 247–259.

Dann, G. (1997) The green, green grass of home: Nature and nurture in rural England. In S. Wahab and J. Pigram (eds) *Tourism Development and Growth: The Challenge of Sustainability* (pp. 257–273). London: Routledge.

Dann, G. (1998a) The pomo promo of tourism. *Tourism, Culture and Communication* 1 (1), 1–16.

Dann, G. (1998b) The dark side of tourism. *Etudes et Rapports,* serie L (14).

Dann, G. (2000a) Differentiating destinations in the language of tourism: Harmless hype or promotional irresponsibility? *Tourism Recreation Research* 25 (2), 63–75.

Dann, G. (2000b) National tourist offices and the language of differentiation. In W. Gartner and D. Lime (eds) *Trends in Outdoor Recreation, Leisure and Tourism* (pp. 335–345). Wallingford: CAB International.

Dann, G. (2000c) Overseas holiday hotels for the elderly: Total bliss or total institution? In M. Robinson, P. Long, N. Evans, R. Sharpley and J. Swarbrooke (eds) *Motivations, Behaviour and Tourist Types: Reflections on International Tourism* (pp. 83–94). Newcastle and Sunderland: Centre for Travel and Tourism and Business Education Publishers.

Dann, G. (2001a) Self-admitted use of cliché in the language of tourism. *Tourism, Culture and Communication* 3 (1), 1–14.

Dann, G. (2001b) Targeting seniors through the language of tourism. *Journal of Hospitality and Leisure Marketing* 8 (3/4), 5–35.

Dann, G. (2002) La Serenissima: Dreams, love and death in Venice. In M. Robinson and H. Andersen (eds) *Literature and Tourism: Reading and Writing Tourism Texts* (pp. 239–278). London: Continuum.

Dann, G. (2003) Noticing notices. Tourism to order. *Annals of Tourism Research* 30(2), 465–484.

Dann, G. and Potter, R. (1990) Yellowman in the yellow pages: Sex and race typing in the Barbados telephone directory. *Bulletin of Eastern Caribbean Affairs* 15, 1–15.

Dann, G., Nash, D. and Pearce, P. (1988) Methodology in tourism research. *Annals of Tourism Research* 15 (1), 1–28.

Denzin, N. (1989) *The Research Act* (3rd edn). Englewood Cliffs, NJ: Prentice Hall.

Dooley, D. (1984) *Social Research Methods.* Englewood Cliffs, NJ: Prentice Hall.

Døvring, K. (1954–1955) Quantitative semantics in 18th century Sweden. *Public Opinion Quarterly* 18 (4), 389–394.

Dunn, D. (1998) Home truths from abroad: Television representations of the tourist destination. Unpublished Ph.D. dissertation, University of Birmingham.

Durkheim, E. (1964) [1895] *The Rules of the Sociological Method* (G. Carlin, ed.; S. Solovay and J. Mueller, trans.). New York: Free Press.

Echtner, C. (1999) The semiotic paradigm: Implications for tourism research. *Tourism Management* 20 (1), 47–57.

Echtner, C. (2000) The representation of the Third World in tourism marketing. Unpublished Ph.D. dissertation, University of Calgary, Canada.

Edwards, E. (1996) Postcards: Greetings from another world. In T. Selwyn (ed.) *The Tourist Image: Myths and Myth Making in Tourism* (pp. 197–221). Chichester: Wiley.

Fine, E. and Speer, J. (1985) Tour guide performances as sight sacralization. *Annals of Tourism Research* 12 (1), 73–95.

Fjellman, S. (1992) *Vinyl Leaves: Walt Disney World and America*. Boulder, CO: Westview Press.

Gamradt, J. (1995) Jamaican children's representations of tourism. *Annals of Tourism Research* 22(4), 735–762.

George, A. (1959) *Propaganda Analysis: A Study of Inferences Made from Nazi Propaganda in World War II*. Evanston, IL: Row, Peterson.

Gerbner, G. (1969) Toward "cultural indicators": The analysis of mass mediated public message systems. In G. Gerbner, O. Holsti, K. Krippendorff, W. Paisley and P. Stone (eds) *The Analysis of Communication Content: Developments in Scientific Theories and Computer Techniques* (pp. 123–132). New York: Wiley.

Gerbner, G., Holsti, O., Krippendorff, K., Paisley, W. and Stone, P. (eds) (1969) *The Analysis of Communication Content: Developments in Scientific Theories and Computer Techniques*. New York: Wiley.

Gerbner, G., Gross, L., Signorielli, N., Morgan, M. and Jackson-Beeck, M. (1979) Violence profile no. 10: Trends in network television drama and view conceptions of social reality 1967–1978. Annenberg School of Communications, University of Pennsylvania (mimeo).

Glaser, B. and Strauss, A. (1967) *The Discovery of Grounded Theory: Strategies for Qualitative Research*. Chicago, IL: Aldine.

Goffman, E. (1979) *Gender Advertisements*. London: Macmillan.

Gottlieb, A. (1982) Americans' vacations. *Annals of Tourism Research* 9 (2), 165–187.

Gritti, J. (1967) Les contenus culturels du Guide Bleu: Monuments et sites "à voir". *Communications* 10, 51–64.

Gruffudd, P. (1994) Selling the countryside: Representations of rural Britain. In J. Gold and S. Ward (eds.) *Place Promotion: The Use of Publicity and Marketing to Sell Towns and Regions* (pp. 247–263). Chichester: Wiley.

Hanefors, M. and Larsson, L. (1993) Video strategies used by tour operators. What is really communicated? *Tourism Management* 14 (1), 27–33.

Hannigan, J. (1980) Reservations cancelled: Consumer complaints in the tourist industry. *Annals of Tourism Research* 7 (3), 366–384.

Holsti, O. (1969) *Content Analysis for the Social Sciences and Humanities*. Reading, MA: Addison-Wesley.

Institute for Propaganda Analysis (1937) How to detect propaganda. *Propaganda Analysis* 1, 5–8.

Jackson, M., White, G. and Schmierer, C. (1996) Tourism experiences within an attributional framework. *Annals of Tourism Research* 23 (4), 798–810.

Katriel, T. (1994a) Sites of memory: Discourses of the past in Israeli pioneering settlement museums. *Quarterly Journal of Speech* 80 (1), 1–20.

Katriel, T. (1994b) Performing the past: Presentational styles in settlement museum interpretation. *Israel Social Science Research* 9 (1/2), 1–26.

Krippendorff, K. (1980) *Content Analysis: An Introduction to its Methodology.* Newbury Park, CA: Sage.

Lasswell, H. (1938) A provisional classification of symbol data. *Psychiatry* 1, 197–204.

Lasswell, H. (1965) Detection: Propaganda detection and the courts. In H. Lasswell, N. Leites *et al.* (eds) *Language of Politics* (pp. 173–232). Cambridge, MA: MIT Press.

Laws, E. (1998) Conceptualizing visitor satisfaction management in heritage settings: An exploratory blueprinting analysis of Leeds Castle, Kent. *Tourism Management* 19 (6), 545–554.

Lew, A. (1991) Place representation in tourist guidebooks. *Singapore Journal of Tropical Geography* 12 (2), 124–137.

Lewis, R. and Chandrasekar, V. (1982) Restaurant advertising: Is anyone listening? *Cornell Hotel and Restaurant Administration Quarterly* 23 (1), 79–84.

Lippmann, W. (1922) *Public Opinion.* New York: Macmillan.

Markoff, J., Shapiro, G. and Weitman, S. (1974) Toward the integration of content analysis and general methodology. In D. Heise (ed.) *Sociological Methodology* (pp. 1–58). San Francisco, CA: Jossey-Bass.

Markwell, K. (1997) Dimensions of photography in a nature-based tour. *Annals of Tourism Research* 24 (1), 131–155.

Markwick, M. (2001) Postcards from Malta: Image, consumption, context. *Annals of Tourism Research* 28 (2), 417–438.

Martin, H. (1936) Nationalism and children's literature. *Library Quarterly* 6, 405–418.

Mathews, B. (1910) A study of a New York daily. *Independent* 68, 82–86.

McDiarmid, J. (1937) Presidential inaugural addresses: A study in verbal symbols. *Public Opinion Quarterly* 1, 79–82.

Mehmetoglu, M. and Dann, G. (2003) Atlas/ti and content/semiotic analysis in tourism research. *Tourism Analysis* 8 (1), 1–13.

Mellinger, W. (1994) Toward a critical analysis of tourism representations. *Annals of Tourism Research* 21 (4), 756–779.

Morgan, N. and Pritchard, A. (1998) *Tourism Promotion and Power: Creating Images, Creating Identities.* Chichester: Wiley.

Moser, C. and Kalton, G. (1986) *Survey Methods in Social Investigation* (2nd edn). Aldershot: Gower.

Nissan, E. and Schmidt, K. (eds) (1994) *From Information to Knowledge: Conceptual and Content Analysis by Computer.* Oxford: Intellect.

O'Barr, M. (1994) *Culture and the Ad: Exploring Otherness in the World of Advertising.* Boulder, CO: Westview Press.

Pearce, D. (1988) Tourist time budgets. *Annals of Tourism Research* 15 (1), 106–121.

Pearce, P. (1977) Mental souvenirs: A study of tourists and their city maps. *Australian Journal of Psychology* 29, 203–210.

Pearce, P. (1991) Travel stories: An analysis of self-disclosure in terms of story structure, valence and audience characteristics. *Australian Psychologist* 26 (3), 172–175.

Pearce, P. and Caltabiano, M. (1983) Inferring travel motivation from travellers' experiences. *Journal of Travel Research* 22, 16–20.

Pearce, P. and Moscardo, G. (1984) Making sense of tourists' complaints. *Tourism Management* 5 (1), 20–23.

Pizam, A. (1993) Using unobtrusive measures in tourism research. Paper presented to the International Academy for the Study of Tourism, Selong Hotel, Seoul, July.

Popping, R. (2000) *Computer-assisted Text Analysis*. Lanham, MD: University Press of America.

Powell, A. (1988) Like a rolling stone: Notions of youth travel and tourism in popular music of the sixties, seventies and eighties. In N. Graburn (ed.) *Kroeber Anthropological Society Papers 67/68*, 28–34.

Pritchard, A. and Morgan, N. (1995) Evaluating vacation destination images: The case of local authorities in Wales. *Journal of Vacation Marketing* 2 (1), 23–38.

Pritchard, A. and Morgan, N. (1996) Selling the Celtic arc to the USA: A comparative analysis of the destination brochure images used in the marketing of Ireland, Scotland and Wales. *Journal of Vacation Marketing* 2 (4), 346–365.

Pritchard, A. and Morgan, N. (2000) Privileging the male gaze: Gendered tourism landscapes. *Annals of Tourism Research* 27 (4), 884–905.

Riley, R. (1994) Movie induced tourism. In A. Seaton *et al.* (eds) *Tourism: The State of the Art* (pp. 453–458). Chichester: Wiley.

Ryan, C. (1995) Learning about tourists from conversations: The over 55s in Majorca. *Tourism Management* 16 (3), 207–215.

Schutz, A. (1944) The stranger: An essay in social psychology. *American Journal of Sociology* 49 (6), 495–507.

Seaton, A. (1994) Tourist maps and the promotion of destination image. In *Proceedings of Research and Academic Papers* (Vol. vi) (pp. 168–184). Society of Educators in Travel and Tourism of America.

Seaton, A. (2000) Content analysis. In J. Jafari (ed.) *Encyclopedia of Tourism* (pp. 106–108). London: Routledge.

Sebeok, T. and Zeps, V. (1958) An analysis of structured content with application of electronic computer research in psycholinguistics. *Language and Speech* 1, 181–193.

Sellitz, C., Jahoda, M., Deutsch, M. and Cook, S. (1959) *Research Methods in Social Relations*. New York: Holt, Rinehart and Winston.

Selwyn, T. (1993) Peter Pan in South-East Asia: Views from the brochures. In M. Hitchcock, V. King and M. Parnwell (eds) *Tourism in South-East Asia* (pp. 117–137). London: Routledge.

Selwyn, T. (1996) Atmospheric notes from the fields: Reflections on myth-collecting tours. In T. Selwyn (ed.) *The Tourist Image: Myths and Myth Making in Tourism* (pp. 147–161). Chichester: Wiley.

Sheldon, P. (1991) An authorship analysis of tourism research. *Annals of Tourism Research* 18 (3), 473–484.

Simmel, G. (1950) *The Sociology of Georg Simmel* (K. Wolff, trans.). New York: Free Press.

Simpson, G. (1934) The negro in the Philadelphia press. Unpublished Ph.D. dissertation, University of Pennsylvania.

Small, J. (1999) Memory work. A method for researching women's tourist experiences. *Tourism Management* 20(1), 25–35.

Smith, H. (1975) *Strategies of Social Research*. Englewood Cliffs, NJ: Prentice Hall.

Speed, G. (1893) Do newspapers now give the news? *Forum* 15, 705–711.

Squire, S. (1994) The cultural values of literary tourism. *Annals of Tourism Research* 21 (1), 103–120.

Stone, P., Dunphy, D., Smith, M. and Ogilvie, D. (1966) *The General Inquirer: A Computer Approach to Content Analysis.* Cambridge, MA: MIT Press.

Street, A. (1909) The truth about newspapers. *Chicago Tribune*, 25 July.

Thompson, S. (1932) *Motif Index of Folk Literature: A Classification of Narrative Elements in Folk Tales, Ballads, Myths, Fables, Medieval Romances, Exempla, Fabliaux, Jest Books and Local Legends.* Bloomington, IN: Indiana University Studies.

Thurot, J. (1981) Tourisme et communication publicitaire. Thèse du doctorat du 3ème cycle, Centre des Hautes Etudes Touristiques, Université de Droit, d'Economie et des Sciences, Aix-en-Provence.

Thurot, J. and Thurot, G. (1983) The ideology of class and tourism: Confronting the discourse of advertising. *Annals of Tourism Research* 10 (1), 173–189.

Urry, J. (1990) *The Tourist Gaze: Leisure and Travel in Contemporary Societies.* London: Sage.

Uzzell, D. (1984) An alternative structuralist approach to the psychology of tourism marketing. *Annals of Tourism Research* 11 (1), 79–99.

van Doren, C. and Heit, M. (1973) Where it's at: A content analysis and appraisal of the Journal of Leisure Research. *Journal of Leisure Research* 5, 67–73.

van Doren, C., Koh, Y. and McCahill, A. (1994) Tourism research: A state-of-the-art citation analysis (1971–1990). In A. Seaton *et al.* (eds) *Tourism: The State of the Art* (pp. 308–315). Chichester: Wiley.

Voase, R. (2000) Explaining the blandness of popular travel journalism: Narrative, cliché and the structure of meaning. In M. Robinson, P. Long, N. Evans, R. Sharpley and J. Swarbrooke (eds) *Expressions of Culture, Identity and Meaning in Tourism* (pp. 413–424). Newcastle and Sunderland: Centre for Travel and Tourism, University of Northumbria and Business Education Publishers.

Walle, A. (1997) Quantitative versus qualitative tourism research. *Annals of Tourism Research* 24 (3), 524–536.

Walworth, A. (1938) *Social Historians at War: A Study of the Treatment of our Wars in the Secondary School History Books of the United States and in those of its Former Enemies.* Cambridge, MA: Harvard University Press.

Webb, E., Campbell, D., Schwarz, R. and Sechrest, L. (1966) *Unobtrusive Measures: Non-Reactive Research in the Social Sciences.* Chicago, IL: Rand McNally.

Weightman, B. (1987) Third world tour landscapes. *Annals of Tourism Research* 14 (2), 227–239.

Weitzman, E. and Milles, M. (1995) *Computer Programs for Qualitative Data Analysis: A Software Sourcebook.* Thousand Oaks, CA: Sage.

West, M. (ed.) (2000a) *Theory, Method and Practice in Computer Content Analysis.* Norwood, NJ: Ablex.

West, M. (ed.) (2000b) *Applications of Computer Content Analysis.* Norwood, NJ: Ablex.

Willey, M. (1926) *The Country Newspaper: A Study of Socialization and Newspaper Content.* Chapel Hill, NC: University of North Carolina Press.

Williamson, J. (1983) *Decoding Advertisements: Ideology and Meaning in Advertising.* London: Marion Boyars.

Wilson, D. (1994) Probably as close as you can get to paradise: Tourism and the changing face of the Seychelles. In A. Seaton *et al.* (eds) *Tourism: The State of the Art* (pp. 765–774). Chichester: Wiley.

Zeppel, H. (1999) Touring Aboriginal cultures: Encounters with Aboriginal peoples in Australian travelogues. *Tourism, Culture and Communication* 2 (2), 123–139.

Chapter 3

Is a Picture Worth a Thousand Words? Snapshots from Tourism Destination Image Research

KELLY J. MACKAY

Pictures are an established means of image building for tourism destinations. The connection between the mental image construct held by tourists and the pictorial representations supplied by destination marketers, however, is not well understood. The purpose of this chapter is to advance understanding of the pictorial element in destination image formation and the factors affecting interpretation of, and memory for visuals used in, tourism promotion. Specifically, tourism destination image research that integrates visual stimuli is presented and synthesized to demonstrate the contributions of picture content elements and individual attributes such as, age, culture, experience, and destination-driven (e.g. by the marketer or researcher) versus tourist-driven (e.g. photo-elicitation) models of image assessment and formation. Quantitative and qualitative image studies that include both specific locations and print advertising from various destinations are examined. The intention of this synthesis is to provide an empirical foundation for integrating visuals into conceptual models of destination image formation.

Introduction

Is a picture really worth a thousand words? While silent on the precise word equivalent, results of advertising-related research indicate that pictorial stimuli are more readily recalled and affect both positive and negative brand/product beliefs and attitudes (Laskey *et al.*, 1994). Enhanced recall has been attributed to pictures stimulating greater cognitive elaboration, which in turn increases information storage and retention (Edell & Staelin, 1983). Additionally, nonverbal cues and visual reinforcement are known to produce superior learning and can be more persuasive than verbal ones (Stewart *et al.*, 1987).

In tourism, which is uniquely visual, pictures are paramount to successfully creating and communicating an image of a destination. In fact, over 75% of the content in most tourism brochures is pictorial (Jenkins, 1999). Despite the dominant use of visuals, be they photographic or video-based, most research on tourist destination image has employed place name or other, more general, word-based approaches to elicit image (Jenkins, 1999). Consequently, with few exceptions (e.g. Dann, 1996; MacKay & Fesenmaier, 1997; Olson *et al.*, 1986; Weaver & McCleary, 1984), tourism research on pictorial content and the influence of visual depictions in the creation of destination image is scarce.

The purpose of the present chapter is to advance understanding of the pictorial element in destination image formation, and the factors affecting interpretation of, and memory for, visuals used in tourism promotion. Given the dominance of visuals in destination promotion and the call for more pluralistic approaches to understanding leisure and tourism behavior (Jenkins, 1999; Samdahl, 1999), a series of image studies conducted by the author that integrate visuals into the method are presented and their implications discussed. The two key questions of interest are: (a) How can visuals be incorporated into the study of tourist destination images? and (b) What is learned from the addition of visuals to studies of destination image? Before addressing these questions it is important to review several seminal works on destination image formation (e.g. Echtner & Ritchie, 1993; Fakeye & Crompton, 1991; Gartner, 1993; Gunn, 1972) that provide background for understanding how destination image is formed and establish the context that supports the inclusion of visuals in the study of image.

Destination Image Models

The term image generally refers to a compilation of beliefs and impressions, based on information processing from a variety of sources over time, that result in an internally accepted mental construct (Assael, 1984; Baloglu & McCleary, 1999; Crompton, 1979; Gartner, 1993). The image construct encompasses cognitive and affective dimensions that weave together various products (attractions) and attributes into an overall impression of a destination. Despite this general understanding, the concept of image has been described as vague (Mazanec & Schweiger, 1981). This ambiguity stems from use of the term image both as the advertised and promoted image of a product or destination, and as the beliefs and expectations held by individuals. When the word image is used to describe a visual/picture, this ambiguity in meaning is further complicated (Jenkins, 1999; Mazanec & Schweiger, 1981).

Typically, image formation models correspond to either person-determined image or destination-determined image (Crompton, 1977). Person-determined image reflects individual differences in information processing and interpretation, whereas destination-determined image reflects the actuality of the destination. The nature of the inputs that contribute to an individual's image of a destination have been classified as organic and induced (Gunn, 1972). Organic inputs are not developed by the destination (e.g. news reports) but include actual experience with a destination. Induced inputs are purposeful, targeted marketing efforts devised by the destination. Extensions on this inputs-based conceptualization of image (Gunn, 1972) have been offered by several researchers who build on the notion of multidimensionality of image portrayal and formation (Echtner & Ritchie, 1993; Fakeye & Crompton, 1991; Gartner, 1993).

Echtner and Ritchie (1993) proposed a comprehensive, multi-dimensional definitional and measurement approach to destination image. Image was described as being comprised of three dimensions: attribute–holistic, functional–psychological, and common–unique. The attribute–holistic dimension is a continuum from individual elements of an image to an overall impression. For example, a destination's image is comprised of beliefs about specific attributes (e.g. climate, accommodations, ease of access), as well as a more integrated or holistic impressions. The functional–psychological dimension distinguishes between the parts of image that are directly observable (e.g. prices) and those that are intangible (e.g. friendliness). The third element, common–unique, recognizes what is similar about a destination and what is distinctive about it. Echtner and Ritchie contend that both symbolic and tangible features play a role in defining image of a place.

Building on the work of Gunn (1972), Gartner (1993) proposed a typology of eight image formation agents that relate to degree of control by the promoter and credibility with the target market. The eight agents suggested to influence image development are: overt induced I, overt induced II, covert induced I, covert induced II, autonomous, unsolicited organic, solicited organic, and organic. Destination marketing organizations have greater control over induced categories. For example, traditional consumer advertising by destinations (i.e. overt induced I) is the most highly controlled but the lowest in audience credibility.

Credibility is increased to some degree by use of a celebrity spokesperson (i.e. covert induced I) in destination advertisements. Information provided by the travel trade is representative of overt induced II. The source of much travel trade information is a destination, so control is medium and credibility is enhanced through the middle party. Familiarization tours, organized by a destination marketing organization for travel media and sponsors, are included in the covert induced II category. Autonomous image formation agents are authoritative and credible. They consist of news and popular culture – widely received sources beyond the destination's control that can swiftly create and change an image. Unsolicited and solicited organic image formation categories refer to information requested from unbiased sources, and information given by knowledgeable others, respectively. Finally, organic image formation is based on past experience with the destination and it is the most credible (Gartner, 1993). Manfredo *et al.* (1992) agreed that source credibility, expertise, and trustworthiness are relevant issues to determining effectiveness of image advertising by destinations.

Gartner (1993) argued that image formation agents differentially affect formation of mental destination images and, therefore, have important implications for creation and change of image by destination marketers. Gartner extended this line of thinking by offering a model that links the process by which image is formed in an individual's mind to destination choice. In this model it is suggested that cognitive, affective, and conative components are hierarchically interrelated elements of image formation. The cognitive aspect of image is constructed from fact and external stimuli, which determine possible destinations to enter the perceived set. Evaluation, which relates an individual's travel motives to perceived images resulting in the choice set, occurs within the affective component. Finally, the conative component of image is formed through the act of visiting, but is dependent upon images derived from previous stages.

Fakeye and Crompton (1991) described a similar process of image development in the context of tourism promotion and destination choice. Image was proposed to evolve through three stages: organic, induced, and complex. In their conceptualization, organic image represents an awareness of the destination that is present before destination promotions are introduced. Induced images are formed when promotions are viewed and evaluated against organic image. Complex image results from actual visitation and experience with the destination. Furthermore, Fakeye and Crompton linked these three types of image to the three functions of promotion, which are to inform, to persuade, and to remind.

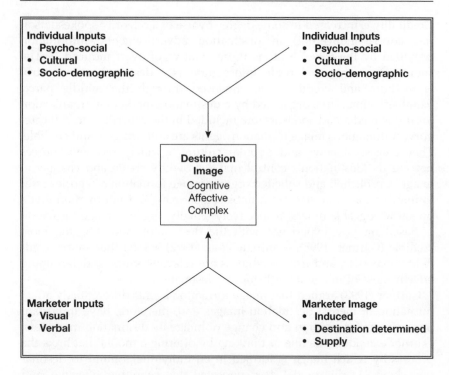

Figure 3.1 Inputs to tourist destination image formation

Informative materials were hypothesized to be most effective at the organic image stage; persuasive materials at the induced image stage; and reminding materials at the complex image stage.

Figure 3.1 illustrates a general model of destination image formation based on Fakeye and Crompton's (1991) and Gardner's (1993) extensions. The figure shows inputs that contribute to individual and marketer images, which are integrated into an overall destination image. The following section elaborates on the visual element in destination image formation from both input perspectives.

Visuals and Destination Image Formation

In tourism advertising and landscape preference literature, it has been suggested that demographic variables (Lyons, 1983; Macia, 1979; Weaver & McCleary, 1984) and familiarity with the destination (Kaplan & Talbot, 1988; Olson *et al.*, 1986; Ulrich, 1983) affect how people judge visuals.

Familiarity, while advanced as both a positive and negative factor in image evaluation, is typically associated with a more realistic impression of a destination that is based on past experience (Gartner & Hunt, 1987; Hunt, 1975). Research has also found a positive correlation between distance from a destination and its image (Telisman-Kosuta, 1989). That is, when the destination is farther away, the image is more likely to be favorable (Crompton, 1979). In other words, the distance factor decreases opportunity for actual visitation and potential negative experiences, which could counter a positive image.

Olson and colleagues (1986) found interaction effects between familiarity and type of pictorial theme, and familiarity and scenery. Familiarity with landmarks implied a less exciting destination, whereas familiarity with natural scenery was associated with more positive ratings. High levels of experience with a natural setting have been found to be associated with symbolic attachments which, in turn, influence visual assessment (Ulrich, 1983).

Weaver and McCleary (1984), who conducted one of the few studies to examine interpretation of visual images in travel advertising, found that age was significant in the interpretation of advertisements relating to company reputation. Macia (1979) and Lyons (1983) investigated effects of age and gender as influences on landscape preferences. These studies found, for example, that children demonstrated higher preference for the landscapes shown than did elderly subjects. Lyons (1983) concluded that landscape preference was dynamic and changed throughout the life cycle. Given that older adults are considered a key leisure travel market segment (Gitelson & Kerstetter, 1990; Lawson, 1991; Rosenfeld, 1986; Weaver & McCleary, 1984), more research is needed to develop effective visual marketing tools to reach this growing segment of travel consumers.

Culture also is purported to influence how people interpret and experience the natural environment (Kaplan & Kaplan, 1989; Kaplan & Talbot, 1988; MacKay & Fesenmaier, 2000; Ulrich, 1983). Consequently, while conveying a consistent image (e.g. landscapes) may be beneficial for marketing implementation, the utilization of standard symbols and images across cultures may result in different connotations that could decrease marketing effectiveness (Hofstede, 1991). With the exception of a few studies on travel motives and vacation choice (Calantone *et al.*, 1989; Richardson & Crompton, 1988; Yuan & McDonald, 1990), cross-cultural market research in tourism is limited (Dimanche, 1994).

In the area of landscape aesthetics and environmental perception research, photographs of scenery have been used to judge preference based on elements such as color, land form, texture, and sense of openness (Kaplan *et al.*, 1989). Kaplan and colleagues classified these elements into four domains: physical attributes, land cover types, informational variables, and perceptual variables. Examples of physical attributes include sky, water, and vegetation. Land cover types refer to broad patterns of physical attributes comprising categories such as agriculture, forests, and cut grassland. Informational variables also have been referred to as cognitive, psychological, and feeling elements by other researchers (Daniel & Vining, 1983; Pitt & Zube, 1987; Zube *et al.*, 1982). These variables depend on the photograph and the perceiver and include coherence, complexity, legibility, and mystery. Perceptual-based variables have been suggested as the most powerful predictors of environmental preference. Variables in this category include openness, smoothness, and locomotion. In summary, there appears to be agreement on certain variables that affect aesthetic preference and interest in natural scenery (Ulrich, 1983). These variables include complexity and structural perspectives such as focality, texture, deflected vistas (mystery), and water. Bernaldez and Parra (1979) classified these variables as "formal" aspects of landscape perception, in contrast to "content" aspects that require an interpretation and/or attribution of significance, as well as perception of the visual scene.

Problem Statement

One of the challenges in tourism image research is that image is frequently measured by examining specific attributes as opposed to the integrated impressions that are acknowledged as the foundation of destination image construction (Jenkins, 1999). Typically destination image is measured using attribute scales and a structured semantic differential and/or Likert-type methodology (Calantone *et al.*, 1989; Crompton, 1977; Gartner & Hunt, 1987; Hunt, 1975; Phelps, 1986; Richardson & Crompton, 1988). While strategies such as these have proved useful in studying the variables that contribute to image, they may not be well suited to examining the highly complex, interrelated factors that ultimately seem to be at work in the formation of destination image. In the general leisure literature, a number of researchers have advanced similar arguments in advocating the need for greater diversity in research methods which enable an integrated, holistic approach to the study of leisure (Henderson, 1991; Mactavish & Schleien, 2000; Samdahl, 1999). Echtner and Ritchie (1993), in their study of destination image, illustrated one of the first examples of such an approach by employing a multidimensional model and a multi-method research design.

Building on calls for more pluralistic approaches to understanding leisure and tourism behaviour, visuals can complement word-based scales and focus group discussions to assist in capturing the holistic elements that are less evident from exclusively verbal designs. The technique of photo elicitation has been espoused as one way to improve the cultural meaningfulness of questions (Harper, 1994). Used as a guide to stimulate discussion, the researcher's interpretation of the pictures (e.g. pre-selected categorizations) is challenged by those asked to interpret them. More specifically, the research participants realize that the researcher does not necessarily share their interpretations (i.e. image evoked) and understanding of the pictures. Visual-based approaches enhance validity of the research and provide a means to explore complex phenomena, such as destination image formation, from different perspectives.

It is argued here that existing literature has not sufficiently connected the mental image construct of the tourist to the pictorial destination image representations supplied by destination marketers. The image models and methods used in this area of study have not embraced the potential use and contribution of visuals in understanding tourism destination image. The research presented in this chapter is a response to the call for expanding traditional approaches to the study of destination image (Jenkins, 1999). Beyond incorporating visuals into traditional survey- and scale-based measurement approaches, the examples herein use multiple pathways and an array of methodological approaches for studying destination image. The first study, a mixed method approach, uses visuals in all phases of the research. The second study employs an experimental design. The third study incorporates visuals in quantitative analysis. The fourth study includes visitor-employed photography as an image assessment technique. Table 3.1 presents an overview of the studies summarized below as "snapshots" in the study of destination image.

Study 1: Snapshots from Riding Mountain National Park

Purpose

In this study the purpose was to advance understanding of the pictorial element in destination image formation and the factors affecting interpretation of visuals used in image advertising. Specifically, the three main research questions were: (1) What are the salient dimensions underlying visual elements of advertisements portraying a destination? (2) How are promotional visuals interpreted as destination image? and (3)

Table 3.1 Summary features of image studies using visuals

Method(s)	Visual phase focus	Sample and data features
Study 1: Snapshots from Riding Mountain National Park		
Rating scales	Categorize attributes; select visual stimuli; for focus group viewing	Convenience sample n = 64; 119 slides rated on 5 attributes: natural scenery, wildlife, people, recreation, manmade landmarks
Focus groups	20 slides viewed to obtain multiple perspectives on how visuals are interpreted in image of Riding Mountain National Park; input for scales in image survey	4–90 minute focus groups: Park visitors Park staff Nonvisitors Chamber of Commerce
Self-administered survey at Park and Mall	Verification of visual classifications; visitor perspective on how pictures relate to Park image; used 20 5 × 7 photos in album with 34 bipolar scales beneath	Quota sample Mall n = 119 Park n = 138
Study 2: Snapshots from Older Adults		
Experimental design	Four destination visuals shown as slides to test memory for pictures as elaborative/attribute based	Random assignment: 90 younger and 90 older adults Encoding instruction: impressions/features/none
Study 3: Snapshots across Cultures		
Rating scales and similarity judgments	Used pairs of destination promotional photographs to elicit underlying image dimensions	36 photo pairs judged by subjects from Taiwan and the USA for MDS analyses of similarities matrix
Study 4: Snapshots from Motherwell National Historic Site Visitors		
Visitor-employed photography and diary	Visitor generated photos to capture image of site	132 Canadian respondents produced 1647 photographs, analysed based on visitors' diary descriptions

Which individual and/or pictorial attributes influence destination image interpretation?

Riding Mountain National Park (RMNP) was the destination setting for the study. It is located in southwestern Manitoba approximately 225 kilometers northwest of Winnipeg. The 2976-square-kilometre park was established in 1933 and boasts a rare ecological interface of three natural regions: plains, plateau, and lowlands (Environment Canada, 1988). Riding Mountain National Park is a year-round park that receives approximately 390,000 visitors per year; 85% of the summer visitors are Manitoba residents (Canadian Heritage, 1994).

Methods

The study design was multi-method and occurred in three phases: stimuli selection, focus groups, and an image survey. In the first phase, stimuli selection, it was imperative to ensure variation in picture content to enable testing of visual effects. Pictures were classified according to predominance of people, recreational activity, natural scenery, wildlife, and manmade landmarks. To ensure variation in picture content, an expanded version of a typology used by Olson *et al.* (1986) in a similar study of vacation advertisements was employed to identify the type of visuals for the study. Slides of RMNP (produced by Parks Canada), which generally fit these categories, were rated on the prominence of five attributes (i.e. natural scenery, people, recreational activity, manmade landmarks, and wildlife). A total of 119 slides were shown for 25 seconds each and rated by 65 university students. Analyses from the visual selection phase resulted in 20 pictures that were used in subsequent phases of the research.

In the second phase, focus groups were conducted as both a distinct data collection stage and as a complement to the stimuli selection and survey phases. Focus groups used free elicitation (Reilly, 1990) with destination visuals to facilitate description of the visuals beyond their general classifications, thereby helping to yield richer information on the relationship of visuals to image. A further purpose of the focus groups was to provide relevant physical and perceptual attributes to be used in constructing scales for the image survey in phase three. Focus groups were comprised as follows: highly familiar Park visitors, persons who had never visited RMNP, members of the chamber of commerce for the town site within the Park (Wasagaming), and Park staff.

The image survey was a culmination of the first two phases. The incorporation of photographs into a self-administered questionnaire provided data for examining the aspects of visuals being evaluated, the images that were being projected by destination visuals, and the individual characteristics and/or visual characteristics that related to the images. The questionnaire was completed by 257 respondents through a mall intercept procedure or through a similar procedure conducted at various sites throughout RMNP. The two locations were to engage respondents who had a range of familiarity with RMNP. Respondents viewed the set of 20 visual stimuli, which were arranged as 5 × 7 inch colour photographs in an album format with one picture per page, and rated them on 34 bipolar attribute scales derived from the focus group phase and relevant literature. For further methodological and analytical details see MacKay and Fesenmaier (1997).

Key findings

For question one (What are the salient dimensions underlying visual elements of advertisements portraying a destination?), the participants paid attention to three underlying visual elements of the pictures: attractiveness, uniqueness, and texture. For question two (How are promotional visuals interpreted as destination image?), four underlying dimensions of destination image emerged. These dimensions were activity (e.g. lots to do, exciting, friendly), familiarity (e.g. tame, safe, urban, familiar), holiday (e.g. affordable, vacation, family-oriented), and atmosphere (e.g. peaceful, pleasant, relaxing, beautiful). Results addressing question three (Which personal and/or pictorial attributes influence destination image interpretation?), are provided in two sections – first the pictorial influence and second the personal factors.

In terms of the relationship between the visual factors and the image dimensions, all three visual elements contributed to the activity and familiarity dimensions but in different ways. For activity, the unusual aspects of the Park and its natural environment contributed to activity (excitement, things to do). Obviously, the more unique a visual, the less familiarity was evoked by it. A texture – viewed as sharp, rough, or dark – elicited activity. The opposite was true for familiarity: pictures seen as smooth and light were familiar. The attractiveness feature (beauty/likability) was salient to both. Only uniqueness of the visual related to a holiday image – specifically, the more unique a destination the less holiday-like it was perceived. For atmosphere, texture that was sharp, hard, or rough suggested an atmosphere that was not peaceful or relaxing. A high degree of uniqueness also produced a nonrelaxing, unpleasant atmosphere. These findings suggest that portraying an optimal level of uniqueness in visuals is key to balancing its positive and negative effects.

As for individual inputs or characteristics, the focus group results shed more light on the effects of familiarity with the destination. Familiarity was found to influence image induced by pictures in a number of ways. Firstly, familiar respondents saw beyond the physical features contained in the pictures. For example, upon viewing a picture of the golf course club house building, some participants exclaimed "fabulous view", or "beautiful lake". They were remarking on the view from inside the club house dining room but not at what was actually contained in the picture. Other findings indicated that familiar visitors linked emotions to the visuals (affective image) and that they held a distinct and varied image of the Park (complex image). In contrast, individuals who were unfamiliar with the Park held a vague or singular image demonstrated by responding only to what was actually present in the picture.

Study 2: Snapshots from Older Adults

Purpose

As a growth market for the leisure travel industry, it is imperative to understand how older travelers respond to highly visual destination advertising. A primary purpose of this study was to explore potential age-related differences in the organization of information in memory as it relates to tourist destination visuals. For this study, the general research question was: When pictures of a tourist destination are viewed, does age and/or encoding instruction affect how this information is encoded and organized in memory? A series of hypotheses based on two age groups (younger and older adults) as well as two encoding instructions (at the features level and at an overall impressions level) and a control (no-goal) encoding instruction were tested in order to answer this research question.

Method

The study gave rise to a 2 (age group) × 3 (encoding instruction) design. Ninety younger adults (between 18 and 25 years of age) and 90 older adults (between 60 and 75 years of age) were recruited as participants for this experiment. Participants first completed a brief questionnaire, which measured demographics, health, and overall travel experience (local, national, and international). Then, participants were assigned randomly to one of the three encoding instructions before viewing the four destination pictures. One third of the subjects were instructed to pay attention to the features in the pictures, one third were instructed to pay attention to their impressions of the pictures, and the final third were instructed to focus exclusively on the pictures. The participants were blind to the purpose of the study but knew that they were going to be asked questions about the pictures that they were about to see. At this point the destinations were not identified. They were then shown each picture from destination marketing promotions in a slide format for 30 seconds. Once the participants had viewed the slides, they completed a 10-minute card-sorting task (Kogan *et al.*, 1980) designed to avoid short-term memory rehearsal of the slides. Following the sorting task, participants were asked to recall, in writing, what they had seen in each photograph. At the top of the response sheet, respondents were prompted as to the location depicted in the slide. There was no time limit on the recall task. Participants completed their task by rating their perceptions of the attractiveness of each picture, their familiarity with each tourist destination, and their travel history to these locations. For complete details on method and analyses see Smith and MacKay (2001).

Key findings

Results of hypotheses testing showed that, under each encoding instruction, there were no significant age differences in the number of features recalled for the pictures. In fact, there were neither main effects for age nor for encoding instructions. The second hypothesis predicted an interaction effect between age and encoding instruction for the number of elaborations in the memory protocols. Again, the results showed that there was no significant difference in the number of elaborations produced by each age group under the various encoding instructions. In addition, no main effects for age or encoding instructions were found.

Although familiarity was statistically controlled as a covariate, a series of analyses was performed to determine whether destination familiarity masked differences between the age groups. These follow-up analyses confirmed that for younger adults there was no significant difference in the number of features recalled based on level of familiarity. The same was true for number of elaborations recalled by high- and low-familiar younger subjects. For older adults, the results again revealed no significant differences for number of features or elaborations based on degree of familiarity. Even when controlling for education and familiarity with the tourist destinations, as well as checking for differences between sexes and direct experience with these destinations, no age-related differences were detected.

Study 3: Snapshots across Cultures

Purpose

The propensity of destinations to utilize standard features (e.g. mountains, beaches) or "hooks" to lure tourists to their destinations, and the variety of cultures represented by target market countries, make the issue of meaning plurality in tourist image perception paramount. The purpose of this study was to proffer multidimensional scaling (MDS) analyses as an effective technique for examining cross-cultural image perception based on visual stimuli. To frame the exercise, two null hypotheses were advanced that focussed on the number and meaning of image dimensions evoked by the visuals across two distinct cultural groups.

Method

This study employed a research design that is methodologically consistent with quantitatively-based cross-cultural research. The success of MDS in the fields of tourism and cross-cultural psychology stimulated this work to explore the utility of this technique in the area of cross-cultural tourism study using visuals. Graduate students from the United States and Taiwan completed a self-administered questionnaire that included paired comparisons of common promotional images used in destination marketing. Previous research by Hofstede (1991) that examined cultural distinctiveness between these countries has shown that Taiwanese people tend to be more collectivist with scores higher on indices of power distance and uncertainty avoidance. In contrast, people from the United States tend to be highly individualist, masculine, and less influenced by uncertainty avoidance (Hofstede, 1991). Destination images used in this study were of Alberta, Canada, but not identified to the subjects. Thirty-six paired comparison similarity ratings were made, by each subject, based on whatever characteristics they thought relevant. Since similarity ratings alone may result in hard-to-interpret dimensions, subjects also rated the images on seven seven-point semantic differential-type scales derived from previous research in landscape perception (Zube & Pitt, 1981; Zube *et al.*, 1982). Descriptions of the analysis procedures can be found in MacKay and Fesenmaier (2000).

Key findings

A three-dimensional solution for the Taiwanese group and a two-dimensional solution for the American group were proposed as the number of image dimensions underlying the visual comparisons. The three dimensions of image suggested by the Taiwanese subjects' assessments of the pictures (as interpreted by a Taiwanese colleague) were: spiritual nature, comfortable risk, and wilderness. Spiritual nature was dominated by nature, peacefulness, that which is known, and the presence of water in photographs. Comfortable risk was related to the scales of smooth, human-made, and unknown. Wilderness was characterized as rough and was associated with the presence of mountains in the pictures.

The two dimensions of image suggested by the Americans' assessments of the pictures were familiarity and spiritual nature. Familiarity referred to the simple, smooth, similar-to-home ends of the scales in contrast to complex, rough, and not similar to home. Spiritual nature was dominated by nature, that which is unknown, and the presence of water in pictures. These findings show that the two groups attended to different aspects of the visuals, which was demonstrated by differences in the number of underlying image dimensions found, and by the composition of those dimensions. Although one dimension, based on a landscape feature (i.e. water), was similarly interpreted, the meaning associated with it was comprised of opposite ends of the known–unknown scale.

Common to both cultures was the saliency of water (as a dimension) in the visuals. It was the most salient for the Taiwanese group, but emerged in the second dimension for the American group. The inclusion of attribute scales in this study facilitated a more comprehensive look, beyond the physical characteristics of visuals, at the psychological and perceptual properties associated with the pictures. For example, water for the Taiwanese subjects also related to nature, peacefulness, and that which is known. A relationship between water and spirituality (knowing and getting close to God) was suggested by a Taiwanese research associate. For the Americans, water was linked to the unknown and natural, which may also relate to a spirituality factor. Interestingly, this Western perception of spirituality included "unknown", whereas the Eastern perception included the "known". This provides a key example of how a similar dimension (e.g. water) can be differentially constituted and evaluated, and why interpretations should be made (or aided) by researchers of the culture under study.

Study 4: Snapshots from Motherwell National Historic Site

Purpose

The overarching goal of this study was to explore the influence of Canadians' cultural backgrounds on place image as conveyed through visual representations of heritage tourism sites, and to explore this in relation to domestic heritage tourism promotion and participation. The focus for the purposes of this chapter, however, is to examine the utility of visitor-employed photography as a method used to elicit destination (site) image. See Couldwell and MacKay (2001) for further discussion.

Method

The study occurred at Motherwell Homestead National Historic Site (NHS) in the province of Saskatchewan. Motherwell Homestead was designated as an NHS because it represents a typical prairie homestead of the early 20th century. It commemorates W.R. Motherwell's role in the development of agriculture on the prairies as well as agriculture settlement patterns. On 42 randomly selected sample days throughout the two-month study period, a cluster sample of all visitors was taken. A total of 136 photo image surveys, consisting of disposable cameras and diaries, were distributed. Visitors were requested to photograph scenes that contributed most to their image of the site. In addition, they were asked to record in their diaries the main subject of their picture and the main reason they took the picture. The diary also contained a brief series of visitor profile questions. Cameras were returned on-site at the exit. Participating visitors were sent a copy of their photographs as an incentive/reward. Photographs were content analyzed based on visitors' descriptions of pictorial content. Descriptive statistics were used to profile respondents, and reveal dominant image subject matter and rationales for selection. Subsequent analyses of diary data and follow-up focus group data will examine the relationship of cultural background to image assessment that are not covered here.

Key findings

Results from 132 photo diaries (97% response rate) suggested three major subject themes (i.e. infrastructure, animation, personalization), and two underlying rationales for the photographs taken (i.e. aesthetics and nostalgia). These themes emerged from seven main categories which, in order of photographic frequency, were: exterior buildings, interior house, demonstration of way of life, farm equipment, animals, grounds, and people (family/friends). The two most frequent photographic subjects featured building exteriors. The facade of the site was suggested as the most salient visual imagery. Reasons for selecting particular subjects that contribute most to site image range from the idiosyncratic "It reminded me of mom's summer kitchen, especially the smells" to the predictable and very frequent "because I like it". In general, themes that emerged regarding why respondents took their pictures pertained to aesthetics or nostalgia. Aesthetics related to the design or tangible elements of the subject matter. Nostalgia related to both representation of a way of life, thereby supporting the historical significance of the site as germane to its visual representation, as well as to a reminder of personal memories, linking historical and personal significance.

Discussion and Implications

Two key questions formed the basis of this chapter: (a) How can visuals be incorporated into the study of tourism destination images? and (b) What would this add to our base of knowledge in the area? The "snapshots" of four studies provided examples of a variety of methods that incorporated visuals into the design. The questions remains: What was learned from the addition of visuals that may not have been otherwise? The results of the four studies suggest that there was indeed value added by using visuals and insights into components of various image models that might not have emerged without them. Although the results presented are not comprehensive or conclusive, several issues are highlighted for consideration and future investigation.

Image theory presents destination image as multidimensional, which was confirmed by the studies reviewed in this chapter. The image dimensions generated from visuals in Study 1, Riding Mountain National Park (attractiveness, uniqueness, and texture) were important in conveying the underlying dimensional structure of tourist destination image: psychological–functional, common–unique, and attribute–holistic elements.

Tourist destination image formation was described as a composite of individual inputs and marketer inputs. Study 1 findings support that, for every case except the holiday image, dimensions of the visual were the most significant predictors of destination image. Respondents were indeed keying their image of the destination from the visual dimensions: attractiveness, uniqueness, and texture. Individual characteristic variables were much weaker predictors of destination image. Age and marital status did not influence the interpretation of visuals as destination image. Income and sex of respondents were significant only for certain types of images. Familiarity was the one consistently significant input variable across all image dimensions. Focus group results provided valuable insights into the nature of its influence. A more affective evaluation of visuals was linked to experience with the destination, whereas a more cognitive evaluation of visuals was linked to lack of experience with the destination.

High levels of experience with a natural setting were associated with symbolic attachments to the visuals. Participants with high levels of familiarity also projected beyond what was presented in the pictorial stimuli. This suggests that more familiar individuals hold destination images closer to the holistic, psychological, and unique ends of the Echtner and Ritchie (1993) image dimension continua. Conversely, individuals unfamiliar with a destination fall closer to the attribute, functional, and common ends of the image dimension continua. In the focus group phase, the nature of the task was more conceptual – identifying attributes of the visuals. In the survey phase, the nature of the task was more judgmental – rating visuals on the attributes. In this research it was the nature not the number of attributes produced by the focus groups which surfaced as a familiarity issue.

The lack of age-related differences in memory for pictures of tourist destinations found in Study 2 (snapshots from older adults) is interesting. The majority of previous memory research has focused on text and this literature was the basis for the hypotheses tested. Evidence in this literature points to age differences in the processing of text-based information. The findings of Study 2, with its use of visuals, however, may be due to the fact that younger and older adults may process pictures in a similar manner. Further, the recall of attractive pictures related to vacation destinations could be considered a relevant social-cognitive task in contrast to past research that used text passages that may not have been meaningful to people. Thus, this study may be a piece that can help to complete a picture of how the aging memory system functions in everyday life. For destination marketers using visual lure advertisements to build image and enhance destination awareness, the results of Study 2 suggest that the same visuals will be remembered equally well by older and younger target markets. This can aid in more efficient use of advertising dollars which account for a large proportion of destination marketing budgets.

It has been contended that different cultures have different aesthetic tastes. As revealed in Study 3 (snapshots across cultures), visual symbols such as water can have different meanings and image evaluations across cultures. Both attention to, and exclusion of, certain destination attributes can, therefore, play a part in how destination promotional visuals contribute to images evoked.

The photo image findings from Study 4 (Motherwell NHS) suggested three major subject themes: infrastructure, animation, and personalization; and two underlying rationales for the photographs taken: aesthetics and nostalgia. Conceptually, these findings support image multidimensionality, including the attribute–holistic, functional–psychological, and common–unique continua espoused by Echtner and Ritchie (1993). More practically, the visitor-employed photography (VEP) method provides highly visual records of what best captures the image of the site and should be compared to the pictures currently used in promotional efforts. It can be used to combine person-determined image with destination-determined image in a meaningful way. The challenges associated with VEP included logistics of site visitors managing more than one camera if they brought their own; control over respondent versus travel party image (whose idea was the picture?); cost of cameras, developing, and mailing; and the sheer volume of pictures/data generated. These drawbacks could be addressed by requesting fewer photographs, or by distributing fewer cameras based on response saturation (of photograph subject and reasons) as the photographs were developed and analysis occurred. An extremely high response rate (97%), unprompted visitor-generated themes and visuals, and enjoyment expressed by respondents are benefits to using the VEP method that support its utility for image assessment.

Using visuals in research leads to several practical implications indicated by the studies reviewed here. Firstly, visuals selected for promotional efforts by marketers who are familiar with the destination are likely to be interpreted differently by travel markets with no/low destination familiarity or experience, or of a different culture. Results also suggest that incorporating the emotional responses of individuals familiar with a destination may be effective in building image in unfamiliar markets. Visuals are important for tourism marketing (both lure and planning) aimed at older adults. Further, it is important to consider the interaction of picture characteristics (e.g. attractiveness, uniqueness, texture,) *and* target market characteristics (culture, familiarity, age) when using visuals to build destination image. Finally, Studies 1, 2, and 3 employed destination-generated visuals and a combination of researcher- and respondent-generated descriptors for these visuals. In contrast, Study 4 featured examples of visitor-generated visuals instead of those provided by a destination/marketer. Coupled with the visitor-produced visuals were descriptions that the visitors generated themselves. This is a departure from researcher- or destination marketer-generated images that may not capture images as perceived by visitors. The examples of destination image research offered in this chapter point to many possible future research avenues toward employing visuals in the design of destination image studies. More pressing, however, is the need to use insights gained from such expanded methodological inquiry to integrate visuals into conceptual models of destination image formation. This chapter is intended to provide a basis for undertaking that next challenge.

References

Assael, H. (1984) *Consumer Behavior and Marketing Action*. Boston, MA: Kent Publishing.

Baloglu, S. and McCleary, K. (1999) A model of destination image formation. *Annals of Tourism Research* 26 (4), 868–897.

Bernaldez, F. and Parra, F. (1979) Dimensions of landscape preferences from pairwise comparisons. In G. Elsner and T. Smardon (eds) *Our National Landscape Conference Proceedings* (pp. 256–262). California: USDA Forest Service.

Calantone, R., DiBenedetto, A., Hakam, A., and Bojanic, D. (1989) Multiple multi-national tourism positioning using correspondence analysis. *Journal of Travel Research* 28 (2), 25–32.

Canadian Heritage (1994) *Guiding Principles and Operational Policies*. Ottawa: Ministry of Supply and Services Canada.

Couldwell, C. and MacKay, K. (2001) Using visitor employed photography to investigate image of a heritage attraction. In *Travel and Tourism Research Association Conference Proceedings* (pp. 332–336). Fort Meyers, FL: TTRA.

Crompton, J. (1977) A systems model of the tourist's destination selection process with particular reference to the role of image and perceived constraints. Unpublished doctoral dissertation, Texas A&M University, College Station, Texas.

Crompton, J. (1979) Motivations for pleasure travel. *Annals of Tourism Research* 6 (4), 408–424.

Daniel, T. and Vining, J. (1983) Methodological issues in assessment of landscape quality. In I. Altman and J. Wohlwill (eds) *Behavior in Natural Environments*. New York: Plenum.

Dann, G. (1996) Tourists' images of a destination: An alternative analysis. *Journal of Travel and Tourism Marketing* 5, 41–55.

Dimanche, F. (1994) Cross-cultural tourism marketing research: An assessment and recommendations for future studies. *Journal of International Consumer Marketing* 6, 123–134.

Echtner, C. and Ritchie, B. (1993) The measurement of destination image: An empirical assessment. *Journal of Travel Research* 31 (4), 3–14.

Edell, J. and Staelin, R. (1983) The information processing of picture in print advertisements. *Journal of Consumer Research* 10, 45–61.

Environment Canada (1988) *Riding Mountain National Park*. Ottawa: Ministry of Supply and Services.

Fakeye, P. and Crompton, J. (1991) Image differences between prospective first-time and repeat visitors to the Lower Rio Grande Valley. *Journal of Travel Research* 30 (2), 10–16.

Gartner, W. (1993) Image formation process. *Journal of Travel and Tourism Marketing* 2, 191–216.

Gartner, W. and Hunt, J. (1987) An analysis of state image change over a twelve year period 1971–1983. *Journal of Travel Research* 16 (2), 15–19.

Gitelson, R. and Kerstetter, D. (1990) The relationship between socio-demographic variables, benefits sought and subsequent vacation behavior: A case study. *Journal of Travel Research* 28 (3), 24–29.

Gunn, C. (1972) *Vacationscape: Designing Tourist Environments*. Austin, TX: University of Texas.

Harper, D. (1994) On the authority of the image: Visual methods at the cross-roads. Rethinking critical theory and qualitative research. In N. Denzin and Y. Lincoln (eds) *Handbook of Qualitative Research* (pp. 403–412). Thousand Oaks, CA: Sage Publications Inc.

Henderson, K.A. (1991) *Dimensions of Choice: A Qualitative Approach to Recreation, Parks and Leisure Research*. State College, PA: Venture.

Hofstede, G. (1991) *Cultures and Organizations: Software of the Mind*. London: McGraw-Hill.

Hunt, J. (1975) Image as a factor in tourism development. *Journal of Travel Research* 13 (3),1–7.

Jenkins, O. (1999) Understanding and measuring tourist destination images. *International Journal of Tourism Research* 1 (1), 1–15.

Kaplan, S. and Kaplan, R. (1989) *The Experience of Nature: A Psychological Perspective*. Cambridge: Cambridge University Press.

Kaplan, R. and Talbot, J. (1988) Ethnicity and preference for natural settings: A review and recent findings. *Landscape and Urban Planning* 15, 107–117.

Kaplan, R., Kaplan, S., and Brown, T. (1989) Environmental preference: A comparison of four domains of predictors. *Environment and Behavior* 21, 509–530.

Kogan, D.A., Connor, K., Gross, A., and Fava, D. (1980) Understanding visual metaphor: Development and individual differences. *Monographs of the Society for Research in Child Development* 45 (Serial No. 183).

Laskey, H., Seaton, B., and Nicholls, J. (1994) Effects of strategy and pictures in travel agency advertising. *Journal of Travel Research* 32 (4), 13–19.

Lawson, R. (1991) Patterns of tourist expenditure and types of vacation across the family life cycle. *Journal of Travel Research* 29 (4), 12–18.

Lyons, E. (1983) Demographic correlates of landscape preference. *Environment and Behavior* 15, 487–511.

Macia, A. (1979) Visual perception of landscape: Sex and personality differences. In G. Elsner and T. Smardon (eds) *Our National Landscape* (pp. 279–285). California: USDA Forest Service.

MacKay, K. and Fesenmaier, D. (1997) Pictorial element of destination in image formation. *Annals of Tourism Research* 24 (3), 537–565.

MacKay, K. and Fesenmaier, D. (2000) An exploration of cross-cultural destination image assessment, *Journal of Travel Research* 38 (4), 417–423.

Mactavish, J. and Schleien, S. (2000) Beyond qualitative and quantitative data linking: An example from a mixed method study of family recreation. *Therapeutic Recreation Journal* 34, 154–163.

Manfredo, M., Bright, A., and Haas, G. (1992) Research in tourism advertising. In M. Manfredo (ed.) *Influencing Human Behavior* (pp. 327–368). Champaign, IL: Sagamore.

Mazanec, J. and Schweiger, G. (1981) Improved marketing efficiency through multiproduct brand names? An empirical investigation of image transfer. *European Research* 9, 32–44.

Olson, J., McAlexander, J., and Roberts, S. (1986) The impact of the visual content of advertisements upon the perceived vacation experience. In W. Joseph, L. Moutinho, and I. Vernon (eds) *Tourism Services Marketing: Advances in Theory and Practice* (Vol. 2) (pp. 260–269). AMA: Cleveland State University.

Phelps, A. (1986) Holiday destination image: The problem of assessment. An example developed in Menorca. *Tourism Management* (Sept.), 168–180.

Pitt, D. and Zube, E. (1987) Management of natural resources. In D. Stokols and I. Altman (eds) *Handbook of Environmental Psychology*. New York: Wiley.

Reilly, M. (1990) Free elicitation of descriptive adjectives for tourism image assessment. *Journal of Travel Research* 28 (4), 21–26.

Richardson, S. and Crompton, J. (1988) Cultural variations in perceptions of vacation attributes. *Tourism Management* 9 (2), 128–136.

Rosenfeld, J. (1986) Demographics on vacation. *American Demographics* (Jan.), 38–58.

Samdahl, D.M. (1999) Epistemological and methodological issues in leisure research. In E.L. Jackson and T.L. Burton (eds) *Leisure Studies: Prospects for the Twenty-first Century* (pp. 119–133). State College, PA: Venture.

Smith, M. and MacKay, K. (2001) The organization of information in memory for pictures of tourist destinations: Are there age-related differences? *Journal of Travel Research* 39 (3), 261–266.

Stewart, D., Hecker, S., and Graham, J. (1987) It's more than what you say: Assessing the influence of nonverbal communication in marketing. *Psychology and Marketing* 4, 303–322.

Telisman-Kosuta, N. (1989) Tourist destination image. In S. Witt and L. Moutinho (eds) *Tourism Marketing and Management Handbook* (pp. 555–561). London: Prentice Hall.

Ulrich, R. (1983) Aesthetic and affective response to natural environments. *Behavior and the Natural Environment* 6, 85–125.

Weaver, P. and McCleary, K. (1984) A market segmentation study to determine the appropriate ad/model format for travel advertising. *Journal of Travel Research* 22 (1), 12–16.

Yuan, S. and McDonald, C. (1990) Motivational determinants of international pleasure time. *Journal of Travel Research* 29 (1), 42–44.

Zube, E. and Pitt, D. (1981) Cross-cultural perceptions of scenic and heritage landscapes. *Landscape Planning* 8, 69–87.

Zube, E., Sell, J., and Taylor, J. (1982) Landscape perception: Research, application and theory. *Landscape Planning* 9, 1–33.

Chapter 4

Entrepreneurial Leadership in Times of Uncertainty: Implications for Tourism Research and Education

ROSLYN RUSSELL AND PETER MURPHY

Introduction

The turn of the new century has brought changes that have been unpredictable and irreversible for many business sectors. Even prior to the disastrous events of September 11, the characteristics of the new economy were such that different perspectives were urgently being sought to help us manage the implications of uncertainty. The dramatic increase in complexity brought about by globalization, unprecedented technological advances, discontinuous change and unpredictability calls for different management and educational tools than were required in the past.

The terrorist attacks on the USA and indeed the fear of terrorism in places once assumed to be "terrorist immune" have resulted in an overall global unrest that has brought a harsh reminder of the volatile nature of tourism and its associated industries. The impacts on travel were immediate. *The Economist* (2002: 5) reports that "immediately after September 11th, hotels around the world looked as if they had been evacuated", with occupancy rates in New York declining by 20 points and in London by 15 points. This decline was despite a reduction in the average New York room rate of 27% and a similar reduction in London. "After the terrorist attacks almost nobody wanted to fly any more, which meant the airline industry faced the worst crisis in its history" (*The Economist*, 2002: 5). As a result airlines heavily dependent on North Atlantic routes, such as British Airways and Virgin Atlantic, experienced traffic declines of over 35%, and national airlines like Swissair and Sabena collapsed into bankruptcy, as did Australia's Ansett Airlines.

Tourism bodies and governments have since undertaken emergency tactical actions in an attempt to mitigate the negative effects. All activities, especially tourism, are now operating under exigencies that cannot be managed by consulting the rulebooks of the past. Indeed, the only condition we can be certain of is that of uncertainty. When this chapter was first written (2001) its authors claimed it was time to formally recognize this environment of uncertainty in tourism research and in educational programmes. Now with the hindsight of the September 11 experience it is essential.

The most vital ingredient needed in such uncertain times is effective leadership. However, the nature of the environment we are now operating in requires leadership qualities that are different from those that worked best under the more stable and predictable conditions of the past. Characteristics such as adaptability, being able to act with certainty in the face of uncertainty, risk-taking and creativity are the qualities needed by leaders – the qualities that have traditionally been used to identify entrepreneurs. In the past entrepreneurial-type people were considered unsuitable for leadership positions in the conservative business world, but now they are highly sought after because they are best suited for the turbulent conditions of today (Maccoby, 2001). Indeed the new global economy is often referred to as an "entrepreneurial economy" (Zahra, 1999; Morrison *et al.*, 1999) where "entrepreneurial leadership will take center stage" (Zahra, 1999). Prior studies (Hambrick *et al.*, 1993; Geletkanycz & Black, 2001) have indicated that the leaders who are most effective in today's environment are those who have experienced a variety of industry backgrounds. Hence, due to the multi-disciplined nature of tourism, the leaders in this sector may have a distinct advantage. Their acquired instincts for survival in an enterprise environment more turbulent than most may have equipped them well with superior adaptive creativity.

However, it is not enough to leave to chance the emergence of effective leaders in the tourism industry. We, as researchers and educators, need to ensure that our efforts in research and teaching efforts are addressing these changing needs. But an ad hoc, scattergun approach that overlooks the legacy of accumulated wisdom cannot substitute for systematic, purposeful inventiveness. Consequently, this chapter will present a discussion on the issues surrounding the changes we are experiencing and suggest some action signposts to future research and teaching.

The history of tourism has provided some ideal examples of leaders from whom we can extract cogent lessons applicable to the dynamic environment experienced today. Leaders with global significance, such as Thomas Cook and Walt Disney, point the way to developing tourism in our uncertain environment, as do some lesser known regional leaders like Tom O'Toole and Paul Miller, who are discussed in more detail later in the chapter. These business leaders have demonstrated entrepreneurial qualities, such as the exploitation of change, creativity and risk-taking, that have made their businesses benchmarks for success in a changing and competitive business environment. Learning from these examples can provide insights into entrepreneurial processes that need to be brought to the forefront of research and teaching in the classroom.

Implications for Research: The Era of Uncertainty

"Uncertainty – in the economy, society, politics – has become so great as to render futile, if not counterproductive, the kind of planning most companies still practice: forecasting based on probabilities" (Drucker, 1995: 39). In order for appropriate and relevant planning to be carried out in tourism, research and education systems have to recognize the true nature of tourism systems (Faulkner, 2000). This may mean giving up prior belief systems that have underpinned much of the research to date – systems that have presumed stability and averages (Russell & Faulkner, 1999). Tourism systems are not closed, are seldom stable (McKercher, 1999) and are certainly not immune to either exogenous or endogenous impacts. One outcome of the September 11 disaster has meant that no one can now ignore the existence and the far-reaching impacts of unpredictable, exogenous triggers on the global, national and regional tourism systems. While most media coverage of this event and others like it, such as the UK's foot-and-mouth outbreak in 2001 (see Butler & Airey, Chapter 10, this volume), has focused on the negative factors and "losers", there has been evidence that, out of this turbulence, some tourism "winners" have emerged. One winner of the September 11 experience in Australia was domestic tourism, as more Australians stayed home or went on regional vacations within the country.

The uncertainty we are experiencing will be a constant in the future. This is not to say that we should necessarily expect ongoing events of the scale of the 2001 US terrorist attacks. But the increasing speed of change generally will naturally bring with it much uncertainty to all industry sectors. Endemic nervousness is lingering and compounding. However, what will hopefully change is how we deal with it. Once uncertainty is integrated into research as being a major variable, techniques can be adapted accordingly. So too with the content and methods used in teaching. There is an obligation to equip students, and future tourism leaders, with attitudes and learning patterns that can utilize uncertainty to create opportunities. Langer has proposed two ways of dealing with change – either in a "mindful" manner that is to actively seek it, create new perspectives and develop new management approaches; or in a "mindless" way with the "application of yesterday's business solutions to today's problems" (Langer, 1989: 152). This chapter is advocating a "mindful" approach towards uncertainty and change.

With an acceptance of uncertainty into the researcher's rubric, we should formally recognize uncertainty as a distinct era in the tourism discipline and add another platform to Jafari's (1990) four research platforms that have recognized similar changes of emphasis in past stages of the tourism discipline's development. Jafari identifies four platforms to which we can add a fifth, uncertainty:

- Advocacy: emphasizes the positive economic and other benefits associated with tourism development.
- Cautionary: challenges overly enthusiastic stances of the advocacy platform by highlighting the evidence.
- Adaptancy: focuses on alternative forms of tourism that were expected to avoid the principal problems of mass tourism.
- Knowledge-based: a multi-disciplinary approach, positioning itself on scientific foundations.
- Uncertainty: a period when the old rules and expectations no longer apply automatically and the opportunities for entrepreneurial leadership become significant.

To develop the fifth platform will require leadership, from within both academia and industry.

Leadership

Leadership studies in the management discipline have, over time, surged and waned in popularity (Meindl, 1990). Due to the dramatic environmental changes of this new era, focus has once again turned to the area of leadership as we investigate who will have "what it takes" to successfully handle the challenges and opportunities presented. While it is not appropriate to provide a chronological development of leadership theories in this chapter, a brief overview of the relevant approaches is provided in order to set the scene for later observations.

Like all research arenas, leadership has been approached from different perspectives, one of the earliest being leadership traits. This perspective suggested that leaders have a certain appearance and specific traits that can be distinguished from ordinary people. It is a useful strategy only if qualified by cautious reservations. More recent research has shown it is not that easy to categorize leaders, and that there is a wide variety of leadership types. However, Ghiselli (1971) identified six traits that appear to be common in effective leadership:

- Supervisory ability.
- Need for occupational achievement.
- Intelligence.
- Decisiveness.
- Self-assurance.
- Initiative.

More recent leadership trait research has suggested that a high degree of "emotional intelligence" is the most significant ingredient of successful leadership (Goleman, 1998: 94) with emotional intelligence consisting of self-awareness, self-regulation, motivation, empathy and social skills.

Leadership has also been investigated as a function of interaction between different situations and with different people. Hersey and Blanchard (1974) proposed a situational theory of leadership which recognized that different styles of leadership are required at different times depending on the circumstances.

In all the perspectives of leadership, though, most would argue that the major responsibility of a leader is to make key strategic decisions (Finkelstein & Hambrick, 1996). A leader is expected to "monitor external developments and set a strategic course for the firm" (Geletkanycz & Black, 2001). If there is a dynamic, unpredictable external environment, then a leader needs to not only accurately read the changes, but to be suitably flexible, creative and adaptable in order to make decisions which will exploit those changes to the advantage of the organization.

Recognizing the increasing pace of change being experienced now and most likely in the future, recent leadership studies are investigating the type of characteristics that are best suited to dealing with the implications of major technological, economic and social changes (Geletkanycz & Black, 2001; Hambrick *et al.*, 1993). A number of studies have found that one of the inhibiting factors for decision makers operating in a dynamic environment is a strong commitment to the status quo (CSQ) (Hambrick *et al.*, 1993). Early theoretical arguments by March and Simon (1958) argued that our perspectives are "bounded" by our prior experiences and knowledge, and hence it is quite logical that the way we approach decision-making is based on what has worked for us in the past. Hambrick *et al.*'s (1993) and Geletkanycz and Black's (2001) studies suggested that those who have a high CSQ measure are less likely to be ready for change – they will like things to remain the same and will most likely continue using the same strategies that have worked in the past. Using Langer's (1989) description, they will operate in a "mindless" fashion – using yesterday's strategies to fix today's problems.

Interestingly, these same studies investigating CSQ have also found a positive correlation with the effects on a specific industry and also tenure within an organization. Hambrick *et al.* (1993) found that lengthy experience within traditional disciplines, such as finance, marketing, law and general management, built a greater commitment to the status quo and hence could decrease a leader's effectiveness in changing environmental conditions. Conversely, functional diversity has been shown to have a negative correlation with CSQ. So leaders who have experienced a variety of industry sectors are considered to be better equipped for change than those who have not.

Regardless of the approach taken by leaders, they will be forced to consider changes as the world and its political-economic systems change. Concepcion and Lomba (2000) have developed an interesting grid to illustrate how change in the global environment has occurred over time at different levels. They match the different world eras with the various characteristics, i.e. change, intelligence, science, thinking, information and worldviews, that dominated the stages of history. Table 4.1 shows

Table 4.1 Levels and characteristics of dynamic change

Level	1 Barbarian to Hellenic culture	2 Renaissance to the Industrial Revolution	3 Scientific management revolution	4 Information revolution
Change	Static	Volatile	Normal	Dynamic
Intelligence	Analytic	Practical	Social	Creative
Science	Mathematics	Chemistry	Physics	Biology
Thinking	Ancient era	Industrial Revolution	Scientific management	Information era
Information	Writing	Editing	Publishing	Computing
World	Rational	Pragmatic	Humanism	Holistic

Source: Concepcion and Lomba, 2000

their depiction of the levels and characteristics of dynamic change. The increasing rate of change is noted with these time periods being proportioned at a ratio of 100:30:10:1 (Concepcion & Lomba, 2000).

In drawing attention to Stage 4, we notice the recognition of an era that is characterized by dynamic change, creative intelligence, biotechnology advances and an holistic worldview. If change is occurring at a multi-dimensional level then the implication is that leaders who recognize these changes and readily adapt to the different needs and conditions will fare better than those who are "stuck" in Level 3 when "order, predictability, conformity and homogeneity were valued" (Coulson-Thomas, 1999: 28). This is congruent with Hambrick *et al.*'s (1993) findings, which suggested those leaders who have experienced lengthy periods of time in traditional sectors (which emerged during Level 3) do not like change.

While those leaders who are entrenched in traditional sectors could be potentially disadvantaged, it is suggested that leaders within relatively newer industry sectors such as tourism may have less of a propensity for CSQ and hence a distinct advantage in the new economy. Because tourism research has emerged from a variety of disciplines, those working within it are found to have diverse but people-related backgrounds, and thus-geographers, economists, psychologists, anthropologists and sociologists are often leaders in the field of tourism research. However, over the past decade or so more people with formal training and degrees in tourism are beginning to emerge.

Entrepreneurial Leadership

Entrepreneurial leadership is leadership with a propensity to exploit change and utilize creativity and includes risk-making and risk-taking. It is more than just managing, implementing, allocating and goal-setting (Larson, 1999) with mechanical rigidity. Entrepreneurial leaders create and combine resources so the "whole is greater than the sum of its parts". The entrepreneurial leader is "the aggressive catalyst for change in the world of business. He or she is an independent thinker who dares to be different in a background of common events" (Kuratko & Hodgetts, 1998: 30). These leaders will "stimulate diversity and reward innovation" (Coulson-Thomas, 1999: 28).

Concepcion and Lomba (2000) have also found that the more successful leaders in this current era are entrepreneurial leaders. The qualities they found entrepreneurial-type leaders to have are logical or analytical and spatial or creative characteristics, as well as a strong results and risk orientation. Below is a list of typical qualities attributed to entrepreneurs.

This particular set is taken from the works of Schumpeter (1934), McClelland (1961), Baty (1990) and Chell *et al.* (1991). While many of these qualities are shared by traditional leaders and entrepreneurs alike, the qualities of creativity, risk-taking and versatility are now recognized as crucial entrepreneurial leadership ingredients:

- Alertness to opportunities.
- Inner locus of control.
- Creativity.
- Innovatory tendency.
- Self-motivation.
- Versatility.
- Decisiveness.
- Risk-taking propensity.
- Self-confidence.
- Flair and vision.
- Self-realization through action.
- Independent nature.
- Leadership aspirations.

Of particular relevance to the issue of tourism research is the area of risk-taking. Research is needed to understand the more volatile mix of today's political-economic situation and its effect on tourism, and to prepare for future market directions and priorities.

As President John F. Kennedy once stated about the USA's commitment to reach the moon:

> while we cannot guarantee that we shall one day be first, we can guarantee that any failure to make this effort will make us last. We face an additional risk by making it in full view of the world, but ... this very risk enhances our stature when we are successful. (Cited in Taffinder, 1995: 39)

This is the essence of risk. Entrepreneurial leaders not only take risks but they make risks. Risk-making is the creation of opportunity and risk-taking converts the opportunity into results (Taffinder, 1995). Taffinder also makes the distinction between managers and leaders: "managers control risk; leaders take risks" (p. 40). Opportunities are risks and entrepreneurial leaders do not sit back and wait for opportunities/risks to fall into their laps – they set about creating risk in order to find opportunity. The leader who does his best to ensure a safe and secure path will find it will only ever lead at best to mediocrity and at worst to failure. However, visionaries must dream rationally rather than with suicidal capriciousness.

The Need for Unpredictability

How do entrepreneurial leaders find risks or opportunity? Taffinder (1995) claims they do it by utilizing change and unpredictability. If there isn't enough change and unpredictability naturally present, they will create it artificially, knowing it is from this that true entrepreneurial spirit can flourish. Taffinder (1995) notes that, throughout history, it is in times of turbulence, such as war, that most technological progress was made. "But the intellectual force behind the industrial revolution was not just about logic, structure and predictability. Entrepreneurial spirit, inventiveness, risks – the unpredictable – were the true hallmarks of technological and industrial advance" (p. 77). In utilizing unpredictability, the leader must be prepared to step outside the pattern and go against the norm. Some leaders think of it as "adventure". Taffinder quotes one prominent leader as saying "If there aren't any threats or impending disasters – I create them" (Hans Boom, in Taffinder, 1995: 79). "Adventure" provides a trigger for change. Entrepreneurial leaders "institutionalize change" to ensure a ripe environment for creativity and innovation.

This is not to say that wild uncontrolled chaos is the desired outcome. Successful leaders have found that the most crucial time for great things to happen is at the point where change is imminent – the brink. Chaos theory describes this point as being at the "edge of chaos" (Gleick, 1987), where a system is brought to a tenuous state leaving it vulnerable for triggers which can cause the system to change direction or collapse. This "edge of chaos" state brings enough uncertainty to the environment that enables leaders to bring about change.

Incidentally but not coincidentally, it is the very same conditions that have been found to be the most significant in the evolution of tourist destinations. In the lifecycle of a tourist destination (Butler, 1980), it is the transition stages in the lifecycle, e.g. between exploration and involvement; involvement and development; and stagnation and rejuvenation/decline, that have been found to be the most fertile for entrepreneurial activity (Russell & Faulkner, 1999). These stages possess "edge of chaos" characteristics, being just turbulent enough to create opportunity and encourage creative activity but not wildly uncontrollable. The intended aim is to have a system that is stable yet alive, or in "dynamic equilibrium", which allows it to be flexible and therefore able to utilize unpredictability to bring about change for the purpose of inspiring innovation. Finding the right mix of uncertainty and stability is the difficulty.

In understanding the vital role of risk and unpredictability in successful leadership for today's environment, we can look at recent events that have caused such uncertainty for the tourism sector (and others) and, instead of feeling a sense of doom, we can say that the time is perfect for creating enormous opportunity for innovation and progress. In a sense, the tourism industry is always primed to absorbing "shocks", as it has experienced fast and turbulent growth during its history and has always been vulnerable to external triggers, which gives it an inbuilt state of "readiness" for change. For example, with the first major oil crisis of the 1970s the airline industry responded by introducing fuel-saving measures as elementary as using push-back togs rather than reverse thrust, and aircraft manufacturers introduced more fuel-efficient engines and airframes requiring fewer engines. More recently the budget airlines (Southwest Airlines, EasyJet and Ryan Air) have been able to profit from strategies like point-to-point service, using cheaper second-tier airports and offering no-frills service, while the larger national carriers have been caught in the expensive and bureaucratic structure of the hub and spoke system. Significantly, tourism opportunities are already being recognized in the surge of the inquisitiveness concerning New York. In another example, Afghanistan has become a tourist destination in the area of "dark tourism" (see Smith, Chapter 13, this volume).

Entrepreneurial Leadership in Tourism

While many industries are now discovering the necessity of encouraging entrepreneurial activity, entrepreneurship has always been present in the development of tourism. From the early beginnings of mass tourism there have been individuals like Thomas Cook and Walt Disney who, with their creativity and passion, exploited the technological changes going on around them to shape the nature of their tourism enterprises. Their innovations at crucial stages in tourism's history – the industrial revolution and the "consumer revolution" – have left a global legacy. Entrepreneurial initiative can be found in all tourism destinations and at a variety of scales, and in many cases it has been the driving force behind a destination's success (Russell & Faulkner, 1999).

The nature of environmental conditions that impact on tourism and its associated industries ensures a predominance of entrepreneurial activity – a case of survival of the fittest. The volatility of the market and the multi-sector nature of tourism are natural attractors to those with entrepreneurial tendencies. In addition, the tourist market is continually being sliced into smaller niches, all requiring new and innovative experiences (Poon, 1993) that generally are best provided by smaller operators who are able to react more quickly to changing market needs. Note with what haste such petty appendages to tourism, such as T-shirt and small flag printing, responded to September 11.

With much tourism research to date focusing mostly on the demand side, including the characteristics and motivations of visitors, there has been an imbalance in the attention given to the supply side of the industry (Smith, 1995). With the supply side of tourism being comprised mainly of small business ventures (Edgell, 1993; Shaw & Williams, 1990), this is where much of the leadership and direction within the tourism industry inevitably originates. However, most attention has focused on the structure rather than on the process, and the research has predominantly explored small business trends and characteristics rather than the entrepreneurial process and behaviour (Shaw & Williams, 1990).

To illustrate the significance of entrepreneurial leadership in the development of tourism, two historical examples will be discussed as well as two regional examples from different countries to provide some points of comparison.

Global Entrepreneurs

Two examples of entrepreneurial leaders who have had a global impact on tourism are Thomas Cook and Walt Disney. Thomas Cook saw opportunity in the new technological advances of the 19th century to bring travel to the masses. His extraordinary vision and ability to combine concepts to create something new illustrates the skills and attitude we need to magnify in research and education. Walt Disney, whose achievements in the movie industry are legendary, successfully crossed over into the tourism industry in the post-war consumer years, and his company is now involved with four of the world's most successful global theme parks.

Thomas Cook

Thomas Cook, often heralded as the "Father of mass tourism" has undoubtedly been the most significant global entrepreneur in the tourism industry. While most introductory texts note his importance and contribution to modern tourism, few focus on his entrepreneurial characteristics as being a major factor in his achievements. The case of Cook remains a powerful model of entrepreneurial leadership demonstrating the rewards of exploiting change, the use of creativity and a unique combination of resources which truly produced a "whole being greater than the sum of its parts". His achievements brought economic vitality to many industry sectors and set new social and cultural standards. In terms of scale, Cook's influence had global implications.

In bringing travel to the masses, Cook paved the way for those other than the rich to see and learn from the world. Cook had a vision of tourism being a "means of emancipation for large numbers of people whose work was drudgery" (Brendon, 1991: 13). Like entrepreneurs before and after him, Cook utilized changes in technology and society to create an opportunity. He saw the steam engine as a tool that enabled him to achieve a dream. The steam locomotive engine wasn't invented for the purpose of tourism, which was probably the furthest thing from the minds of Watts and Stephenson. However, as with most entrepreneurs, Cook saw its potential and extended its use and benefits to a wider market. He wasn't the inventor of the new technology and he wasn't the first to offer an organized tour, but what he did do was spot an opportunity to uniquely combine a number of existing concepts to create something new.

The huge success of his initial excursions only whetted his appetite to further provide what the public needed. He continually looked for ways of overcoming obstacles to travel, simplifying it for the tourist. He found ways of overcoming the currency barriers by introducing the precursor to the traveller's cheque; he introduced what was known as a "circular ticket", which combined a range of tickets for different modes of transport that covered a specific itinerary but different routes for one price. This provided independence and freedom to travellers without the fuss. He also made it not only possible but enjoyable for women to travel safely on their own for the first time (Withey, 1997).

A symbiotic relationship evolved between Thomas Cook and tourism. His concept gave birth to mass tourism by "simplifying, popularizing and cheapening travel" (Brendon, 1991: 17). Upon Cook's death, tributes to him mirrored definitions of current-day entrepreneurship:

> The late Mr Thomas Cook . . . was a typical middle-class nineteenth-century Englishman. Starting from very small beginnings, he had the good luck and the insight to discover a new want, and to provide for it. He saw that the great new invention of the railway might be made, by the help of a new organization, to provide large numbers of people with pleasanter, cheaper, and more varied holidays than they had ever been able to enjoy before. (in Pudney, 1953: 19)

Walt Disney

Walt Disney is another entrepreneurial pioneer who exploited changing technology and social expectations to leave an indelible print on modern entertainment through his creative genius as manifested in his films, cartoon characters, theme parks, merchandise, organizational management and resort planning. The empire he created still lives and operates and is just as pervasive in western culture, if not more so, since his death. As with all entrepreneurs, it was Disney's exceptional ability to conceptualize in a magical way that made him different. Where most people saw a rodent, he saw a talking mouse with red shorts and yellow shoes called Mickey. Elephants could fly, and children should always be happy. "From the beginning, it was Walt, with his intuitive knack for storytelling, who created the magic" (Grover, 1991: 7). Bryman classes Disney as a "member of a fairly select band of individuals who have not simply built organizations, but who inculcate high levels of enthusiasm in themselves and in their goals among those who work for them" (1995: 14).

Disney set new standards in tourist attractions. Disneyland and Walt Disney World were outstanding examples of Disney's ability to conceptualize. Like Thomas Cook before him, he was gifted in providing a unique combination or "package" of concepts to meet the needs of the tourists, before they even knew they needed them. Their entrepreneurial visions fed the relentless drive to actualize them with an enthusiasm that swept others along with them. The term "integrated values" is supposed to be a modern marketing technique, although people like Disney and Cook were doing this decades, and in Cook's case, a century before the term was even invented.

So, while the achievements of those like Cook and Disney have been a major influence on tourism as we now know it, it is surprising how little significance has been placed on the investigation of their entrepreneurial qualities in research efforts. Equally lacking is the encouragement and development of these traits in the academic curriculum.

Disney exhibited the ability to break down sectoral boundaries, extending his movie magic into a new arena and in the process transforming funfairs into theme parks. Such innovation presented typical entrepreneurial barriers even to a successful businessman. Key among these was the funding of the first theme park, Disneyland. Disney had great difficulty raising the cash for his dream and the project was saved by a business deal with the new ABC television network. It is ironic that some 40 years later the Disney Corporation bought its "banker" and now includes the ABC television network in its entertainment stable.

Regional Entrepreneurs

Paul Miller: Victoria Harbour Ferry Company (Canada)

The Victoria Harbour Ferry Company operates a small waterbus system with a tourism rather than a transport emphasis in and around the harbours of Victoria, British Columbia, Canada. It was started by Paul Miller in 1990 and by 1997 consisted of eight small boats and a staff of 32, who handled over 100,000 passengers a year. In the years of its existence, Miller has won several plaudits, including the GEM (Going that Extra Mile) award from the Victoria hospitality society and the presidency of Tourism Victoria (the regional tourism association) in 1999.

To guide his company's strategic management and make it stand out in a crowded marketplace, Miller decided to create a strong and definite mission statement. When he started the ferry business in 1990 his original mission statement was "To become the best loved business in town". This meant it had to be noticed and appreciated, not just by its customers but also by the host community. To achieve this goal, the Victoria Harbour Ferry has taken a very proactive role in its community relations, but nothing compares with the return received from one generous gesture. At one of the Tourism Victoria meetings discussing events and festivals, Miller volunteered to have his fleet of (then five) boats open the spring boating festival with a water ballet. This meant he had to choreograph the performance and provide loudspeaker music to the inner harbour, where the ballet was to be performed, fifteen minutes before the start of his regular schedule. It was such a success it has been repeated on a regular basis since that festival and brought the company much free publicity and financial reward.

The public relations gesture of the water ballet is only one of several innovations that Miller has incorporated into his company. Another is to take advantage of tourism's seasonality factor by using the closed season for repair and maintenance, following the dictum of Covey's (1989) time management matrix. This matrix notes that business managers are particularly pressured by whether an issue is important or urgent, and advises them to place as much of their essential decision-making into the "important, but non-urgent" category. Consequently, Paul Miller's fleet is always in top condition and at times able to come to the rescue of other boaters who have not been so thorough in their preparation and maintenance. The company also uses the actual seasonal conditions to determine the opening and closing of the business's season. Rather than being determined by a fixed calendar date, Miller has adopted a "soft" opening and closing strategy that is guided by local weather conditions – an essential feature for a business that transports people across water that can be both choppy and cold at either end of the summer season.

Associated with the seasonality factor has been Miller's approach to hiring staff. Given his need for seasonal employees, but ones with significant hard skills (master's ticket) and soft skills (interacting with tourists), he has had to seek assistance from a limited labour pool. What he has done is to approach and attract retiring professionals, who would like a pleasant summer occupation that would enable them to retire to a warm location during Canada's winter months. Consequently, among his boat "skippers" are retired naval officers and airline pilots, who "summer" in Victoria and "winter" in Arizona or California. In addition, this form of recruitment has brought him one of the highest staff retention rates in the local industry, which in turn assures that his business can offer a quality experience.

Tom O'Toole: Beechworth Bakery (Australia)

Successful examples of tourism entrepreneurship can occur in the most unlikely places and in activities not generally considered as core tourism businesses, providing tourism research with some interesting lessons in the reality of the tourism market. An example of such a situation has occurred with the Beechworth Bakery, which in a small community of 3000 in the northeast countryside of Victoria, Australia, has developed a business with an annual revenue of approximately A\$4 million (O'Toole with Tarling, 2000). Obviously, in this situation many of its customers have to be tourists and observation soon makes it clear that this bakery has become a principal attraction of this heritage tourism town, with tourists descending on it from dawn to dusk. As a consequence there are several tourism lessons to learn from the success of this small business, both in terms of research and practice.

In terms of research we have been guided by the work of Smith (1995) and others in the development of a supply-side taxonomy, which has frequently formed the basis of industry definitions and satellite account analysis. In such studies the traditional place for service businesses, such as local bakeries, in the tourism product lexicon has been a classification of peripheral or marginal activities, with 25% or less of their business being attributed to tourism. However, in Australia small town bakeries often provide seating capacity that converts them into meeting places and reliable eating shops for the passing traveller. Thus, while few can emulate the tourism business volumes of the Beechworth bakery, they should not be automatically confined to the periphery.

The principal reason for the Beechworth Bakery's success has been the actions of its owner-operator, Tom O'Toole, and his strategies of small business management that have embraced tourism as a key element of his business prosperity. From his successful strategies we can detect business practices that further blur the distinction between locals and tourists in the real marketplace. These strategies are among those revealed in his book *Breadwinner: A Fresh Approach to Rising to the Top* (O'Toole with Tarling, 2000), where he outlines his philosophy and approach to business, and have been selected by the authors as those being most relevant to a tourism analysis. O'Toole outlines 31 principles of entrepreneurship in his book, under the heading "The Gospel of Thomas" (O'Toole with Tarling, 2000: 181–209), of which we will discuss five.

Not surprisingly the first lesson from Tom O'Toole's gospel is to *"Get out of your comfort zone! Take a risk – smile! Shock people!"* In this he supports many of the analysts of entrepreneurship who maintain that this form of business is synonymous with innovation and leadership (Drucker, 1985), e.g. trying something new and different so your business stands out from the crowd. An innovative thought for a baker is to include tourists in his strategic planning. His philosophy is "If I can get them to Beechworth I've got a chance of getting a dollar out of their pockets – but first I've got to get them to Beechworth" (O'Toole with Tarling, 2000). To do this he has made his bakery as welcoming as possible, and has promoted the town and its heritage attributes wherever he can.

Linked to O'Toole's promotional efforts is his *commitment to the community*, which goes beyond the usual support of community groups and festivals, to help those in need:

> We also freeze our own food down at the end of the night – which is a pain in the bum because we have to carry the freezer space – and we give it to disadvantaged groups, single mums, needy people, the prison, and the prisoners' families on special occasions like Father's Day. The prisoners look after us; we've never been broken into yet. When they get out of prison, they come down and cash their cheque at the Bakery. (O'Toole with Tarling, 2000: 195)

Like all successful businesses O'Toole advocates *listening to the customer*, and he encourages customers to let him know what they think of his business and product. But, unlike many other businesses, he doesn't try to please all customers. He feels you can waste so much energy trying to please some customers that it is not worth the effort, and that he is "better off looking after the 98% of the people who are happy coming into my business" (p. 195).

Finally, O'Toole feels that, if a person chooses to run their own business, especially in the tourism arena, then they should *"choose to be happy"*. Becoming an entrepreneur should be a matter of choice, and if the selected business is to contribute to tourist experiences then a happy and enthusiastic workplace will go a long way towards achieving visitor satisfaction. One can certainly see this happiness radiating from the pages of Tom O'Toole's book and in the service received at his bakery.

From this short examination of the Beechworth Bakery it can be seen that suggested guidelines for entrepreneurship and tourism have much in common. There has been a reaffirmation of certain "good business" practices like "listening to the customer" along with the advice of experience that "you cannot please them all, so don't try". In terms of entrepreneurial advice there is the reaffirmation of the need to be innovative, but along with that is the serious advice that it should be fun – for the entrepreneur and the customer. Perhaps the most relevant advice to tourism businesses is that they should look and act beyond the confines of their own business premises. Beechworth Bakery is what it is today because of O'Toole's support of Beechworth as a tourist destination and a caring community. It is this external vision wrapped up in a sense of happiness that can make a business succeed.

Implications for Education

One of the greatest challenges in the new millennium is how to teach entrepreneurship and leadership to university students. Some consider that these qualities are not teachable but are innate. Others feel it necessary to restructure educational delivery. Gibson (1998) believes we need to rethink the relevance of traditional methods of linear thinking and approaching problems with the time-honoured logical reductionist strategies. He asks how such methods can produce valid "solutions" in our increasingly non-linear and unpredictable world. Handy (1998) warns that traditional education can contribute to "de-skilling" (p. 25) if new approaches are not incorporated to represent the change in the environment. If acknowledgement is given to the changes going on around us, these need to be taken into account in curriculum design and research. Charles Handy (1998: 25) claims it is necessary to:

> Change our whole educational system. I believe that we need a totally
> new kind of schooling which is not about learning knowledge and

facts. Those are still necessary of course, but those things are easy to get at now . . . the job of the teacher, then, is to help them to know what to do with all this knowledge, and how to do it.

Odgers (2000) suggests that the goal should be to create an educational environment that encourages and rewards students for developing "attributes" rather than just knowledge that will stand them in good stead for coping with today's environment. Specifically, Odgers is referring to the entrepreneurial attributes like adaptability, creativity and risk-taking. Students need to be aware that reality is often very different to the "textbook". They need to be encouraged to use their intuition when faced with the myriad of exogenous variables that impact on a business. Too often educators take away their "common sense" by encouraging them to stay within the boundaries of the lecture notes and the textbook guidelines. Agor (1986) has developed a research-based framework which highlights the significance of the role of intuition in today's business environment. He found (Agor, 1986: 29) that intuition is a brain skill which is best suited to situations:

- Where there is a high level of uncertainty.
- Where there is little previous precedent.
- Where variables are less scientifically predictable.
- Where "facts" are limited.
- Where facts do not clearly indicate the direction to take.
- When analytical data are of little use (e.g. new trends emerging).
- Where there are several plausible alternative solutions to choose from, with good arguments for each.
- Where time is limited and there is pressure to be right.
- For negotiations and personal decisions.

By encouraging the development and use of such a skill, it is possible to abolish the idea of a "right" answer in student assessment.

Creativity is another crucial attribute that is being sought by employers. Organizations are realizing that the only competitive advantage they can hope to achieve is through their human capital. Therefore it is a process that should feature significantly in education programmes. Unfortunately, the traditional education system does all it can to strip a child of his or her imagination and creativity – forcing all to conform to the "right" answers and the prescribed processes, leaving little scope for a student to expand and develop creative thinking. While there is much emphasis on teaching university students to think analytically or critically, there needs to be just as much if not more significance placed on teaching the techniques of lateral or creative thinking.

So the question remains as to how can these entrepreneurial attitudes and skills be imparted to students in the tourism discipline? A combination of approaches is recommended, utilizing both traditional learning methods and also incorporating a range of other approaches to provide a more holistic and relevant experience for the student. Providing examples and cases is a traditional method which can illustrate to the student how individuals have used entrepreneurial skills to bring about innovation in the tourism industry. Using real examples also provides a far more realistic view of the type of exogenous variables that an entrepreneurial enterprise is likely to face, how the entrepreneur dealt with the unpredictable, their pathways to success and also their experience with failures. For example, instead of just teaching the existence of Thomas Cook as an historical incident in the development of mass tourism, a closer look at Thomas Cook the individual would provide a valuable insight into the importance of entrepreneurial attributes in the rise of tourism as it is today.

One of the realities entrepreneurs are faced with in having their dream realized is having to inspire others and obtain enthusiasm and financial capital from potential investors. It is not enough to just have a "great idea". Students need to acquire the skill of "persuasion". This is also a key attribute of successful leaders. So assessment should take into account not only the content of the business plan, but also the student's creativity, their ability to extend that creativity into an innovation and their persuasive skills in convincing "investors" that their idea is worthwhile.

Learning by doing is a less traditional but highly valuable method of encouraging creative thinking and applying it to a business setting. This can involve having students develop a "real" and viable tourism business initiative, not only applying the theoretical concepts of business planning, SWOT analysis and financial processes, but also incorporating the techniques of creativity and innovation and accepting the existence of risk. When creativity is allowed to emerge educators are always surprised at the level of creative capital that is found in students.

Two examples of student initiative and innovation that the authors are directly familiar with incorporate capstone courses within tourism programmes in Canada and Australia. At the University of Victoria, Canada, students were encouraged to stage an annual conference for the benefit of the industry. By bringing together key issues and prominent speakers, including the best student papers, the students were able to assist the local industry whilst showcasing themselves. Such conferences were managed completely by the students and were designed to make a profit.

At La Trobe University, Australia, students are encouraged to create small event businesses in a Tourism Venture Planning class. In 2001 these events included wine tours, a local river cruise and a cooking demonstration. The combined class profit of A$6000 was donated to cancer research. In the process these students learned how to select an opportunity, develop it into a business plan, risk their time and money to implement the plan and experience the disappointments of failure and the highs of success, each step being a real application of concepts taught throughout the programme and an invaluable lesson in entrepreneurship.

Conclusion

There can be little argument that we are indeed living in an era that is characterized by unprecedented change, bringing with it high levels of uncertainty. The question is whether research and education systems utilize this uncertainty to create opportunities for the tourism industries and tourism students. If research is to provide meaningful information to those who use it, uncertainty must be accounted for in the models developed and the outcomes produced. By adding uncertainty to Jafari's (1990) multi-level research platform, we are formally acknowledging this era and recognizing that conditions are different than before and therefore the underlying principles of research will need to reflect these differences.

One of the distinguishing factors of this era of uncertainty is the type of leadership required for successful tourism businesses. Entrepreneurial leadership is advocated as being most suited to turbulent conditions and dealing with unpredictable circumstances. Entrepreneurial leaders are characterized by their ability to create opportunities out of turbulence. Risk-making, risk-taking and creativity are skills that distinguish entrepreneurial leaders from traditional leaders, and these are the skills needed to be instilled in students to ensure their survival in the marketplace. In doing so, it will be necessary to change current methods and approaches in the classroom, seeking out and highlighting entrepreneurs within the tourism industry – both past and present – to demonstrate how opportunity can come from unpredictable triggers and how entrepreneurs utilize their creativity to bring their dreams to reality. Undoubtedly instances of failure will also be witnessed, but the positive way these failures are dealt with is another distinguishing characteristic of the entrepreneur. Indeed, many successful entrepreneurs have built their success on lessons learned from early failures or partial successes.

A surprising feature may come to light for those of us who are grappling with these dramatic changes mid-career, which is that we might indeed find that the students presently in the education system, especially the Generation Y demographics, will cope with uncertainty and change far better than we do. This group has grown up in turbulent conditions and stability is a condition they are not accustomed to and therefore do not expect. Evolutionary principles tell us that they possess inbuilt adaptive traits. The enormous technological advances being witnessed today do not surprise them, they do not expect to be securely employed and they expect to be rewarded for the innovation they contribute rather than for attaining long-service status. The real challenge is not to convince students they need a different set of skills but for educators to let go of former beliefs and practices and embrace these attributes to help ensure their own survival in the current marketplace.

References

Agor, W.H. (1986) *The Logic of Intuitive Decision Making: A Research Based Approach for Top Management*. New York: Quorum Books.

Baty, G.B. (1990) *Entrepreneurship in the Nineties*. Englewood Cliffs, NJ: Prentice Hall.

Brendon, P. (1991) *Thomas Cook: 150 Years of Popular Tourism*. London: Secker & Warburg.

Bryman, A. (1995) *Disney and His Worlds*. London: Routledge.

Butler, R.W. (1980) The concept of a tourist area cycle of evolution: Implications for management of resources. *The Canadian Geographer* XXIV (1), 5–12.

Chell, E., Haworth, J. and Brearly, S. (1991) *The Entrepreneurial Personality Concept: Cases and Categories*. New York: Routledge.

Concepcion, J. and Lomba, J. (2000) From dynamic leadership to entrepreneur management: Between antimanagement and promanagement. In ASQ (ed.) *54th Quality Congress Proceedings* (pp. 371–376). Anaheim, CA: ASQ.

Coulson-Thomas, C. (1999) Individuals and enterprise: Management services entrepreneurs in the new millennium. *Management Services* (Oct.), 28–30.

Covey, S.R. (189) *The Seven Habits of Highly Effective People*. Melbourne: Business Library.

Drucker, P.F. (1985) *Innovation and Entrepreneurship: Practices and Principles*. New York: Harper & Row.

Drucker, P. (1995) *Managing in a Time of Great Change*. New York: Tourism Talley.

The Economist (2002) Back to basics: A survey of management. March 9 (Supplement).

Edgell, L.D. (1993) *World Tourism at the Millennium*. Washington, DC: USTTA, US Department of Commerce.

Faulkner, B. (2000) The future ain't what is used to be: Coping with change, turbulence and disasters in tourism research and destination management. Professorial lecture, Public Lecture Series, Griffith University, August.

Finkelstein, S. and Hambrick, D. (1996) *Strategic Leadership: Top Executives and Their Effects on Organizations.* Minneapolis/St Paul, MN: West Publishing.

Geletkanycz, M. and Black, S. (2001) Bound by the past? Experience-based effects on commitment to the strategic status quo. *Journal of Management* 27, 3–21.

Ghiselli, E. (1971) *Explorations in Managerial Talent.* Pacific Palisades, CA: Goodyear.

Gibson, R. (ed.) (1998) *Rethinking the Future.* London: Nicholas Brealey Publishing.

Gleick, J. (1987) *Chaos: Making a New Science.* London: Heinemann.

Goleman, D. (1998) What makes a leader? *Harvard Business Review* 76 (6), 93–102.

Grover, R. (1991) *The Disney Touch.* Homewood, IL: Business One Irwin.

Hambrick, D.C., Geletkanycz, M. and Fredickson, J.W. (1993) Executive commitment to the status quo: Some tests of its determinants. *Strategic Management Journal* 14, 401–418.

Handy, C. (1998) Finding sense in uncertainty. In R. Gibson (ed.) *Rethinking the Future* (pp. 17–32). London: Nicholas Brealey Publishing.

Hersey, P. and Blanchard, K. (1974), So you want to know your leadership style? *Training and Development Journal*, February, 22–32.

Jafari, J. (1990) Research and scholarship: The basis of tourism education. *Journal of Tourism Studies* 1 (1), 33–41.

Kuratko, D. and Hodgetts, R. (1998) *Entrepreneurship: A Contemporary Approach.* Forth Worth, TX: The Dryden Press.

Langer, E.J. (1989) *Mindfulness.* Reading, MA: Addison-Wesley.

Larson, P. (1999) A look at leadership. *Montana Business Quarterly* (Summer), 18–20.

Maccoby, M. (2001) The new new boss. *Research Technology Management* (Jan.–Feb.), 59–61.

March, J. and Simon, H. (1958) *Organizations.* New York: Wiley.

McClelland, D. (1961) *The Achieving Society.* Princeton, NJ: Van Nostrand.

McKercher, B. (1999) A chaos approach to tourism. *Tourism Management* 20 (4), 425–434.

Meindl, J. (1990) On leadership: An alternative to the conventional wisdom. *Research in Organisational Behavior* 12, 159–203.

Morrison, A., Rimmington, M. and Williams, C. (1999) *Entrepreneurship in the Hospitality, Tourism and Leisure Industries.* Oxford: Butterworth Heinemann.

Odgers, J. (2000) We all are – or soon will have to become entrepreneurs. Paper presented at the Academy of Business and Administrative Sciences (ABAS) International Conference 2000, Prague, July 9–12.

O'Toole, T. with Tarling, L. (2000) *Breadwinner: A Fresh Approach to Rising to the Top.* Melbourne: Information Australia.

Poon, A. (1993) *Tourism, Technology and Competitive Strategies.* Wallingford: CAP International.

Pudney, J. (1953) *The Thomas Cook Story.* London: Michael Joseph Ltd.

Russell, R. and Faulkner, B. (1999) Movers and shakers: Chaos makers in tourism development. *Tourism Management* 20 (4), 411–423.

Schumpeter, J.A. (1934) *The Theory of Economic Development.* Cambridge, MA: Harvard University Press.

Shaw, G. and Williams, A.M. (1990) Tourism, economic development and the role of entrepreneurial activity. *Progress in Tourism, Recreation and Hospitality Management* 2, 67–81.

Smith, S.L.J. (1995) _Tourism Analysis: A Handbook_ (2nd edn). Harlow: Longman.

Taffinder, P. (1995) _The New Leaders_. London: Kogan Page.

Withey, L. (1997) _Grand Tours and Cook's Tours: A History of Leisure Travel, 1750–1915_. New York: William Morrow and Company.

Zahra, S.A. (1999) The changing rules of global competitiveness in the 21st century. _Academy of Management Executive_ 13 (1), 36–42.

Chapter 5
The Ownership and Evaluation of Visitor Attractions

A visitor attraction is a focus for amusement, recreation and, in part, educational activity undertaken by both day and stay visitors and by local residents. The range of visitor attractions is considerable (though the majority were never designed for visitors) and there are numerous variations in terms of the product concept. It is therefore possible to classify them along a number of different dimensions: ownership, capacity, market or catchment area, permanency and type. The most basic classification by type is to group attractions into those that are gifts of nature and those which are man-made. As with natural resources, such as national/country parks, forests and designated areas of outstanding landscape value, a great many man-made tourist attractions, because of their historical legacy, are not commercially owned. They are owned by central government in the case of national collections, quasi-public bodies which are at an "arm's length" from the government, local government, voluntary bodies in the form of charitable trusts and so on. This raises issues of political involvement in setting objectives, success criteria and the impact of the size of the not-for-profit sector in the market place alongside commercial attractions.

Introduction

A visitor attraction provides a focus for amusement, recreation and, in part, educational activity undertaken by both day and stay visitors that is frequently shared with the local resident population. Every municipality and rural district boasts at least one attraction, adding to its appeal as a destination. Thus, the range of visitor attractions is extensive and there are numerous variations in terms of the product concept or creativity of the design and its appeal, which may be termed the "imagescape" to match the term "imagineers" used by the Disney Corporation to describe its designers (Kirsner, 1988). It is therefore possible to classify them along a number of different dimensions: ownership, capacity, market or catchment area, permanency and type. The concern here is with the nature of ownership and how it affects the funding, operations and evaluation of attractions, but this in turn is linked to type, for which the most basic classification is the grouping of attractions into those that are gifts of nature and those that are man-made. The former include the landscape, climate, vegetation, forests and wildlife, embodied in, say, country parks in Britain, lakes in Canada, mountains in Switzerland, the coast in Spain or game reserves in Africa. The latter are principally the products of historical development of countries and civilisations (Richards, 1994), but also include artificially created entertainment complexes such as theme parks, of which the best known are the Walt Disney parks, originating in California (1955), but now reproduced in Florida, Tokyo and near Paris.

It will be appreciated that the basic classification may be subdivided again into attractions which are site-specific because of the physical location of facilities and therefore act as a destination, and attractions that are temporary because they are events. International events that are regarded as world class normally stand alone as "hallmark" activities, while others may be used to complement site-specific attractions (Getz, 1991, 1997). It is what is happening at the time that is usually more important for events than their location, so mega-events and exhibitions may move around the globe. But some evolve in and become specific to and therefore branded by their location; thus several of the most spectacular events in the form of parades or carnivals have become associated with major cities – for example, the Lord Mayor's Show in London or the Calgary Stampede in Alberta – because cities provide access to a large market and have the economic base to support them. Similarly, important religious festivals are often connected with locations that are considered the foundations of the faith, such as Mecca and Jerusalem. Complementarity may be achieved, for example, by staging a festival of the countryside to enhance the appeal of a country park or markets and fairs in towns and villages of historic interest, and similarly by the performance of a Shakespeare tragedy in the courtyard of an historic castle. Janiskee (1996) examines three event models as suitable attractions for historic houses – community festivals, stand-alone tours and living history portrayals – and deduces that the latter, which include holiday celebrations, ceremonies, rituals and parties, historic re-enactment (Crang 1996) and the learning of vernacular skills, crafts and household "chores", are best suited to such venues. Events are also used to raise awareness and give animation to object-oriented attractions, such as museums, and to encourage new and repeat visitors, particularly in the off-season.

In the main, events are commercial activities, but cultural and sporting proceedings, for example, can raise the image of a destination; a factor which lies behind the very competitive bidding for mega-events such as the Olympic Games, which had a lasting impact on the international perception of Barcelona in 1992. The current view is that the Games held in Sydney in 2000 were equally successful and are perceived as a 10-year marketing investment for Australia. Roche (1994), however, raises a cautionary tale from the 1991 World Student Games in Sheffield, UK, by drawing comparisons between the planning rationality for hallmark events and the political realities concerned with civic pride and city re-imaging, which bypassed, to a considerable extent, the conventional policy processes for such activities, resulting in questionable economics and political division amongst the local representatives.

Attraction Development

The division between natural resources and man-made attractions is not always well defined. Many natural attractions require considerable inputs of infrastructure and management in order for them to be used for tourism purposes – for example, national/country parks, ski resorts and game reserves. This infrastructure may also be put in place to protect the resource from environmental damage. In numerous countries, it is no longer possible to have open public access to many forests. Specific sites are designated for cars, trailers and camping, as well as colour-coded trails for walkers. Attractions that are the legacy of history and culture also share with natural resources the fact that they cannot be reproduced without considerable expense and alterations to their authenticity, unlike attractions designed principally for entertainment. They deserve, therefore, greater protection and management input to guard against excessive use. Such man-made attractions are commonly in the control of the state. A good example is Stonehenge, a prehistoric stone circle in southern Britain, which exhibits all the features of being resource-based and non-reproducible and for some time now has been threatened by too many visitors. Measures to resolve this have been the construction of a new visitor centre some distance from the monument and putting a cordon around the stones to prevent them being further defaced by touching and, in some instances, the chipping of the stones by capricious visitors. The surrounding area is an example of a tourist destination that owes its position on the market to this major attraction, which has uniqueness and appeal that is otherwise not present in the area or in the country. This may particularly be the case in peripheral areas, whereas urban complexes often contain a variety of attractions within their borders. A major resource of this kind is often termed a "flagship" attraction, as it may be regarded as a core tourism asset amongst others that provides a locality with economic benefits over a wide range of businesses. This is, of course, relative to the spatial economic conditions of the region where the attraction is situated. It is for such economic regeneration reasons that governments sponsor tourism developments, although Pearce (1998) notes that public intervention in urban redevelopment in Paris had more to do with broader cultural considerations of image and political opportunism than the immediate economic gains from tourism.

Transcribing the above concepts across the landscape of natural and man-made attractions serves to show that commerciality and consumer choice are rather modern notions in that probably over 70% of today's attractions have not been brought into existence for tourism purposes. The development process is, therefore, a gradation from a situation of no adaptation (but rather controlled management) to visitor attractions that are purpose-built. The reality of this is reflected in the pattern of ownership shown in Box 5.1, which in turn affects the management and development process.

Ownership

As with natural resources, such as national/country parks, forests and designated areas of outstanding landscape value, a great many man-made visitor attractions, because of their historical legacy, are not commercially owned. They are owned by central government (in the case of national collections), quasi-public bodies which are at an "arm's length" from the government, local authorities and voluntary bodies in the form of charitable trusts, which have to be incorporated, and a variety of clubs and societies which are often unincorporated.

Public ownership

Publicly owned attractions may receive all or a substantial part of their funds from general taxation, either directly or via grant-in-aid for quasi-public bodies – for example, public agencies such as English

---

Box 5.1 Ownership

Public
- Central government
- Government agencies
- Local authorities
- State industries

Voluntary organisations
- Charitable trusts (incorporated)
- Private clubs and associations

Private
- Individuals and partnerships
- Private companies
- Corporations

Heritage, which looks after many public monuments and historic properties in England, and Historic Scotland and Cadw (Heritage), which do the same for the rest of Britain. They are thus provided in the manner of a merit good and in so doing impose a degree of coercion on everyone, as individuals are not free to adjust the amounts that are made available. This is shown in Figure 5.1: the supply schedule S S is the quantity of, say, museum services supplied to each person as a result of public provision. The distance $0t$ represents the amount of income foregone per person in terms of tax and A the demand curve of individual A and similarly for B. At a tax cost $0t$, A demands only Qa museum services while B demands Qb. Clearly, the supply of services exceeds A's demand by XY, but falls below B's demand by YZ. Faced with an oversupply, A cannot adopt the market consumer's option to "exit", nor can B purchase more. They can only "voice" their disapproval, from which it follows, therefore, that public provision is likely to generate political debate and lobbying as political parties and individuals try to alter the amounts produced to suit their own agenda or requirements. The political difficulties that this gives rise to can be seen in the UK millennium celebration at the Dome in Greenwich, which received an initial grant of £399 million from the Millennium Commission. Because its financial performance was below target, the Dome had recourse to more funds

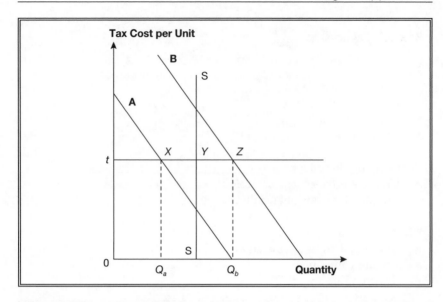

Figure 5.1 Provision of public goods

from the Commission, amounting to an extra £229 million. Although this money was designated as additional to normal state spending on education, health and welfare, the public's perception (encouraged by media reporting), at a time when expenditure on these sectors was not matching need, was that the Government had got its priorities wrong and the Dome did not represent good value for money. The effect of this was to turn the Dome into the classic "political football".

Over time a consensus emerges in any country about the greatest attractions being national assets and therefore being protected through public funding, but this does necessarily imply an agreement on the amount of money given. Thus an almost continual debate goes on about charging for national museums. The trend in the last two decades has been to impose entrance fees in order to cut public expenditure, though there is still firm resistance amongst certain sections of the community, including museum managers, who feel that museums have a public obligation requirement. As a consequence, only voluntary admission donations have been introduced in some instances, with a recommended minimum contribution, while other museums have simply refused to charge for admission. Recent experience in the UK, with the re-election of a Labour Government in 2001, has been to reverse the policy of charging for admission to national museums.

It is evident from the above discussion that the classification of goods and services into public and private provision is by no means clear-cut. It is up to society to decide upon the dividing line through the political process. Nevertheless, governments do have to make everyday decisions on which projects to promote, which is why the UK government, with the establishment of the National Lottery in 1993, set aside a series of funds to disburse some of the proceeds to the arts, sport and cultural heritage (Heritage Lottery Fund), as these causes are normally under-resourced by any government when faced with the competing demands of health, welfare, education and defence. The need for these funds is particularly true of attractions, as they are frequently sponsored by local authorities and voluntary organisations, which look to central government for grant assistance. To aid decision-making, economists have devised the analytical framework of cost-benefit analysis, which takes a wider and longer look at project decisions. The diversity of tourism expenditure is such that the most feasible method of assessing government support is to look at the impact that spending by visitors to the attraction has on local income and employment via the multiplier process. Implicit in this process is the requirement that the normal financial checks will be undertaken to ascertain whether the project is able to sustain itself operationally; if not, then it will need permanent subsidy if it is to proceed.

Voluntary organisations

Many museums and events have arisen out of the collections or interests of a group of enthusiasts who come together to provide for themselves and others collective goods and services which are unlikely to have any widespread commercial appeal (market failure) and are equally unlikely to be of sufficient importance to attract central provision by the state. These organisations are, in economic terms, "clubs" and, because they normally have non-profit aims, they are entitled to claim the status of charities for tax purposes. However, in contrast to the public sector, they are not able to raise funds from taxation and so in the long run must cover their costs out of income. Yet, unlike the private commercial sector, their income is not made up solely from admission charges and visitor spending inside the attraction. Membership fees, gifts, bequests and grants from public bodies (both at national and international level) and charities often take on a far greater significance in the income statement. As a consequence, recruiting new members to share the collective experience is a priority task for these organisations.

The economic analysis of such organisations (Buchanan, 1965) revolves around membership size in which exclusion from consumption is possible. This is unlike public collective goods, where state provision is made because the possibilities of "free riding" imply that, if the good or service is to be provided at all, it has to be made available to everyone without exception, or public merit goods, which have in theory an infinitely large membership. The optimal membership conditions are shown in Figure 5.2. Membership size becomes part of the overall cost function, so that on the one hand adding new members at first reduces the average cost (*AC*) of provision per person, while on the other new members create additional costs and external diseconomies through more crowded facilities. Hence, with a demand schedule *D1 D1*, equilibrium is at point *X*, which satisfies all marginal conditions and the club meets its charitable status by breaking even one year with another through keeping membership at *M1* and charging an annual joining fee of *F1*. Should the demand curve be *D2 D2*, the club may charge members *F2* so as to meet its objectives and make up the required difference in revenue, *F1XYF2* from other sources. It could also charge members *F1* and open the club to non-members. In practice, as already noted, clubs resort to a variety of methods to make up their income, but, mindful of

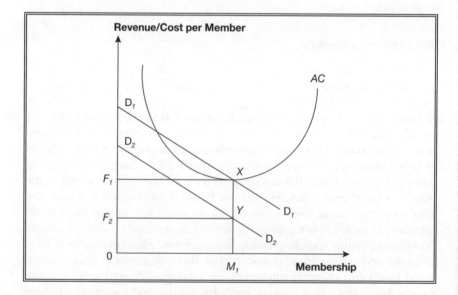

Figure 5.2 Voluntary associations

charitable objectives, they are careful to ensure that their not-for-profit aims are maintained, implying that average cost pricing (so that all benefits are returned to members) is the rule. This classifies them as 'fix-price' organisations, in that, should the demand schedule be higher than $D1$ $D1$, they will tend to accumulate waiting lists for membership and may extend facilities, rather than seek monopoly rents by raising dues.

One of the best-known examples of an economic club in Britain, that is very commercial in its outlook, is the National Trust, which maintains a wide range of historic properties, parks and woodlands, and is an institutional model that has been copied elsewhere. By law, trusts are incorporated for the purposes of education, religion, relief of the poor or the public good (Rose-Ackerman, 1996). This allows them to qualify for public funding and tax relief for capital and revenue expenses. Acquisition has normally been via bequests from previous owners together with substantial endowments that provide the economic foundations for the organisation. Given the breadth of its facilities, with the potential of taking on more, it has a policy of expanding membership, but, as in the case of many other non-profit organisations, the National Trust hedges the demand risk by receiving income as well from admission charges, shops, catering, grants and donations, sponsorship, events and services rendered – for example, lecture programmes. On the cost side, like other voluntary societies, the Trust benefits from some labour inputs and materials being provided free of charge.

Commercial sector

Over and above the man-made attractions left by historical legacy, there are plenty of artificially engineered attractions in the hands of the private sector whose principal role is one of entertainment. These attractions are user-oriented and are purpose-built to draw in and satisfy visitors: they include theme and leisure parks (Corze, 1989; Durlacher, 1994), sporting venues, theatres (Hughes, 1989), all-weather holiday centres and entertainment complexes. They exist in all scales and some are capable of handling thousands of visitors per day. Theme parks may also include an educational function for the benefit of schools – for example, EPCOT in Disney World – as well as providing exciting "white-knuckle" rides in the form of rollercoasters, "runaway" trains, log flumes and oscillating "pirate" ships. But essentially they are about "fun", for such parks are the modern form of the travelling fairs of yesteryear that have been made obsolete by technology, laws on safety and duties of care to the public, and by the increase in leisure expenditure that has reduced the need to travel from one market to another to capture limited spending power.

For the commercial attractions the rules of market economics apply. They are required to make profits so as to contribute a return on the capital invested (Swarbrooke, 2002). In theory this return, at a minimum, should be equal to the going cost of investment funds, and for new or "venture" projects considerably more. In situations where attractions are owned by multi-product firms or conglomerates, the ability of the facility to contribute to the cash flow of the overall business is often given a higher priority than return on capital. Production industries frequently have long lead times between incurring costs and receiving revenues. In these circumstances, the ownership of subsidiaries capable of generating ready cash inflows into the organisation on a daily and weekly basis can contribute greatly to total financial stability.

Cost structure

The principal economic concerns of most commercial attractions are the same ones that face many other tourist enterprises, namely their cost structures and the seasonal nature of demand. Typically the cost structure of visitor attractions is made up of a high level of fixed costs (and therefore unavoidable as they arise principally out of the initial capital investment) in relation to the operational or variable costs of running the enterprise. This is known as a high operating leverage and results in businesses that are very sensitive to variations in demand. The problem is illustrated in Figure 5.3, where it is assumed that there are two concerns that have exactly the same revenue line R and break-even point BEP. However, one attraction has a high operating leverage as shown by the cost line $C1$ $C1$, and the other a low operating leverage represented by $C2$ $C2$. The possible outcomes of these two concerns are shown by $V1$, $V2$ and $V3$. Suppose $V3$ sales are achieved; then it is clear that the enterprise with the high operating leverage makes substantially more profit than the other. This is represented on Figure 5.3 by the difference between the revenue and cost schedules, where it may be seen that $DF>DE$. On the other hand, if the outcome is $V1$ sales then the attraction with the cost structure $C1$ $C1$ will make large losses, $AC>AB$. Given the predominance of the high operating leverage phenomenon in the attraction business, it is not surprising that the collapse of large visitor attraction projects that fail to meet their visitor targets is somewhat "spectacular".

The effects of having high fixed costs also spill over into pricing policy. The difference between the price charged for admission to an attraction and the variable or marginal cost of providing the visitor experience for

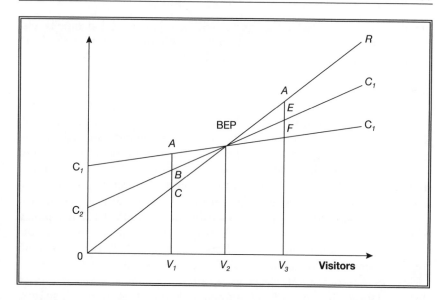

Figure 5.3 Significance of operating leverage

the customer is the contribution margin per customer towards paying the fixed costs and meeting targets on profitability. Where the contribution margin desired is low because fixed costs are low, the marginal cost of supplying an additional unit is relatively high and so provides a good guide to setting the price level. This is known as cost-oriented pricing. On the other hand, where there are high fixed costs, the admission charge has to be set considerably above the marginal cost of provision, in order to ensure a high contribution margin to meet the financial costs of servicing the investment that has been sunk into the attraction. In this instance, the marginal cost of provision is no longer a good guide to pricing and the enterprise is forced to take a market-oriented stance in its pricing policy. The difference between the admissions price and marginal cost is the range of price discretion that the organisation has, for it must cover its operating costs in the short run, but may take a longer-term perspective in terms of how it might cover its fixed costs.

By seeking out a range of different market segments with a variety of different prices, including discounts for volume sales and seasonal ticket holders, the commercial attraction operator will try to optimise the revenue yield on the site's assets. The operator's ability to manage revenue in this way will be constrained by the economic climate surrounding the business, which will include the customers' perceptions of value for money ("what the market will bear"), personal income levels, particularly amounts for discretionary (non-essential) spending, the level of market segmentation possible and the degree of competition.

Seasonality

Seasonality becomes an issue in attractions because the product, the visitor experience, cannot be stored. This being the case, it is peak demand that determines capacity and user-oriented attractions are frequently designed to a standard based on a fixed number of days per annum when capacity is likely to be reached or exceeded. This implies that, at most times of the year, the attraction has too much capacity. The level of investment is therefore more than what would be required if the product was storable. In turn, seasonality can affect pricing policy as presented in Figure 5.4: $S\ S$ is the supply schedule representing the incremental cost of expanding visitor numbers. $D2\ D2$ is the demand for the visitor experience in the main season, while $D1\ D1$ is the off-season demand. Market clearing requires a policy of seasonal price differentiation, charging $P2$ in the main season and $P1$ in the off-season. In any one year attractions have a variety of peaks and troughs, so that strict optimisation would entail a whole range of different price levels.

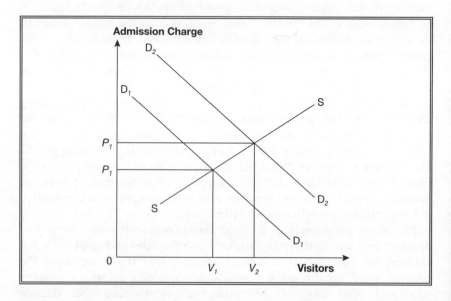

Figure 5.4 Seasonality effects

However, in practice many attraction managers are opposed to seasonal pricing, because, they argue, it simply reacts on customers' perceived value for money in that the public does not respond well to wildly fluctuating prices. Visitors feel that they are being overcharged because they are unable to come in the off-season. To counter this perception problem, attraction operators tend to narrow seasonal price ranges and offer additional product benefits, in the form of free entrance to different parts of the site, to those visitors coming when the attraction is not busy. Similar arguments apply to using price as a regulator of visitor numbers and so all attractions resort to a variety of non-price methods to manage visitor flows, though some theme parks are now using premium ticket pricing to "jump" queue lines for their most popular rides.

Another method of smoothing the difference in prices is to charge a two-part tariff. Instead of the major contribution to fixed costs being borne by main season visitors, the admission price is made up of a fixed charge to meet the requirement to cover fixed costs in the long run and a variable charge depending on the level of usage. While most attractions pay attention to segmented pricing techniques for groups, senior citizens, children and schools, the dictates of revenue management do require operators to address the seasonal and spatial limitations of demand in their pricing policy.

Public Sector Involvement

From a commercial perspective, to paraphrase the famous dictum about hotels that has been attributed to Conrad Hilton: "There are only three things you need to know about attractions: visitors, visitors and visitors!" Again, no better example of this principle can be found in the Millennium Dome at Greenwich. It was designed as a celebration for the year 2000, but was judged by the press as a commercial attraction, so that the out-turn of 6.5 million visitors for the year as against a design budget of 12 million was declared a financial "disaster" in the media and the political arena, and an embarrassment to the Government. Thus, once paying visitors are introduced to attractions in the public and voluntary sectors, then pressure builds up for the visitor experience, in support of admissions, to become the marketed output, as in the commercial sector. This has its own dynamic in terms of fashion and tastes and so creates a momentum for change in the nature or presentation of the product, something that is often resisted by the curatorial side of these attractions, which is rightly concerned about the authenticity of the visitor experience. For example, in the 1980s the Victoria and Albert Museum in London was heavily criticised for using the marketing strap-line: "Ace café with a rather nice museum attached!", although this was not a change in the product but rather a deliberately provocative teaser to stimulate a reappraisal of the museum by the market – something that is quite acceptable today.

As the quest for improving the attraction experience to maintain attendances forces theme and leisure park operators to install more complicated rides and challenging entertainment, so static attractions and object-oriented museums, unless they are national collections, no longer appeal to visitors as they once did (Swarbrooke, 2002). Despite the intrinsic value of historic buildings and collections, presentation, interpretation and good support facilities have become increasingly important, an aspect that not-for-profit organisations have learnt from the commercial sector, driven by the need to understand their customers. Hence living museums, such as Colonial Williamsburg in Virginia and Beamish in the north of England, by using the interpretation and presentation technology of today to create time capsules of yesterday, have crossed the boundary between a theme park and a museum (Prentice, 1994). Similarly, historic properties, museums and gardens change their displays and feature special exhibitions/events to maintain interest. Some of these attractions are fortunate enough to be able to link into themselves regular events aimed at an enthusiast market – for example, automobile rallies – for which demand is more or less continuous.

Regeneration

Where old industrial buildings, disused market halls, railway stations and docks are located close to urban centres, it is fairly widespread to find public sector intervention, both at national and international level (Wanhill, 1995, 1997), to convert them into tourist zones which serve both visitors and residents alike, as in Montreal and Singapore (Chang *et al.*, 1996). Since leisure shopping is an increasingly important visitor and resident activity, there has been a focus on specialty shopping – as in Covent Garden, London – intermingled with hotels, leisure attractions and also business facilities, such as a convention centre, an exhibition hall or trade centre and offices, in order to attract commercial developers. In this way, tourism has replaced manufacturing and distribution industries, which have left the inner core for more spacious and cheaper locations on the outskirts of the city (see Jansen-Verbeke, Chapter 12, this volume).

As evidence of the changing nature of the core for tourism purposes as well as serving local residents, Pearce (1999) cites examples of urban attractions in Paris, namely churches, department stores and even sewers, noting that managers of these sites have become increasingly aware of their multiple identities and have developed visitor strategies for this. Thus tourism has been recognised as a feasible economic option and catalyst for community regeneration – for example, the development of Baltimore's Inner Harbor, or South Street Seaport, New York, or the Albert Dock, Liverpool, UK, or Darling Harbour, Sydney, or the Victoria and Alfred Wharf, Cape Town. In this way, tourism can become the "glue" that holds the area together, particularly where there is little else the local authority can do with such assets. Ownership of regeneration development is mixed, frequently resulting from a private/public sector partnership in which the revenue earning activities are commonly in the hands of the private sector and the rationale for public participation is vested in the wider economic, social and environmental benefits that are bestowed.

Even for commercially desirable urban sites, there is usually a percentage, around 15–20%, devoted to leisure in order to obtain planning permission. However, the leisure development may be drawn from the local authority's "wish list" of amenities for local residents and could be unsuitable for tourism purposes. One aspect that has been difficult to guard against where public authorities are involved is the danger of project inflation in response to civic pride and the vainglory of politicians, either nationally or locally. There seems to be an implicit belief that winning in the electoral marketplace translates itself into the economic marketplace. This results in an exaggeration of employment creation to obtain development grants, increased complexity, which boosts consultants' fees, and substantial capital structures to the benefit of the architects. Several millennium projects in the UK have gone this way and some have had to be closed – for example, the National Centre for Popular Music, Sheffield, the Centre for the Visual Arts, Cardiff, and the Earth Centre, Doncaster, though there are plans to relaunch the latter. The lesson for the Heritage Lottery Fund and the Millennium Commission from these examples is straightforward: major capital projects should not be undertaken unless their market function is clear, visitor displacement has been considered and a "proper" feasibility study has been carried out so that the nature of the risks involved are thoroughly understood and accepted. Commercial developers are also guilty of project inflation in order to obtain the backing of banks for debt capital, which in turn helps to lever in equity.

The core of the attraction product is the imagescape, the purpose of which is to convey the essence of the visitor experience to the potential market. As commercial operators well know, failure to distinguish between the core and peripherals designed to augment the imagescape, or lack of content control as in the case of exhibitions that are made up of a variety of sponsors, or failure to communicate the imagescape to the market, will lead to underperformance and possible project failure. Success comes from having a clear idea of the imagescape, proven management skills and knowledge of the market. This reason explains why the regeneration approach is so risky from a pure attraction (as opposed to a mixed development) perspective, because of the location-led pathway that can result in an "outside-in" project that goes from the physical structure to the imagescape, as opposed to an "inside-out" project that takes as its starting point the imagescape and then creates the structure around it, which is the case of most visitor attractions that appear to be flourishing. The structure of the Dome was finalised long before the content was known, so it had to be designed to give maximum exhibition space. The final 14 zones inside the Dome were the subject of much debate and political interference and were essentially "anticipatory" imagescapes evoking expectations (Denis, 1991), as opposed to "reproductive" imagescapes that evoke known products or events (only the transport zone sponsored by Ford had artefacts). The creativity of the imagescapes and how they were linked together were not effectively communicated to the general public and allowed the media to satirise the project as ersatz and of no substance, even though the satisfaction rating amongst those who actually visited the Dome was well over 80% (National Audit Office, 2000).

Practicalities

The reality of ownership patterns indicates that most attractions are non-corporate, which absolves them from public shareholding constraints, while many are in the non-profit sector (public or voluntary) and so have a myriad of objectives and mixed funding and operating methods arising from different ideals. Mixed ownership patterns may also apply – for example, the Big Pit Mining Museum in Blaenafon, South Wales (Wanhill, 2000), where mine visits were the province of a charitable trust for educational purposes, while all other aspects were dealt with by the commercial subsidiary, Matchtake Ltd, because in order to survive financially the Trust had to undertake commercial activities that were not in accordance with its charitable objectives. Structured in this way, a museum that is a registered charity, with its buildings protected as public monuments, does not leave much scope for development, since it has no assets upon which to raise capital and therefore has to resort to grants and donations for any future projects, and whatever it can generate from visitor attendances. Suffice to say that the Big Pit was doomed to struggle for its existence, since it did not achieve its planned threshold visitor numbers and was on the point of closure in 1998, when a rescue package wound up the existing ownership structure, so that it could be absorbed by the state-run National Museums and Galleries of Wales (NMGW) in 2000 to conserve it for posterity.

The British Government with the Private Finance Initiative (PFI) has positively supported mixed organisational structures similar to that of the Big Pit. The thread of the argument for PFI deals runs as follows: funding constraints inhibit those responsible for national museums and galleries from meeting their statutory duties of displaying objects to the public to showing no more than a fraction of the entire collection. The private sector understands the market and, if it could be brought in to contribute to the capital costs of a new development as well as taking care of the revenue operations, there would be a net gain to the economy at large, particularly if there were regeneration benefits from the project.

However, although commercialisation brings the public and voluntary sectors closer to the market, their mixture of ideological objectives, such as conservation, authenticity and education, and their charitable status and sunk capital costs, plus regeneration aspects, implies that they cannot be compared to commercially established attractions that are seeking a return on capital invested and attempting to maintain a strong, if not dominant (Braun *et al.*, 1992), position in their marketplace. It is also politically difficult, in the case of national collections, to accept insolvency: for example, the Royal Armouries Museum in Leeds, UK, which was opened under a PFI deal in 1996, had to be bailed out with public money in 1999 when visitor numbers fell to less than half of the break-even volume and considerably below the design forecasts, thus transferring the demand risks back to the state sector (National Audit Office, 2001). Instances of this kind rightly raise scorn from commercial operators who argue that, if public funding and project inflation results in a situation where there is no relationship between the cost of delivering and what the customer actually pays, then this is a case of predatory pricing in an oversupplied market that is likely to harm them commercially. Governments are sensitive to this kind of criticism and as a rule avoid trying to compete "head on" with the private sector.

Winning Attractions

When dealing with visitor attractions it will be readily appreciated that the number of permutations to do with the variety in ownership patterns, imagescapes and ways of classifying attractions is immense. With such a wide setting, it is a debatable point as to whether anything can be concluded as to what constitutes "successful" development, particularly when most attractions are non-corporate, which absolves them from public shareholding constraints, while many are in the non-profit sector and so have a myriad of objectives arising from different ideals. However, noting that, for the majority of attractions their location is already restricted by circumstances, which limits their ability to reach out to the market, there are a number of aspects to consider that may throw some light on understanding the make-up of a successful attraction project.

Market–imagescape mix

When presenting the core of the attraction product, the diversity of imagescape themes is beyond doubt extensive, though, essentially, there is very little new in what draws visitors: the main attractions are still the wonders of the natural and physical world and the endeavours of human society, including, but to a much smaller extent, dark subjects that deal with what are considered to be behaviour inversions, such as the grim consequences of war (Smith, 1998), crime and punishment (Foley & Lennon, 1996) and the erotic (Ryan & Kinder, 1996). On the presumption that visitor numbers are performance targets, then, whatever the imagescape, it is important to realise that it is inextricably bound up with the market assessment, as indicated in Figure 5.5, and vice versa. Thus, while there is a clear demand for entertainment attractions, success is related to the creativity of the design and its appeal. What is also significant is the scale, thus small attractions may offer only a single imagescape, often proscribed by the resource base, while created attractions like theme parks promote multiple imagescapes structured around different rides and features in order to achieve the required market penetration rates.

"Me too" attractions

The common attraction experience is linked to the first quadrant (Q I) of Figure 5.5, since this involves least risk, which in turn has implications for finance and operational viability. It involves least risk because it is possible to look at parallel projects to the one in question and see whether they are successful or not. It should also be possible to obtain reliable data to be combined with overall market trends to see what the market absorption capacity is likely to be. "Me tooism" is a favourite

Image Market	Current	New or future
Current	Q I "Me too" attraction	Q II "Grand inspiration" attraction
New or **future**	Q III "New version" attraction	Q IV "Wonder" attraction

Figure 5.5 The attraction market–imagescape mix

occupation of local politicians who see a political opportunity arising from the location of the project in their constituency. They can always justify this on the basis of the need for the project in their area, but whether it is possible to turn need into demand at a price, which will make the project financially viable, is another question! There is always a danger that the "me too" approach can saturate the market and can result in non-viable attractions that end up wasting resources. For example, due to the repetition of mining attractions in the South Wales area in response to political pressure, the time path taken by the Big Pit museum discussed earlier has been from Quadrant II into Quadrant I, leaving the NMGW with the task of moving it into Quadrant III by rejuvenating the product. Surveys undertaken at the mine indicated that only 7% of visitors would be likely to go to a similar attraction so it is not surprising that the mine lost market share. This is symptomatic of a lack of vision in the creation of new attractions through acting in isolation and not relating the imagescape to the market.

"New version" attractions

The development process here may be the opening up of new market opportunities while preserving the existing imagescape in content and format, rejuvenating the existing attraction because the current public has become too familiar with the product and the market has moved on, or a combination of the two. Spatial division of markets can be important, thus old concepts can work in new destinations while new concepts are needed to move forward in established destinations. Corporate examples of the former can be found in Disney, Universal Studios and Lego, who have sought to increase their global presence through park development, tailoring them to local needs so as not to be too formulaic in design.

Replication may also serve to raise the standing of the original park to sacralisation status amongst enthusiasts (MacCannell, 1989), because it is considered the natural home of the product. Heritage associations may partake of this by acquiring new properties and adapting them to visitors in areas where there is an undersupply of castles, palaces and stately homes open to the public. Clearly, such developments are supply-led, as they are generating demand in spatial terms where it has not been previously, so there is a need for substantial market research and forecasting to take account of both the short-term conditions (economy, financial climate and the political situation) and the longer-term ones (demographics, social values and lifestyle, technology, climate and environment).

Product rejuvenation is a defensive strategy to retain existing attendances that requires careful monitoring of key market trends. It is readily apparent that current markets in themselves are not static, so the key question for "new version" attractions is whether, for example, by their use of new technology for better visual interpretation, experiences and sales, they are leading the market or simply catching up in respect of product formulation, the communications proposition and the channels of communication. Meeting the needs of new and future markets may require a much greater leap forward in terms of imagescape development for the new version to be successful, something that was achieved by the opening in 2000 of the Tate Modern gallery in the old South Bank Power Station on the River Thames in London.

"Grand inspiration" attractions

One of the difficulties of starting attractions in this quadrant is assessing whether the "grand inspiration" will work in relation to the imagescape or whether it is simply the "single genius" approach to project development, which could be an indulgence that is unnecessarily or unrealistically costly in terms of what the market can afford. A common strategy in this area is to try to reverse the project evaluation sequence by estimating the volume of visitors needed to make the project both feasible and viable at a price the market is prepared to pay. In terms of the Big Pit example used earlier, the Joint Steering Group did try to turn the project "upside down" by estimating the volume of visitors needed to make the project feasible. But they felt that there was sufficient margin of safety and so did not go into major details of operating costs and revenues (Wales Tourist Board, 1979). Instead they concentrated on the capital requirements needed to start the project.

An important aspect of delivering projects in this quadrant is the track record of proposers in order to be able to raise finance and obtain various planning consents. In a European context and near major cities in North America, the latter is a "minefield" of issues, as most sites are under local authority control and local government culture is not noted for being receptive to new ideas or being able to think in 10–15-year trends. Equally, many developers have experienced and recognised the ability of local pressure groups to "kill off" sound project proposals.

"Wonder" attractions

The term "'wonder" attraction is used here to describe those very large projects that have major economic impacts on their location and are eagerly sought after as "flagship" enterprises, for successful projects of this kind lay down the architecture of the industry (Abernathy and Clark, 1985) and the new framework in which competition will occur and develop, setting future standards for some time to come. Maximum uncertainty holds in this quadrant because of the number of unknowns and often the scale of the project, which on the one hand deters competition, but on the other increases financial exposure. However, this quadrant only applies to relatively few projects: past examples being Disneyland in California, EPCOT (1982), the Sydney Opera House (1973), Baltimore's Inner Harbor (developed form the 1960s onwards) and the Millennium Dome. This is because data on attractions drawn from around the world will show that the majority are geared to fewer than 200,000 visitors, which minimises the risk of scale. The very large attraction operators, such as the Disney Corporation, or major corporations with a leisure interest, are the ones who fund commercial projects of this kind, but even here they are careful to limit their financial exposure, as in the case of Disneyland Paris.

Usually "wonder" projects proceed with public sector support, both in terms of kind (land) and cash, so as to spread the risks and help draw in external finance. Their downfall on the financial side has commonly come from:

- Too large a capital cost making the project unaffordable from the standpoint of raising equity to match debt – for example, Wonderworld (at the old steel works in Corby) and the Battersea (to be based at the redundant power station situated on the south bank of the River Thames) in the UK, which came forward to the City of London for finance during the 1980s.
- Delays in building or underestimation of construction costs that lead to serious cost overruns and the need for refinancing, as in

the case of the Sydney Opera House in the 1960s and Brighton Marina in the UK during the 1970s.
- Ignoring funders' demands by bringing them in at the end of all the feasibility work, when it would have been more appropriate to have them in at the beginning.

Alternatively, money may come from public or quasi-public funds. The spate of "millennium vision" attractions sponsored by the Heritage Lottery Fund in the UK fall into this category, though not necessarily, as noted earlier, to good effect. In Europe, many large projects have been initiated through the European Regional Development Fund and most members of the European Union offer some form of investment support to new tourism projects (Wanhill, 1997), in addition to the many other ways where the public sector has tried to set the "right climate" for tourism development (Wanhill, 1995).

Unfortunately, market assessment for such unique attractions is notoriously difficult; for example, the estimates of visitor numbers for the Millennium Dome in London ranged from 9 to 17 million. Twelve million was the figure that the Government was prepared to accept and budget for, on the basis that it was meant to be a public festival, so that everyone who might want to come should be able to do so. In these circumstances, there is a need to build up a large database of market trends in different leisure activities, make future change assumptions (predictions) and consider the project in a "with and without" situation. Developing project scenarios so as to give a thorough understanding of what is being proposed and the risks involved is more important than the actual projections, though the latter are required to give dimensions to the project and to assess its impact on the economy.

Repeat visits

The essence of the core of the attraction product and its development is the encouragement of repeat visits, unless the market for the experience is global, which therefore provides a catchment population that is to all intents and purposes infinite in size, since it is continually being replenished. Figure 5.6 shows two product life cycles derived from logistic generating processes for visitors (Lundtorp and Wanhill, 2001). They illustrate what happens when the market matures to a steady state of continual repeat visits and conversely when the attraction is a "once-only visit", so that, when the optimum market penetration rate is reached, demand falls away. Entertainment attractions, such as cinemas and

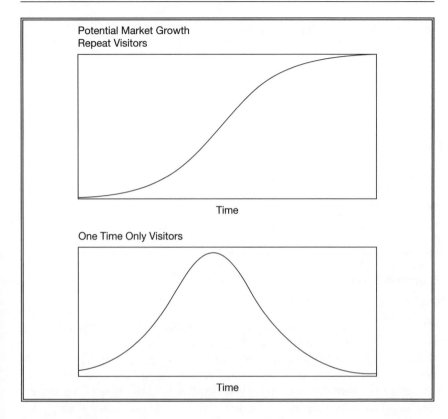

Figure 5.6 The attraction life cycle

theatres, are able to survive on once-only purchases of the experience, because they continually change the core, while theme parks embody thrill rides for which there is a repetitive demand that they reinforce with a rolling programme of replacement and re-theming to persuade their customers to return. Similarly, leisure-shopping facilities continually replace their merchandise in line with fashion.

However, for the majority of visitor attractions that were not built for such purposes, their ability to maintain attendances is functionally related to the size and dynamics of their market, and their capacity to alter the core imagescape and supplement it by special events and other supporting features. To this extent, national museums are at a considerable advantage because of the size of their collections; for example, the Victoria and Albert Museum, mentioned earlier, has only about

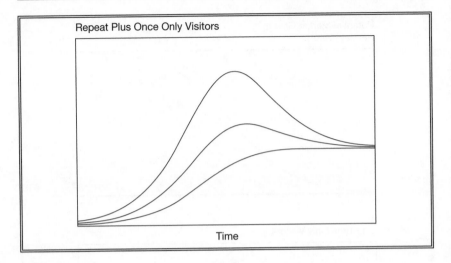

Figure 5.7 The mixed-market life cycle

3% of more than four million objects on public display, although more are accessible in its reading, study and print rooms.

Figure 5.7 shows the combined market for once-only and repeat visitors: most attractions pass through a celebratory phase, either because there is a pent-up demand to see a collection as in the case of a museum or the project offers the newest experience in its field. Hence, theme park developers apply a rule that bases forecasted attendances on around 80–85% of the launch year. The higher the proportion of once-only visitors in the market, the more peaked is the cycle and the greater is the drop to a sustainable level, a factor which affects many smaller attractions in the not-for-profit sector who only have limited collections to display.

Reverse product development

The imagescape does not have to be revolutionary in design: in fact, few are, but it needs to be flexible if the attraction has to rely on repeat visits to meet its performance targets. The creation of imagescapes suggests that, in those sectors of the economy where the marketed output is experiences, the transformation of ideas to innovation cannot be compared to the processes seen in manufacturing. It appears that some of the most successful attractions are those that have followed a reverse product development cycle to that normally understood in the production of commodities (Barras, 1986). For commodities, development starts with product innovation (invention and introduction of the product), then qualitative process innovation (the setting up of the manufacturing systems, which is "capital widening") and finally quantitative process innovation (improvements and rationalisation of the production system for mass supply, which on balance displaces employment through "capital deepening"). Services start with the quantitative process innovation by taking established products and using them to increase the efficiency of current service production, which, in turn, leads to qualitative changes in the production system and then wholly transformed or entirely new service products.

Thus, for attractions, existing products that are at the end of the production chain, which have been developed for other purposes and in other industries, are adapted to provide a visitor experience with the aid of new communication techniques. For example, the Lego brick was well established as a toy long before the creation of the parks and, similarly, the Disney characters were well known in the entertainment industry and as toys before the development at Anaheim. Many commercial organisations are now going down this "post-Fordist" road of building on their customers' association with their products to stretch their brands into industrial tourism.

Museums and galleries also follow this formula by marking (MacCannell, 1989) and presenting objects and works, many of which may already have a high intrinsic value and association in the public's mind, in ever more stimulating ways. From an economic perspective, the fact that commodities from the past are still regarded today, despite belonging to different vintages of taste, arises from the rarity value bestowed by their antiquity, so that ownership, either in the private or public domain, conveys prestige. In essence, when applied to visitor attractions, the reverse product development model is trying to minimise the risks of failure through reproductive imagescapes that generate a ready awareness in public perceptions. For many cultural resources, monuments and works of art, this was not always so: thus, one of the best loved of Verdi's operas, La Traviata, was not that well received when it was first performed, there was fierce opposition to the Eiffel Tower and Van Gogh only ever sold one painting in his lifetime, because the audience had no prior perceptual experience of the creativity put before them and marking as to its acceptability. This supports the view that an avant-garde or anticipatory imagescape is difficult to evaluate in the marketplace, because there is no recognition at large of its value and so it runs the risk, as in the case of the Millennium Dome, of being lampooned as the

Emperor's new clothes, or causing public outrage when it runs counter to what is considered to be good taste. Taste balances the desire to conform against the desire to be different and so, while all attractions aim to achieve an element of surprise, it is important for general public acceptance that the content of an imagescape conforms to styles that are characteristic of the time so as not to exceed the bounds of taste, unless it is a commercial attraction, such as the London Dungeon (a macabre exposition of medieval crime and punishment), which is designed to shock and appeal to the voyeur and lovers of the bizarre, something that would not normally be acceptable in the public domain. By way of contrast, a millennium project in the UK that has been very successful is the London Eye, which is a giant Ferris wheel on the southern bank of the river Thames, near the Houses of Parliament. It is selling a tried and tested product in a setting of superb quality.

Economic evaluation

Noting that the price elasticity of demand for attractions tends to be inelastic over the relevant range, because what matters is a "good day out", commercial operators bemoan the poor revenue management of the non-profit sector. However, this once again begs the question as to what is meant by "success", given the multitude of objectives in this sector. Figure 5.8 illustrates the normative economics of the pricing rule that is to be followed. Market economics dictate that private operators should attempt to optimise profitability, which is achieved by equating marginal revenue (MR) to marginal cost (MC), setting an admission charge of $P1$ and attracting $V1$ visitors. The public sector is faced with two economically efficient choices: free at the point of use, which results in a demand level of $V4$, or setting admission equal to MC, implying a charge $P2$ for $V2$ visitors. On the other hand, the appropriate policy for the voluntary sector, if it wants to distribute maximum benefits to its members or visitors, is to set fees equal to AC, setting a price $P3$ to generate $V3$ users. Thus through pricing policy, the pattern of ownership can alter the financial outcomes of an attraction.

A valid criticism of the not-for-profit sector, whether it is public or voluntary, is that it has the tendency to try and do too much, because the management tries to meet perceived needs rather than the market demand schedule, the latter being the primary concern of the private sector. To take a simple analogy: if people are asked if they want more of a collective good, then, in the absence of a price system, they will surely vote "Yes" and the public sector is likely to try and meet such

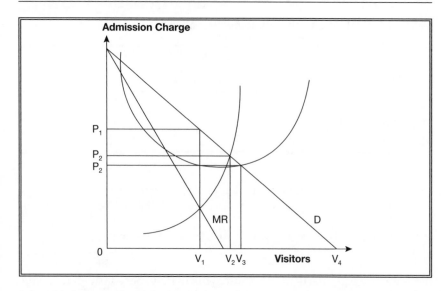

Figure 5.8 Pricing rules

needs as there is a political incentive to do so. For example, the Big Pit
was conceived as a public merit good but was expected to operate as a
commercial attraction, yet it would never have come into existence on
the latter terms alone. On the other hand, in any public discussion of
the Big Pit prior to its absorption by the NMGW, the Trust usually laid
stress on the achievements of the mine in acting as a "flagship" project
to attract visitors to a peripheral area such as Blaenafon. The museum
generates export revenues and jobs, in a location where there are few
alternatives other than living on public welfare, the latter giving rise to
a low-income economy. This raises questions as to matching the evaluation of attractions in the non-profit sector to their objectives. Clearly, it
makes no sense to appraise the Big Pit on commercial grounds if that
is not its purpose. The best that can be hoped for in financial terms is
a percentage of cost recovery.

Table 5.1 presents a broad summary of some evaluation methods that
can be applied to not-for-profit attractions, including those in the voluntary sector that receive grant support, and indicates where conflicts might
arise. Thus, if the objective is to create a viable tourist attraction from
the public sector standpoint, then assessing the economic impact, with
financial conditions, appears most appropriate. Economic yardsticks are
only one way of allocating resources and the case for many cultural or

Table 5.1 Evaluation methodologies for attractions

Evaluation	Project objective		
	Tourism	*Local heritage*	*Avant-garde*
Economic impact	3	3 7	7
Contingent valuation	3 7	3	3 7
Socio-political assessment	7	3 7	3

Notes:

  3 = method makes major contribution to project objective
3 7 = method partly contributes to project objective but can be partly at variance with it
  7 = method likely to be at variance with project objective

heritage projects, particularly those which may be considered avant-garde, is often made in terms of qualitative evaluation through a panel of experts, which transcends the economic calculus of utilitarianism. Advocacy in such cases can range from the visionary "big idea", through philosophical and ideological values, community pride and prestige, to barely concealed electoral calculations. In respect of the latter, it is always a matter of some agitation to public servants, during the preparatory months before a general election, as to how many projects, which fail economic hurdles but have a high visibility, will receive permission to go ahead. In this way, the socio-political assessment may run counter to the project objective of building a viable tourist attraction, as in the case of the Millennium Dome, where the amount of political interference was legion. What this indicates is how democracy relaxes one of the constraints in Arrow's famous Possibility Theorem (1951) to make social choices; namely, intensity of preferences do matter in the final ordering of projects selected.

Similarly, the point has been made earlier that many museums, gardens, sports stadiums, opera houses and market square or harbour developments are offered as public merit goods for the purposes of economic regeneration and so normal commercial criteria apply only in part. Their evaluation may be based principally on their economic impact in order to assess their contribution in stimulating the local economy, though this may not necessarily reflect their intrinsic value as contributing to the "cultural stock" of the nation. Thus, an avant-garde art museum, such as the Louisiana in Copenhagen, may only come about through a socio-political decision that draws in both the state and wealthy patrons. What is important to consider is the "bequest" value of attractions of this kind and contingent valuation is the only technique capable of measuring total economic worth by estimating the public's willingness to pay (Bille Hansen *et al.*, 1998). In sum, as Table 5.1 indicates, where there are conflicting objectives in the development of an attraction, the operation is unlikely to maximise any of them but rather to optimise between them. Therefore, it is bound to underperform on any single success factor. Thus the Dome brought considerable regeneration benefits to Greenwich, given that it was established on what was considered one of the most polluted industrial sites in Europe. From a "standing start" it achieved in one year about three times as many visitors as any other paid attraction in Britain, but it fell well short of its design capacity and was ridiculed by the media because of it, while the politicians tried to distance themselves from the project. Of course, economic calculus cannot cover all aspects of the evaluation process. If it were to, then there would be no need for a "decision-maker". Thus, in the final analysis, all public projects are subject to socio-political assessment to some degree, but the lessons from the Dome experience are threefold:

- In a democratic country, where there is a viable opposition, there is a need for cross-party support for the creation of national attractions.
- Political opportunism has to be tempered with realism to prevent project inflation.
- Major attractions of this kind that have international significance (Greenwich is the "home" of time), if they are to be undertaken at all, must be done well, almost regardless of cost, because the "eyes of the world will be looking upon them".

Conclusions

From the discussion that has taken place, it will be readily appreciated that the ways of classifying and evaluating attractions are immense. From a development standpoint, a useful classification is the placing of attractions on a scale that has, at one end, those that have been built or designed for visitor purposes, which are in the minority, and, at the other, resources and facilities that are neither for visitors nor can be adapted for them, with the bulk of attractions spread out between these two poles. This, in turn, is linked to the pattern of ownership and the multiple objectives that beset different ownership structures. Once attractions in the not-for-profit sector have been adapted for visitors, then weight builds up to interpret success in terms of the quality of the experience, visitor numbers (to capture the spillover benefits of visitor expenditure) and, where admission is charged, some level of financial viability, which brings this sector closer to the workings of commercial operators, for whom economic objectives of profitability are normally paramount. However, with public and voluntary attractions it is important to balance outcomes against the priorities assigned to the various objectives and to eliminate, as far as possible, conflicts. Failure to do so is the source of frequent misunderstandings and inappropriate evaluations of such attractions.

Given that visitor numbers are a performance target and noting that, for the majority of attractions, their location is already proscribed (means restricted from natural causes) by circumstances, the Market–Imagescape mix (Figure 5.5) plays a pivotal role, with the need to develop an imagescape, at whatever level of the attraction, for which demand is more or less continuous through the universality of its popularity. While this is readily accepted in the case of entertainment attractions, in the museum world the commitment to popularising the product has raised concerns about over-staging the experience, in the sense of being too technologically driven, which overemphasises the media rather than the message embodied in the resource base. Within the commercial sector, attractions that are flourishing are, as a rule, those that have followed the reverse product development sequence, namely the creation of reproductive imagescapes from products designed for other purposes and in other industries. Similarly, in the not-for-profit sector, the reverse product development model supports the observation that award-winning attractions are those that have a strong resource base and use technology to add value to the experience. To take the technology route alone is to embark on a fashion cycle that may be unsustainable in the longer term, which was the principle reason for the closure of Tussaud's Rock Circus in London's Piccadilly Circus in 2001, in that the attraction was unable to keep up with the investment required and the pace of change demanded by the "pop" music world. Successful visitor generation requires, in the main, the creation of imagescapes that have strong associations, are different, but not too different, and are flexible enough to encourage visitors to return, the delivery of which requires clear objectives, proven management skills and knowledge of the target audience. Avant-garde or anticipatory imagescapes have a high probability of economic failure, both commercially and also in the wider sense of attracting visitor expenditure to an area, but they may be judged to have significant cultural values. This implies that non-market models of resource allocation are needed for many such attraction developments to occur.

Note

1. The author gratefully acknowledges the funding support from the Danish Social Science Foundation via the Danish Centre for Tourism Research.

References

Abernathy, W. and Clark, K. (1985) Innovation: Mapping the winds of creative destruction. *Research Policy* 14, 3–22.

Arrow, K. (1952) *Social Choice and Individual Values*. New York: Wiley.

Barras, R. (1986) Towards a theory of innovation in services. *Research Policy* 15, 161–173.

Bille Hansen, T., Christoffersen, H. and Wanhill, S. (1998) The economic evaluation of cultural and heritage projects: Conflicting methodologies. *Tourism, Culture & Communication* 1 (1), 27–48.

Braun, B., Soskin, M. and Cernicky, M. (1992) Central Florida theme park pricing: Following the mouse. *Annals of Tourism Research* 19 (1), 131–135.

Buchanan, J. (1965) An economic theory of clubs. *Economica* (Feb.), 1–14.

Chang, T., Milne, S., Fallon, D. and Pohlmann, C. (1996) Urban heritage tourism: The global–local nexus. *Annals of Tourism Research* 23 (1), 284–305.

Crang, M. (1996) Magic Kingdom or a quixotic quest for authenticity. *Annals of Tourism Research* 23 (2), 414–431.

Corze, J. (1989) Theme and leisure parks. In S. Witt and L. Moutinho (eds) *Tourism Marketing and Management Handbook* (pp. 459–462). Hemel Hempstead: Prentice Hall.

Denis, M. (1991) *Image and Cognition*. New York: Harvester.

Durlacher, D. (1994) Theme parks. In S. Witt and L. Moutinho (eds) *Tourism Marketing and Management Handbook* (2nd edn) (pp. 14–18). Hemel Hempstead: Prentice Hall.

Foley, M. and Lennon, J. (1996) JFK and dark tourism: Heart of darkness. *Journal of International Heritage Studies* 2 (2), 195–197.

Getz, D. (1991) *Festivals, Special Events and Tourism*. New York: Van Nostrand Reinhold.

Getz, D. (1997) *Event Management and Event Tourism*. New York: Cognizant Communication Corporation.

Hughes, H. (1989) Entertainment. In S. Witt and L. Moutinho (eds) *Tourism Marketing and Management Handbook* (pp. 127–130). Hemel Hempstead: Prentice Hall.

Janiskee, R. (1996) Historic houses and special events. *Annals of Tourism Research* 23 (2), 398–414.

Kirsner, S. (1998) Hack the magic: The exclusive underground tour of Disney World. *Wired* (March), 162–168 and 186–189.

Lundtorp, S. and Wanhill, S. (2001) Resort life cycle theory: Generating processes and estimation. *Annals of Tourism Research* 28 (4), 947–964.

MacCannell, D. (1989) *The Tourist: A New Theory of the Leisure Class* (2nd edn). New York: Schocken Books.

National Audit Office (2000) *The Millennium Dome*. London: The Stationery Office.

National Audit Office (2001) *The Re-negotiation of the PFI-type Deal for the Royal Armouries Museum in Leeds*. London: The Stationery Office.

Pearce, D. (1998) Tourism development in Paris: Public intervention. *Annals of Tourism Research* 25 (2), 457–476.

Pearce, D. (1999) Tourism in Paris: Studies at the microscale. *Annals of Tourism Research* 26 (1), 77–97.

Prentice, R. (1994) Heritage: A key sector of the "new" tourism. In C. Cooper and A. Lockwood (eds) *Progress in Tourism, Recreation and Hospitality Management* (Vol. 5) (pp. 309–324). Chichester: Wiley.

Richards, G. (1994) Cultural tourism in Europe. In C. Cooper and A. Lockwood (eds) *Progress in Tourism, Recreation and Hospitality Management* (Vol. 5) (pp. 99–115). Chichester: Wiley.

Roche, M. (1994) Mega-events and urban policy. *Annals of Tourism Research* 21 (1), 1–19.

Rose-Ackerman, S. (1996) Altruism, nonprofits, and economic theory. *Journal of Economic Literature* 34 (2), 701–728.

Ryan, C. and Kinder, R. (1996) Sex, tourism and sex tourism: Fulfilling similar needs? *Tourism Management* 17 (7), 507–518.

Smith, V. (1998) War and tourism: An American ethnography. *Annals of Tourism Research* 25 (2), 202–227.

Swarbrooke, J. (2002) *The Development and Management of Visitor Attractions* (2nd edn). Oxford: Butterworth-Heinemann.

Wales Tourist Board (1979) *The Tourism Potential of the Big Pit, Blaenafon*. Cardiff: WTB.

Wanhill, S. (1995) Some fundamentals of destination development. *Revista Portuguesa de Gestao* 2/3, 19–33.

Wanhill, S. (1997) Peripheral area tourism: A European perspective. *Progress in Tourism and Hospitality Research* 3 (1), 47–70.

Wanhill, S. (2000) Mines – a tourist attraction: Coal mining in industrial South Wales. *Journal of Travel Research* 39 (1), 60–69.

Part 3: A Vulnerable Industry: Global and National Issues

Part 3 Introduction

A Vulnerable Industry: Global and National Issues

The focus of the second section of the volume deals with aspects of the nature and effect of tourism in different situations. It is one of the characteristics of the study of tourism in recent years that the subject has been examined and criticized in terms of the effect which it has had upon destination areas by many authors. It is perhaps ironic that it is only in the very recent past that researchers have turned their attention to the vulnerability of tourism to exogenous forces and the way in which tourism itself has been affected by many other agents of change. Despite the massive dimensions of tourism, it always has, and will probably always remain, peculiarly vulnerable to the effects of events and policies rarely directly concerned with its operations and existence.

In the first chapter in this section, Julio Aramberri reviews and discusses the questions of how global tourism is and what exactly its dimensions are. For many years researchers, politicians, planners and others have been told, with little hard reliable evidence, that tourism is the largest item in world trade, and/or the largest industry in the world, and that it employs many millions of people and contributes high proportions of the value of many nations' gross product. For an equal period of time many critics of tourism and disinterested observers have remained sceptical about such claims. The creation of the *Tourism Satellite Accounts* was intended to provide more robust and directly comparable statistics between countries that would be able to answer more convincingly questions about the size and value of the tourism industry. As tourism has become ever more global, such issues have been assuming increasing importance and influencing investments and development policies.

In his chapter, Aramberri casts a critical eye upon some of the claims and generalities which have been made, particularly in the context of the structure of world tourism, the relative importance of international and domestic tourism and the issue of economic leakage. He demonstrates convincingly that tourism is not as global as may initially appear, with marked concentrations of tourism visitation and expenditure in a very limited number of countries. While the phenomenon is truly global, its economic significance is highly concentrated. When examining the international and domestic elements of tourism, it becomes clear that, despite the great attention which is paid to the international flows of tourists, especially by bodies such as the World Tourism Organization and World Travel and Tourism Council, the vast proportion of the movement of tourists is domestic – within their own countries – and that this is not likely to change in the conceivable future. Finally, he addresses the complex aspect of leakages – the escaping of tourist expenditures out of the initial receiving country – a consideration of considerable concern to many "developing" countries which rely heavily on tourism for foreign exchange. While he shows that leakage certainly does exist and that it is highest in many small, often insular, countries, in fact the level of that leakage is not as high as might have been thought from some of the criticisms that have been made about the possible benefits and costs of tourism.

Stephen Smith, in his analysis of the geographical structure of tourism in Canada (Chapter 7), deals with some of these issues at a national level. He examines the dimensions, structure and distribution of tourism within Canada, revealing that the industry, as in other countries, is dominated small and medium-sized operations. He argues, however, that, contrary to common perception, in the Canadian context at least this pattern is not as dominant as that for all other industries. Smith argues against the general description of tourism as an industry, noting that it is better described, in his terms, as an "economic constellation", with the common factor being the services provided to travellers. Taking a true geographical approach, he analyses national and sub-national data to discuss the pattern of tourism by sector and by political unit (province and territory), how the pattern varies by region and what variables are related to these variations.

He confirms, in the case of Canada, as Aramberri does at the global scale, the importance of tourism to the overall economy, and goes on to argue convincingly the fact that tourism is a much more complex phenomenon than generally accepted.

Perhaps because of the economic significance of tourism, as shown in the above two chapters, much attention is focused on the impacts of such a large industry on destination regions. One example is the fact that tour operators are often heavily criticized for their domination of tourism in what might be termed "new" tourism destinations and countries. They are commonly portrayed as restricting local development by exerting control over key aspects such as transportation and marketing and forcing small local operators to accept unrealistically low prices for accommodation and services, while restricting direct access to the large "developed" country markets.

Nevenka Čavlek (Chapter 8) takes a different approach and examines the influence of tour operators on tourism development at the international scale. She reviews the role played by tour operators and argues for acceptance of the fact that it may well be appropriate to subdivide the development of tourism in specific destinations in such a way as to reflect the stages in development of the relevant tour operators to those areas. Given the importance of tour operators in modern-day tourism, they have to be acknowledged as one the major players in tourism, adding to the dynamism of the industry and playing a major role in the nature, scale and rate of development of destinations. She examines two of the major European markets, the German and the British, in order to illustrate her arguments, and divides the development of tour operators serving these markets into four stages: introductory, take-off, maturity and mass consumption. She concludes with the need for further investigation of the role of tour operators and the examination of other markets to broaden the implications of the research.

It is often ignored or unappreciated how vulnerable even an industry as large as tourism can be to other factors. The fourth chapter in this section by Anton Gosar (Chapter 9) deals with the response and potential weakness of tourism to external forces, in this case the process of political development and the establishment of two nation states (Slovenia and Croatia) in the Balkan peninsula of Istria. The development of tourism in this northern Adriatic region followed the pattern laid down in many European countries, of being initiated by the development of railway services and the patronization of the elite of the surrounding countries. The complicated political situation in the Balkan region following the Second World War did not seriously hinder the development of tourism in this region and, despite the constant probability of political unrest that would follow the break-up of Yugoslavia, tourism was successful in the region until the conflict of the early 1990s. Gosar discusses the divergent tourism strategies which followed the disintegration of Yugoslavia into five states – in particular Slovenia and Croatia, which controlled Istria. The origin of visitors changed markedly and neither country has yet managed to achieve visitor numbers comparable to those which existed in the 1980s. While the trend in recent years has been upward, confused images, continuing uncertainty in customers' minds over security and inconsistency in policy have all combined to slow the restoration of visitor numbers to previous levels. Gosar's chapter is a clear statement of the effect of radical political change on tourism, even in an area with a successful history of previous development and many inherent attractions.

The vulnerability of tourism to exogenous forces and political uncertainty is also the theme of the final chapter in this section, by Richard Butler and Airey (Chapter 10). They examine the effects and implications of the outbreak of foot-and-mouth in 2001 in the UK. Despite its relatively minor consequences for humans, the image created by the response to the outbreak was severe enough to deter large numbers of tourists from visiting Britain and altered, albeit temporarily, the domestic tourist patterns within Britain also. Butler and Airey outline the changing responses of the British government to the outbreak, demonstrating the lack of awareness of the value and significance of tourism to the British economy. The official response was confused and inconsistent, and, combined with the extremely negative images which were carried by the media, served to not only confuse but deter potential visitors to the United Kingdom. They conclude that the full effects of the outbreak are unlikely to be determined because of other events which occurred in 2001, including the attack on the twin towers in New York in September. They note the continuing reluctance among government departments and ministers to accept the reality of the importance of tourism, and the priority given to agriculture, particularly in the early months of the outbreak. They conclude that the episode is further evidence of the poor appreciation of tourism in many countries and the vulnerability of the industry to forces outside its control. Their depressing conclusion is that little has changed despite government restructuring, and the response to another outbreak is likely to be the same as that in 2001, with similar, if not more severe, damage to an already vulnerable tourism industry in the UK.

The issue of the relative importance given to tourism by governments in different countries is a key one with respect to the priority given to tourism in times of crisis. At this point at the beginning of the 21st century, tourism, along with other elements of the world's economy is facing a series of crises. Just how well it will survive and in what form remains to be seen.

Chapter 6
How Global Is Tourism?

JULIO ARAMBERRI

Introduction

Like the proverbial elephant by a group of blind men, tourism is described in many different ways and from different perspectives. However, no matter what or where we touch, when it comes to economics, we know that we are dealing with something humongous in proportion. At least, this is what current statistics show and the recent estimation of a system of Tourism Satellite Accounts (TSA) for 160 countries and territories by the World Travel and Tourism Council (WTTC) has only begun to give us some accurate idea of the sheer size of this 800-pound gorilla.

This chapter is based on that simulation. It is not meant to discuss its general value as a statistical tool, nor its internal details or coherence. It will not argue its merits relative to the work that the World Tourism Organization (WTO) has endeavored to complete for the same subject (TSA). It will deliberately abstain from such discussions and will take the WTTC database at face value with the same leap of faith that is usually taken in relation to other statistical instruments. The WTTC database may be faulted in many respects and we will learn more about them once it is more widely used. However, until a better tool is available, WTTC data allow us to go beyond the well-known limits of WTO statistics.

Up to now, WTO statistics have covered mainly two sides of the field – international arrivals and international receipts. The first of these two series is affected by some substantial disadvantages. Firstly, it leaves out of the picture any tourist exchanges that did not happen in the international arena, thus turning the different nations into the main protagonists in this field. Soon, the ranking of the world's top destinations became a kind of Olympic Games, the scene where obscure passions were deployed, as though there was a mysterious relation between the number of international arrivals into a given country and some corresponding amount of national prestige. In this way we have witnessed the efforts of some countries to increase their numbers by hook or crook.

For instance, in the 1960s and 1970s, Spain, then under General Franco's dictatorship, exhibited the increasing number of foreign visitors as a token of the political legitimacy that it was lacking in the political arena. In the authorities' view, the growing inflow of tourists proved that the country was enjoyed and accepted as any other by those sheer numbers, in spite of its being different from the European democracies. After the country found a new democratic framework, international tourist arrivals were exhibited as an approval mark for the country's new course and the inertia to inflate the numbers remained until recently, for once you have an historical series, no matter how bogus, changing it becomes difficult and everyone feels the need to remain a consistent liar.

Around 1989, in a tribute to the bicentennial of the French revolution, France, unhappy at lagging behind some other tourist powers, decided to refurbish its arrivals count and, all of a sudden, the country surpassed in a fell swoop all its previous rivals. Grandeur was well served once again.

In both cases, however, those prestigious numbers came to the detriment of the bottom line. According to WTO data, in 1998 France reached 70 million international arrivals and earned US$29.9 billion in international receipts; in 1999, they were 73 and US$31.7 billion, with an average expenditure per visitor of US$427 and US$434 respectively. For Spain, the amounts were 47.4 million visitors and US$29.74 billion in 1998 and 51.4 million visitors and US$32.91 billion in 1999. They spent an average of US$627 and 635 in each of these years. Italy, however, with fewer arrivals, registered expenses per visitor of US$855 and 785; in the UK, they were US$814 and 815; and, in the US, US$1535.

If, instead of a ranking of international arrivals, a ranking of economic success is devised, among the 144 countries reporting to WTO in 1998, France was number 101 in 1998 and number 64 in 1999 (with reports for only 96 countries at the time of writing this chapter). Spain fared a bit better with position 73 in 1998 and 48 in 1999. But both were amply surpassed by countries as varied as the US, Australia, Italy, Cambodia, Denmark, Brazil, India and many other allegedly lesser tourist powers.

The second main flaw affecting WTO arrival figures is that only international arrivals are counted, that is, those trips where border crossings take place. This creates a bias in favor of geographic areas like Europe that count many and relatively small countries. With just a little bit of hype one could maintain that in many a European country one needs a passport to reach the final stop of the nearest bus route. No accident then that this region will carve the lion's share in the distribution of international arrivals, and, even though Europe has been losing market share over the years, in 1999 it still accounted for 59.3% of all international arrivals. France and Spain alone had a joint share of the world market to the tune of 18.8%.

However, it was another story when international receipts were taken into account. In 1998 Europe had a market share of 52.7% of world receipts, while the Americas reached 26.8% and the East Asia and the Pacific (EAP) regions 15.4%. Again, as soon as profitability was considered, the picture was vastly changed. According to WTO data, the average in expenditures per international arrival in Europe was US$605 in 1998 and 595 in 1999, while in the Americas it reached US$983 in 1998 and 995 in 1999 (in North America the respective numbers were US$1041 and 1052) and in the EAP countries US$789 and 753. Europe may have the highest numbers of arrivals and the main share in receipts, but it is clearly less profitable than the other two more developed tourist regions of the world.

The data used in the rest of this chapter come from a different source – the simulation initially made public by WTTC in its website in the summer of 2001, taking the year 2000 as its starting point. Those data have subsequently been revised and reorganized in the same site, but here it has been preferred to maintain them in their initial version. Private checks on the new data show that our analysis would not have changed significantly if the latter figures had been selected.

The WTTC database was cross-referenced with other databases to substantiate the conclusions of the chapter. Again, here our method was far from perfect, as many times those checks were incomplete or referred to different years. But in an issue where statistical punctiliousness often rules out more general arguments, daring may be welcome. At any rate, it can help in furthering the discussion of some conventional wisdom that is all too often taken for granted. Even if the conclusions are deemed excessive or unwarranted, they may succeed in sharpening a long delayed and overdue discussion.

The chapter's goal is modest. Even though its title includes the ominous G-word (global, as in globalization), it will refrain from the heated discussions that surround this matter. The recent arguments around the existence of a trend toward a global economy and about its social and cultural impacts are too heated and usually all encompassing.

Often the term globalization is used in a restrictive way, meaning the diffusion of production techniques, organizational methods and financial practices that favor quick productivity increases. In this way, globalization is no different from the old mechanism of cultural diffusion that has favored the dissemination of productive innovations since the oldest of times. However, it is also a special case thereof, for today these techniques and practices can be easily reproduced in almost any region of the globe, and their transfer has grown at warp speed thanks to specific mechanisms and institutions (such as IT technologies, just-in-time production and distribution, unified financial markets and the Internet) that rearranged the world economy only 10 years or so ago. Globalization in this sense is above all an economic process and so it was perceived until recently.

However, since an assortment of groups with different goals and ideologies succeeded in blocking the World Trade Organization Assembly in Seattle at the end of 1999, and tried to repeat the feat in Washington DC, Prague, Genoa and other scenes of World Bank, IMF or G-7 meetings in successive years, the discussion about globalization has become not only multimedia but also multidimensional, and includes many other aspects beyond its initially economic boundaries, in fields such as culture, education, health and international relations.

At the same time, globalization has also grown into a lightning rod that attracts a critical discharge of radical energies differing in scope and aims. Since the end of the Soviet Union and its empire around 1990 and until Seattle, there had been many scattered criticisms of the new world order, but they lacked a unifying theme. Since Seattle, however, the old witticisms on things such as the Trilateral Commission or the new world economy have been recycled as invectives against globalization, that alleged conspiracy of some cosmic powers, as arcane and murky as their own acronyms (WTO, IMF, Spectra, whatever), while the scattered attacks against the rush of those who wanted to declare an end to history, the dismay caused by environmental abuses, the critique of neo-liberalism (in its European meaning) or, in the peerlessly synthetic French way, *la pensée unique*, have coalesced thanks to the catalyzing pleasures of pure action. Some optimists on the left seem to think that, with globalization defeated, history will finally excuse itself for its inconstancy in keeping some previous appointments with them, and many others consider it bad manners to see the slightest positive feature in it. Thus globalization has morphed into a secular version of the old Roman Catholic hell – that mixture of all evils without a glimmer of good.

As stated, the goal of this chapter is considerably more modest than those general propositions. It will be limited to assessing and appreciating how the TSA system recently provided by WTTC affects some accepted thought frameworks. In spite of the many methodological problems that the use of the database poses, it provides us with the opportunity to go a bit deeper into some areas of the tourism system that remained in a twilight zone due to the lack of relevant data.

WTTC-TSA data allow us to start negotiating those pitfalls as they focus on the sheer economic dimensions of the tourism system. At the same time, they may help us start a discussion of many interesting aspects of this industry. This chapter will address three such issues, widely held in our conventional wisdom, usually among anthropologists (Nash, 1996; 2000) and sociologists (Crick, 1996; Ireland, 1996; Urry, 1996).

The first refers to the structure of world tourism. It is often assumed that the global tourism system pits the developed North against a backward South (De Kadt, 1979). The picture, however, seems a bit more complicated. Once the relevant numbers are taken into consideration, there is no such thing as a tourist South, to the exception of a few island states or assimilated territories (small territorial enclaves in continental landscapes). In fact, the tourist South is close to non-existent.

In a second stretch, it will be maintained that the travel and tourism economy has a low global component in the sense that international arrivals and receipts pale before the magnitude of domestic or national tourism (Archer, 1974; Smith, 1985; Smith, 1989). This runs counter to a school of thought for which its international dimension is the main ingredient of modern tourism.

Finally, in close connection with the first two arguments, the chapter will plumb the so-called leakage issue (Archer, 1977, 2000). It is often said that, for those southern destinations which are in fact recognized tourist meccas, tourism might be closer to blight than to blessing. Most of the money they pocket in international receipts leaves the country in the form of import outlays that only cater to the needs of international travelers and do not add to the welfare of the residents. According to our interpretation of the data, nothing could be farther from the truth. In fact, it is so-called over-par tourist destinations that are mostly affected by leakages or, to put it in another way, southern tourist countries and resorts spend less in tourist imports than does the industrialized North.

The Amazingly Shrinking Global Tourist System

The *CIA World Factbook 1999* (2001) states that the combined GDP (at purchasing power parity or PPP) of the 160 countries and territories included in the WTTC-TSA database reached some US$39.4 trillion for the year. On its side, WTTC simulated a global production of tourism- and travel-related services exceeding US$4.5 trillion in 2000. This amounts to about 11.5% of the total GDP estimated by the *CIA Factbook*. It is indeed a very significant area of economic activity.

However, it does not mean that it is equally spread all over the world. Table 6.1 shows that the world's top 15 producers of tourism services, both directly and indirectly, contribute nearly four-fifths of this figure. Tourism may be a global economic activity in the sense that it is conducted in nearly all areas of the planet, but the lion's share is generated in less than a tenth of the countries and territories under study.

This group of top producers is mainly composed of industrialized countries with high per capita income. Only China and the former Soviet Union are exceptions to this rule, but the sheer size of their own general economies gains them entry to this club. For the rest, the club is made up of the most productive world economies (as is the case for the US, Japan, Germany, France, the United Kingdom, Canada and the Netherlands) plus some other developed countries that are also well-known interna-

Table 6.1 World's top 15 travel and tourism economies

Rank	Country	Value (US$ billions)	Global market share (%)
1.	USA	1293.02	28.54
2.	Japan	510.83	11.28
3.	Germany	330.27	7.29
4.	France	246.92	5.45
5.	UK	242.10	5.34
6.	Italy	216.19	4.77
7.	Spain	147.02	3.25
8.	Canada	122.87	2.71
9.	China	111.84	2.47
10.	Netherlands	75.85	1.67
11.	Australia	70.29	1.55
12.	Former SU	58.27	1.29
13.	Switzerland	56.60	1.25
14.	Austria	56.12	1.24
15.	Belgium	51.02	1.13
Total		3589.21	79.23

Source: Author's elaboration on WTTC, 2001

tional tourist destinations (such as Spain, Australia, Switzerland and Austria).

The club coincides to a great extent with the world's top 15 destinations and top 15 foreign currency earners (see Tables 6.2 and 6.3) as per WTO data. However, some tourist powerhouses according to the latter data are left behind when their respective total tourism economies are considered. Mexico, Poland, Greece, the Czech Republic and Hungary may be popular international destinations, but in the WTTC ranking they respectively come in positions 16, 27, 45, 46 and 28.

On the other hand, Japan, which is not included in any of the high-ranking positions when it comes to international tourism, is number 2 when the whole industry is considered. Something similar happens in the case of Germany, whose global market share is much higher than

Table 6.2 World's top 15 tourism destinations

Rank		*International tourist arrivals (millions)*		*Change 1999/1998 (%)*	*Market share 1999*
		1998	*1999*		
1.	France	70.0	73.0	4.3	11.0
2.	Spain	47.4	51.8	9.2	7.8
3.	United States	46.4	48.5	4.5	7.3
4.	Italy	34.9	36.1	3.3	5.4
5.	China	25.1	27.0	7.9	4.1
6.	United Kingdom	25.7	25.7	0.0	3.9
7.	Canada	18.9	19.6	3.7	2.9
8.	Mexico	19.8	19.2	–2.9	2.9
9.	Russian Fed	15.8	18.5	17.0	2.8
10.	Poland	18.8	18.0	–4.4	2.7
11.	Austria	17.4	17.5	0.7	2.6
12.	Germany	16.5	17.1	3.7	2.6
13.	Czech Rep	16.3	16.0	–1.8	2.4
14.	Hungary	15.0	12.9	–13.8	1.9
15.	Greece	10.9	12.0	9.9	1.8

Source: WTO, 2000

Table 6.3 World's top 15 tourism earners

Rank		International tourist receipts (US$ billions)		Change 1999/1998 (%)	Market share 1999
		1998	*1999*		
1.	United States	71.3	74.4	4.5	16.4
2.	Spain	29.7	32.9	10.7	7.2
3.	France	29.9	31.7	5.9	7.0
4.	Italy	29.9	28.4	–5.1	6.2
5.	United Kingdom	21.0	21.0	0.0	4.6
6.	Germany	16.4	16.8	2.4	3.7
7.	China	12.6	14.1	11.9	3.1
8.	Austria	11.2	11.1	–0.9	2.4
9.	Canada	9.4	10.0	6.7	2.2
10.	Greece	6.2	8.8	41.6	1.9
11.	Russian Fed	6.5	7.8	19.4	1.7
12.	Mexico	7.9	7.6	–3.9	1.7
13.	Australia	7.3	7.5	2.6	1.7
14.	Switzerland	7.8	7.4	–5.9	1.6
15.	China, Hong Kong SAR	7.1	7.2	1.8	1.6

Source: WTO, 2000

those of France and Spain, though being outranked by them in the numbers of international arrivals and receipts. Finally, one should mention the overwhelming position of the US as a tourism powerhouse, which reflects the fact that, even usually coming second or third in the WTO data for international arrivals, its 280-odd million inhabitants maintain a thriving tourist economy inside their own country.

The same pattern appears when comparisons are made between geographic regions instead of single countries. World tourism is not evenly spread among them all. On the other hand, the picture that appears when this dimension is taken into account is also one of imbalances. While some regions are heavy producers of tourist services, others make a minimal contribution to the global tourism economy. Three areas (North

America, the European Union and East Asia account for the greater share of the total tourism economy. Altogether they generate 83.74% of it. The three larger spheres in Figure 6.1 correspond to these three areas and provide a user-friendly vision of their overwhelming weight in the world's production of tourism.

Does it mean that there are no other important countries or regions for tourism in the world? This would be the wrong conclusion. It is possible to devise a way to assess the relative weight of the tourism sector within each one of all those economies and build some categories that can give us a better understanding of the relative importance of tourism for some countries whose small physical and economic size does not assure them a seat in the big leagues.

This goal may be reached by assessing the relative importance of their travel and tourism GDP in relation to their own national GDP. As the typical ratio for the world is 11.5%, we have devised three categories to classify the WTTC countries and territories into over-par, on-par and under-par tourism economies. The par category includes all those countries whose ratios are contained between the typical 11.5% and twice this figure at 23%. All tourist economies that exceed this ratio will be considered over-par, while those below 11.5% will be labeled as under-par.

The results of this classification offer a clear pattern. There are only a few countries and territories, just 22, which can be counted in the first

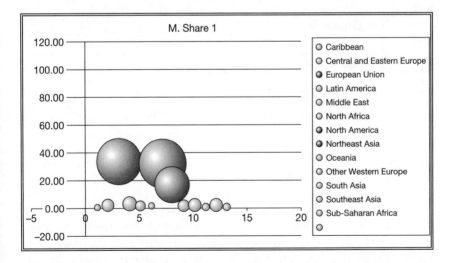

Figure 6.1 Market share of the different world regions

Table 6.4 League of over-par tourist countries

Rank	Country	TTGDP/GDP
1.	British VI	96.43
2.	Aruba	76.88
3.	St Lucia	67.69
4.	Macau	61.44
5.	Maldives	61.11
6.	Antigua- Barbuda	57.69
7.	Anguilla	55.56
8.	Cayman Islands	50.54
9.	St Kitts and Nevis	45.83
10.	Vanuatu	45.83
11.	Seychelles	44.07
12.	Bahamas	42.83
13.	Barbados	40.00
14.	St Vincent and the Grenadines	40.00
15.	Bermuda	36.00
16.	Iceland	33.96
17.	Burma	31.58
18.	Cyprus	31.36
19.	Grenada	27.78
20.	Jamaica	24.09
21.	Sao Tome	23.53
22.	Malta	23.40

Source: Author's elaboration on WTTC, 2001; CIA, 2001

category, as per Table 6.4. Leaving aside the oddity of Burma, whose very high tourism and travel GDP is difficult to explain, all of these countries and territories, but Macau, are island economies that have bet heavily on tourism as their main economic activity. Most of them (13) are in the Caribbean, and the rest are scattered all over the globe. Some other Caribbean destinations do not appear in this ranking of over-par tourist incidence, but this may be due to problems caused by the rounding of their GDP to billions of US dollars.

The on-par group consists of an additional 33 countries. Most of the top 15 producers (Switzerland, Austria, Spain, UK, Japan, Italy, the Netherlands, Australia, France, Germany, the US and Belgium) are in this category, which also includes some other members of the EU, plus again some Caribbean and South Pacific destinations.

There is finally the sub-par category and 101 countries and territories belong to it. Most of Latin America and practically all of South East Asia, the Middle East and Africa can be found here. Mexico is a big surprise with only 3.21% of its total GDP in provenance from tourism. Something similar happens in the Czech Republic (6.47%), Turkey (5.7%), Poland (5.65%), South Korea (5.21%), China (2.1%) and India (1.32%). The lowest tourism incidence can be found in Algeria (0.15%), where the influence of tourism is close to zero.

It is not easy to understand the reasons behind these results and one can only advance some hypotheses that will possibly be falsified soon by better explanations. Let's start with the over-par tourism countries. Almost all of them are islands (Macau can be considered as one to this effect), and all of them but Iceland have small territories that cannot be easily put to many different economic uses. In the past most of these islands developed a very specialized economy based on the production of a few products that have been complemented with tourism in the present. With small populations and low per capita incomes, they have become destinations dependent almost exclusively on the international tourism that provides most of their income. They have added another form of monoculture on top of the previous ones.

With some exceptions that should be analyzed more closely, the second group of countries (on-par tourist destinations) seems to be well developed and diversified economies that enjoy the vicinity of other similar nations. Tourism is an important part of their economies, but it is complemented with the production of many other goods and services. High per capita incomes create an important domestic market for tourism, only to some extent dependent on international arrivals. Most domestic tourism industry is supported by the national population, while international travel and tourism are also thriving.

The third group is to some extent and with many exceptions the reverse of the on-par countries. Tourism, both domestic and international, is still quite undeveloped in most of those countries and does not constitute a main source of income. Even in those cases like China or, to a lesser extent, India that have a high number of international arrivals, the relatively low living standards of their populations do not allow for the development of a thriving domestic tourism sector. It will, therefore, take some time before they are able to offer their own nationals the opportunity to support a dynamic tourism industry that reaches the typical world ratio for travel and tourism demand as compared to GDP.

In this light, one should reassess the standard notion about the world tourist system. The idea that the latter consists of a developed North that enjoys and consumes the products and services provided by the nations of the less developed South does not seem to hold. Most regions of the world are only barely touched by international tourist flows and many countries, including Mexico, the Czech Republic or Turkey, cannot be considered primary tourist destinations. This may seem counterintuitive, given the visibility of places like Cancún, Prague or some Aegean resorts, but figures do not necessarily coincide with bright images. In fact, international tourist exchanges seldom follow the North–South pattern, and only the few islands just named can be described as genuinely tourist focused. On the other hand, most tourist activities happen almost exclusively within the so-called countries of the North, along with the former Soviet Union and China.

Home, Sweet Home

Leaving aside the case of the so-called over-par countries, most tourist activities are caused by internal demand. This is where we will turn now.

There are a few different ways of assessing the relation between what can be seen as the global or international tourism component in a given economy and its domestic elements. One can measure the ratio between tourist exports (that is, international visitor receipts) in a given economic unit and its GDP. Or the exports can be related to the tourism and travel GDP (total production of tourism goods and services minus imports). Or one can find the share of exports within the more restricted category of travel and tourism industry GDP (only that part of the industry that caters to the need of domestic travelers, whether individuals or business, plus travel by government officials and incoming international tourism).

According to WTTC methodology, one can count three main types of tourism related exports in an economy. The first one, called Visitor Exports (VE), is the amount (measured in US dollars) of expenditures by non-residents in a given country or territory. The second, called Other Exports (OE), is the amount of US dollars generated by the sale of goods and services to foreign tourist companies. Finally, the item Total Exports (TE) is the sum of the two previous categories and the most comprehensive of all.

However, one has to be careful when using TE, for the two categories it mixes (VE and OE) tend to be different animals. In many cases some countries that receive a high number of receipts from VE have a low amount of OE and vice versa. For instance, most Caribbean islands make few OE, as most of their GDP originates with non-resident expenditures or VE. On the other hand, some Middle East countries with low inflows of foreign visitors are high on OE as they sell their oil for tourism-related purposes (for instance, as fuel for commercial aircraft).

For each of these categories one can rank the total of countries and territories along the same classification of over-par, on-par and under-par used in the previous section. Our first task will be to provide a rank of the different countries according to the share of their TE in their respective GDP. This might be called their globalization index, measuring how dependent they are on their tourist exports. The WTTC world amount of TE in the simulation for the year 2000 reaches US$976 billion, divided into US$561 billion in VE and US$415 billion in OE.

Using the data provided in the *CIA Factbook*, the world average in this dimension (TE/GDP) is 2.5%. If, as in Table 6.5, we take the first 25 countries in the ranking, whose ratio is around at least five times this percentage, we find 16 Caribbean destinations, some other islands (Kiribati, Vanuatu, Seychelles, Cyprus, Malta and Cape Verde), Hong Kong, Macau and Belize. These are our over-par international or global destinations, and they coincide substantially with the list of over-par tourist economies in Table 6.4.

At the opposite end, 62 countries are below the typical ratio, but there is no single reason why they should find themselves there. One finds among them some of the main international tourist destinations (US, Japan, Mexico, Argentina, Brazil, China and India) together with many others that appeared among the under-par tourism producers. In the first cases, the reason may be that, even though they receive consider-able flows of international tourists, those are still few in comparison with their domestic demand. For the others, the laggards, their international or global tourist product is still low in proportion to a domestic demand that, in spite of its feebleness, well exceeds their international desir-ability. The same can be said for the mid section or on-par group of 68 countries, where main producers such as Austria, France, UK, Spain, Germany, the Netherlands and the Dominican Republic are joined by Zambia, Taiwan, Tanzania, Kuwait or Saudi Arabia. Future statistical refinement, future increases in GDP and more attention to changes in international fads or, on the other hand, counteracting forces may make our understanding of those dissonances better.

Table 6.5 Top global destinations and Total Tourism exports vs. GDP

Rank	Destination	TE/GDP (%)
1.	British VI	120.3*
2.	Anguilla	88.9
3.	Antigua-Barbuda	68.1
4.	Aruba	58.1
5.	St Lucia	52.7
6.	Cayman Islands	46.7
7.	Macau	42.4
8.	Maldives	42.0
9.	St Kitts and Nevis	34.6
10.	Seychelles	33.2
11.	Bahamas	29.8
12.	St Vincent and the Grenadines	29.7
13.	Barbados	29.5
14.	Reunion	28.6
15.	Cyprus	27.1
16.	Bermuda	27.0
17.	Vanuatu	26.7
18.	Guadeloupe	21.2
19.	Grenada	20.6
20.	Malta	19.7
21.	Jamaica	18.1
22.	Hong Kong	14.4
23.	Belize	13.9
24.	Martinique	13.3
25.	Cuba	13.1

Source: Author's elaboration on WTTC, 2001; CIA, 2001
Note: * Exceeds 100 due to rounding

Table 6.6 Top global destinations and Visitor Exports vs. GDP

Rank	Countries	VE/GDP (%)
1.	British VI	114.3*
2.	Anguilla	88.9
3.	Antigua- Barbuda	67.3
4.	Aruba	53.8
5.	St Lucia	50.8
6.	Cayman Islands	43.0
7.	Maldives	40.7
8.	Macau	38.4
9.	St Kitts and Nevis	33.3
10.	Bahamas	29.2
11.	Seychelles	28.8
12.	Barbados	28.6
13.	St Vincent and the Grenadines	26.7
14.	Cyprus	26.3
15.	Vanuatu	25.0
16.	Bermuda	24.0
17.	Grenada	19.4
18.	Guadeloupe	18.6
19.	Malta	18.1
20.	Jamaica	17.0
21.	Kiribati	12.5
22.	Belize	12.2
23.	Cape Verde	11.3
24.	Martinique	11.2
25.	Cuba	11.1

Source: Author's elaboration on WTTC, 2001; CIA, 2001
Note: * Exceeds 100 due to rounding

Concentrating on VE does not change the picture much, as in Table 6.6. Here the typical ratio between the world VE and the GDP for the countries in the WTTC database is 1.5%. Once again we find 16 Caribbean destinations among the top 25 (six times over the 1.5 mark), plus a few of the islands already mentioned and Macau. No clear trend can again be found at the other side of the spectrum, where top producers mix again with many under-par countries. The picture is quite similar when TE and VE exports are related to the T&T Economy GDP and the T&T Industry GDP.

The WTO database of international receipts comes in handy here to cross-reference the previous classifications (see Table 6.7). Dividing WTO foreign receipts of each one of the countries in the WTTC database by the previous categories of GDP, T&T Economy GDP and T&T Industry GDP can show whether the outcomes are consistent with this picture. Though the base years for each one of them are different (WTO data are for 1998 while the *CIA Factbook* data are for 1999), if the results coincide largely with the former, one can assume that the classification is reliable, though the figures for both global VE and each individual country may differ. In fact, the ranking is quite similar. A classification based on WTO data also counts 15 Caribbean destinations among the top performers, while including the US, the UK, Japan, Canada and Brazil in the bottom 42 countries.

Box 6.1 includes the 21 destinations with the highest T&T GDP global index, as they appear in all of the lists we have elaborated. These are the real Top of the Pops in the global dimension of tourism. The "island" factor accounts for most of this outcome. We are facing countries and territories with relatively low populations that receive relatively high numbers of incoming tourists. Therefore it stands to reason that the ratio between these two factors should favor the international or global component of their tourism industry. On the other hand, destinations with higher demographics dilute this impact. They may accommodate many more tourists in absolute numbers than do those Top Global Destinations, but their proportion in relation to their domestic markets still remains low.

In fact, the most striking facts are found at the other side of the spectrum, as the number of international arrivals worldwide pales before the number of tourists who prefer to remain within their own countries for their vacations or business trips. As a matter of fact, far from looking for the pleasures of home away from home, most tourists simply decide that the best destination remains home, sweet home. Again it would be too easy to explain their behavior by a single factor such as low incomes.

This may be the case for a number of tourists in countries such as China, India or Brazil, but it cannot exclusively account for the fact the most tourists in well-developed countries prefer to stay at home. A look at two top tourist countries, US and Germany, stresses the point.

Table 6.7 Top global destinations and international tourist receipts vs. GDP

Rank	Countries	Tourist receipts/GDP (%)
1.	Anguilla	66.7
2.	Maldives	55.6
3.	Antigua-Barbuda	50.0
4.	Cayman Islands	48.4
5.	St Lucia	44.6
6.	Aruba	44.4
7.	Macau	34.5
8.	St Kitts and Nevis	33.3
9.	Uganda	32.3
10.	Bahamas	25.3
11.	Bermuda	24.5
12.	Barbados	24.1
13.	St Vincent and the Grenadines	23.3
14.	Vanuatu	20.8
15.	Cambodia	20.4
16.	Seychelles	18.6
17.	Dominica	18.2
18.	Cyprus	17.0
19.	Grenada	16.7
20.	British VI	14.3
21.	Slovakia	14.2
22.	Jamaica	13.6
23.	Belize	13.5
24.	Guadeloupe	12.7
25.	Malta	12.5

Source: Author's elaboration on WTO, 2001; CIA, 2001

**Box 6.1 Top of the pops: Highest T&T GDP
(in alphabetical order)**

Anguilla	Guadeloupe
Antigua-Barbuda	Jamaica
Aruba	Macau
Bahamas	Maldives
Barbados	Malta
Belize	St Kitts and Nevis
Bermuda	St Lucia
British VI	St Vincent and the Grenadines
Cayman Islands	Seychelles
Cyprus	Vanuatu
Grenada	

Source: Author's elaboration based on WTTC (2001)

Total Tourism and Travel Exports in relation to the US GDP are just 1.86%, while US Visitor Exports reach a mere 1% of GDP (WTTC, 2001: 122), in spite of the fact that it made over US$71 billion in 1998 on this side (WTO data) and was by far the highest beneficiary of international tourist receipts for the year. The overwhelming majority of Americans stay within their country when they travel, and most of them prefer the home turf in spite of their high per capita incomes.

Something similar can be said of Germany, the country where propensity to travel is higher than anywhere else (75.3% in 1999). According to *Reiseanalyse 2000* (FUR, 2001), one of the main databases on German vacation trips, in 1999 German nationals 14 years and older went on 62.6 million vacation trips (5+ days) with 17.2% of them taking more than one holiday trip during the year. On average, each German traveler took 1.3 long vacations in 1999. On top of this, Germans had 54 million short vacations (2–4 days) coming to a total figure of more than one billion vacation days. Most vacationers went for an international destination in their trip, altogether 44.5 million or 71% of all vacations. However, Germany itself remained the top vacation land for most German tourists (18.2 million vacationing in the country as against 9.2 million traveling to Spain, the next most popular destination).

However, according to another database (IPK International, 2000), in 1999 Germans (population 15+ years) took 192 million trips with over-night stays (including long and short vacations, private and business trips). Of them, roughly 60% had Germany as their goal, while the outbound market accounted for just 40%. In the vacation market itself, outbound vacations accounted for 59 million trips while domestic ones reached 55 million. However, Germany itself, with 33% of the trips, remains the top destination for Germans. Spain (accounting for 6% of the German vacation market) is the main international destination, but it only reached the fifth position after four German regions (Bavaria, Nord-Rheinland Westphalen, Niedersaxe and Baden-Württemberg).

No Need To Call the Plumber

In tourism economics, the substantive *leak* or *leakage* describes "that part of national income which is not spent on domestically produced goods or services". Archer (2000) names taxes, savings and imports as the main sources of leakage in tourism. As a matter of fact, it is imports that have become the focal point of this discussion (De Kadt, 1979; Eadington, 1992), as they are a permanent loss of revenue and appear as a deficit in the balance of payments. Other researchers go a step further in turning the eventual leakages into one of the reasons why international tourism is not the source of economic benefits that its supporters imagine or, even more, why it may become a dangerous road for those countries that follow it (Smith and Brent, 2001).

The discussion of leakages, however, has not been documented in detail, making mostly room for estimates that may vary wildly. Archer, for instance, states that "leakages out of national economies vary from as little as 10% to as much as 80%" (2000). The same broad boundaries are accepted in the still limited literature on the question.

The WTTC database offers the possibility of addressing some of these issues in a more substantive way. The database itself does not provide figures for the tourism imports of the different economies, but they can be inferred. WTTC defines the total production of tourist goods and services for a given country as its Travel and Tourism Economy (T&TE). This magnitude is made of the T&T GDP plus the T&T Imports. Subtracting a given country's T&T GDP from its T&TE should provide the amount of the T&T Imports for each case.

Once those amounts have been determined, it is possible to estimate the percentage of leakage for each individual tourism economy by dividing the total amount of tourism imports by the *CIA Factbook* GDP data. The leakage ranking for the top 25 countries can be seen in Table 6.8.

The presence of Sweden, Austria and Belgium notwithstanding, most of the countries in this list coincide with the 25 top destinations with a higher global index of tourism in their GDP. There are again 15 Caribbean islands among them and most of the rest are also islands or assimilated enclaves.

Table 6.8 Top 25 leaking countries

Rank	Country	I/GDP (%)
1.	Antigua-Barbuda	61.5
2.	British VI	57.1
3.	Anguilla	55.6
4.	Reunion	44.1
5.	Comoros	39.0
6.	Guadeloupe	20.5
7.	Martinique	19.5
8.	Aruba	17.5
9.	Cuba	17.2
10.	St Kitts and Nevis	16.7
11.	Bermuda	16.5
12.	St Lucia	15.4
13.	Cayman Islands	15.0
14.	St Vincent and the Grenadines	13.3
15.	Maldives	13.0
16.	Hong Kong	12.8
17.	Seychelles	11.9
18.	Bahamas	10.2
19.	Iceland	10.1
20.	Kuwait	10.0
21.	Barbados	9.7
22.	Belgium	9.1
23.	Sweden	8.9
24.	Puerto Rico	8.8
25.	Austria	8.7

Source: Author's elaboration on WTTC, 2001; CIA, 2001

The relevant issue, however, is that the leakage percentage is higher than 25% only for the first five destinations, while the rest remain well below this amount. Even more, from Kuwait (position number 20) down, the rest of the 160 countries and territories have a leakage index below 10%, which is definitely not high. Compared with the leakages that affect, for instance, the 15 main T&T producers (see Table 6.9) those leakages do not seem excessive. Puerto Rico has a lower percentage of leakages than Sweden or Belgium, and Barbados is close to them. Only seven countries in Table 6.8 leak more than double the percentage of Belgium, the top leaking country among the top producers. It seems that reports on the importance of leakages have been seriously overstated.

There is another way of looking at the issue – the balance of payments standpoint. It may be true that some tourist countries and destinations pay a high price in imports to increase their foreign exchange. But, on the other hand, what really matters is whether their benefits on this side are significant. The importing effort that they have to make may be

Table 6.9 Leakages in the top 15 tourism economies

Rank	Country	I/GDP (%)
1.	Belgium	9.1
2.	Austria	8.7
3.	Netherlands	6.7
4.	Switzerland	5.9
5.	Canada	5.7
6.	Germany	5.4
7.	France	4.3
8.	Spain	3.8
9.	Australia	3.1
10.	Italy	3.0
11.	UK	2.4
12.	Former SU	2.3
13.	Japan	2.3
14.	USA	2.0
15.	China	0.3

Source: Author's elaboration on WTTC, 2001

highly rewarded by the amount of their tourist exports. This is what we should discuss now.

Again, one should be aware of some pitfalls. The best way to reach a conclusion on whether leakages make sense seems to relate the total amount of tourist imports made by the different countries to their

Table 6.10 Top 25 least leaking destinations

Rank	Country	I/TE (%)
1.	Macau	12.9
2.	Vanuatu	15.6
3.	Fiji	19.3
4.	Cyprus	25.2
5.	Thailand	28.1
6.	St Lucia	29.2
7.	Laos	30.1
8.	Aruba	30.1
9.	Maldives	30.8
10.	Mauritius	31.1
11.	Cayman Islands	32.3
12.	Barbados	32.7
13.	Jamaica	33.9
14.	Bahamas	34.3
15.	Namibia	34.5
16.	Greece	35.7
17.	Seychelles	35.7
18.	Tunisia	37.1
19.	Ethiopia	39.1
20.	Benin	39.6
21.	Malta	40.3
22.	Cambodia	44.6
23.	Paraguay	44.6
24.	St Vincent and the Grenadines	44.9
25.	Morocco	45.1

Source: Author's elaboration on WTTC, 2001

total tourist exports (Table 6.10), as the WTTC database does not make a difference between what we might call Visitor Imports (VI) and Other Imports (OI). VI would be the money spent by the nationals of a given country or territory while abroad. OI refer to the purchase of foreign goods or services to be employed for tourism purposes locally. As we shall see, ignoring the difference makes odd bedfellows, with developed economies that are important generating markets rivaling in leakages with less developed countries. However, there is no way to refine the issue, as we should, by comparing VI to VE and OI to OE, and we will have to limit our comparison to Total Imports (TI) versus Total Exports (TE).

Seven Caribbean destinations, plus a number of other islands or enclaves (Macau) and some well-known tourist destinations (Greece, Tunisia, Thailand and Morocco) are among the least leaking destinations in the world. The odd presence in the list of some countries with a low global T&T economy, such as Benin, Laos, Ethiopia or Paraguay, may be due to the fact that their Other Exports are high, as compared with their imports. For instance, after rounding, Benin's TE reach US$100 million, but half of them are OE. Something similar happens in the case of Paraguay. That situation contrasts with that of the world main tourism producers, as seen in Table 6.11.

In order to achieve their high performance as producers, all these countries have to spend many resources importing goods and services that will allow them to meet their tourist demand, while, at the same time, they are key generating markets. Taking these two factors into consideration, international tourism seems to be more onerous for well-developed tourism economies than for many less developed destinations. For every US$100 that the UK makes in tourism exports, it has to pay US$57.74 in imports. Five top producers are in the red as tourism goes. In the case of Japan, the country has to import for tourism nearly twice as much as it makes from its tourist exports. In this particular case, however, tourism deficits lessen the huge surplus that the country shows in general exports, and the Japanese government has consistently encouraged travel abroad by its nationals to achieve this goal.

At any rate, we should not be surprised that leakages are part and parcel of international tourism, for it is a case of international trade and trade always demands a relation between imports and exports. The key factor lies elsewhere. When measured by the relation between imports and GDP as well as imports and exports, the most globalized world-tourism destinations fare quite well. Only a handful of the latter (mostly islands and similar enclaves) have significant leaks, while at the same time most of them reap remarkable benefits in terms of foreign exchange.

Table 6.11 Leakages in the top 15 T&T producers

Rank	*Country*	*I/TE (%)*
1.	Japan	196.1
2.	Germany	147.0
3.	Belgium	125.1
4.	Canada	110.5
5.	USA	108.3
6.	France	91.6
7.	Austria	89.2
8.	Netherlands	86.5
9.	Australia	77.2
10.	Switzerland	75.1
11.	China	69.5
12.	Italy	67.7
13.	Spain	66.1
14.	Former SU	58.3
15.	UK	57.7

Source: Author's elaboration on WTTC data

Conclusion

As stated, this chapter's goal is modest. It has avoided a general discussion of the benefits and the pitfalls of globalization as such and has only endeavored to assess some acquired ideas on the macroeconomic effects of global tourism. At this level it has resisted the promises of a well-established trinity – to wit, that:

- Global tourism is a system made of the opposition between the developed North and the less developed South.
- International tourism is the main component of that tourist system.
- Eventual economic benefits derived by less developed countries from this system tend to be deceptive, as they are accompanied by a high degree of irretrievable leakages.

In opposition, our discussion has tried to establish that, at a macroeconomic level:

- The alleged global tourist system is difficult to pin down, as an overwhelming number of countries scarcely have a significant T&T economy in comparison to their GDP.
- With the exception of a handful of global destinations, domestic tourism is more significant and productive than international travel.
- On top of being necessary to any trading system, leakages in the global tourism industry affect less developed countries only superficially.
- When it comes to leakages as measured by the national balances of payments, developed countries tend to have a higher leakage percentage than global tourist destinations.

In so doing, the present chapter only aims at refocusing the discussion at this systemic level. It does not profess to have any answers to the other dimensions (cultural, social and microeconomic) of the big elephant whose shape and size will still be a matter for squabbles in the foreseeable future.

References

Archer, B. (1973) *The Impact of Domestic Tourism*. Bangor: University of Wales Press.

Archer, B. (1974) *Tourism Multipliers: The State of the Art*. Bangor: University of Wales Press.

Archer, B. (2000) Leakage. In J. Jafari (ed.) *Encyclopedia of Tourism*. London and New York: Routledge.

CIA (2001) *The CIA World Factbook*. At http://www.odci.gov/cia/publications/factbook.

Crick, M. (1996) Representations of international tourism in the social sciences: Sun, sex, savings, and servility. In Y. Apostolopoulos, S. Leivadi and A. Yiannakis (eds) *The Sociology of Tourism: Theoretical and Empirical Investigations*. London and New York: Routledge.

De Kadt, E.J. (1979) *Tourism: Passport to Development? Perspectives on the Social and Cultural Effects of Tourism in Developing Countries*. New York: Oxford University Press.

Eadington, W.R. (1992) *Tourism Alternatives: Potentials and Problems in the Development of Tourism*. Philadelphia, PA: The University of Pennsylvania Press.

FUR Hamburg (2000) *Reiseanalyse 1999*. Press release, Berlin, March 3.

IPK International (2000) *European Travel Monitor 1999*. Press release, March 2.

Ireland, M. (ed.) (1996) Gender and class relations in tourism employment. In Y. Apostolopoulos, S. Leivadi and A. Yiannakis (eds) *The Sociology of Tourism: Theoretical and Empirical Investigations*. London and New York: Routledge.

Nash, D. (1996) *Anthropology of Tourism*. Oxford: Pergamon.

Nash, D. (2000) Imperialism. In J. Jafari (ed.) *Encyclopedia of Tourism*. London and New York: Routledge.

Smith, V. (1985) Introduction. *Annals of Tourism Research* 13, 329–330.

Smith, V. (1989) Introduction. In V. Smith (ed.) *Hosts and Guests: The Anthropology of Tourism*. Philadelphia, PA: The University of Pennsylvania Press.

Smith, V. and M. Brent (eds) (2000) *Hosts and Guests Revisited: Tourism Issues in the 21st Century*. New York, Sydney and Tokyo: Cognizant Communications Co.

Urry, J. (1996) Tourism, culture and social inequality. In Y. Apostolopoulos, S. Leivadi and A. Yiannakis (eds) *The Sociology of Tourism: Theoretical and Empirical Investigations*. London and New York: Routledge.

WTO (2000) *Tourism Highlights 2000*. At http://www.world-tourism.org.

WTTC (2002) *Tourism Satellite Accounts*. At http://www.wttc.org.

Chapter 7

The Geographical Structure of Canadian Tourism

STEPHEN L.J. SMITH

Introduction

The popularity of the phrase "tourism industry" in both scholarly and industry publications implies there really is such an industry. However, this is not the case. "Industry" denotes a group of businesses that produce essentially the same product using a common technology and whose output is substantial enough to be readily captured by a System of National Accounts. With respect to a homogeneous product and a common technology, tourism clearly is not a conventional industry. For example, both accommodation and transportation establishments are part of the "tourism industry". In the case of accommodation, the product is a place to stay; for transportation, the product is movement. Although the notion of a "homogeneous product" is somewhat elastic – an accommodation product can be as precise as a hotel; combined with motels, B&Bs, and similar establishments as "roofed accommodation"; or more generally combined with campgrounds as "accommodation services" – combining accommodation and transportation into a single product strains logic to the breaking point.

Tourism is better thought of as an "economic constellation" – a grouping of numerous industries in the transportation, accommodation, food service, recreation and entertainment, and travel trade sectors that creates a picture of something more than the simple collection of the parts. The phenomenon that links these industries is that all are services used by people engaged in activities temporarily away from their usual environment. Thus, whereas industries are characterized by the products that businesses produce, tourism is characterized by the activities of consumers.

While one cannot speak of a tourism industry per se, one can speak of tourism industries. Simply put, a tourism industry is any industry that produces a tourism commodity. A tourism commodity, in turn, is any commodity for which a substantial portion of demand comes from persons taking a tourism trip (a trip for virtually any purpose, other than routine commuting, taking a person temporarily outside his usual environment – WTO, 1999).

Tourism industries have several characteristics that shape the magnitude, nature, and distribution of their economic, social, and environ-mental impacts as well as pose significant challenges for effective planning, development, marketing, and management. One of the most frequently mentioned qualities is that tourism consists primarily of small and medium-sized establishments (SMEs). For example, the World Travel and Tourism Council (WTTC, 2001a, 2001b) estimates that 95% of the world's tourism firms are SMEs (which the WTTC defined as establishments with fewer than 10 employees).

Further, while tourism establishments are found in virtually every region and every community in industrialized nations, there is substantial variation in the concentration of tourism activity among regions. While these observations could be considered to be almost common sense, there has been little empirical analysis of their actual magnitude and pattern. This chapter examines these two characteristics using national and sub-national data. Specifically, it attempts to answer the following questions in the context of Canadian tourism:

(1) What proportion of tourism establishments can be classified as small or medium-sized – by sector and by province/territory?
(2) How does the absolute and relative magnitude of each sector vary by province/territory?
(3) What demographic or economic variables appear to contribute to the variations in the size and mix of tourism establishments by province/territory?

Definitions and Data Sources

As noted previously, an industry conceptually can be defined as a group of businesses meeting three criteria: (1) they produce essentially the same product, (2) they use essentially the same technology, and (3) the value of their combined output exceeds a specified threshold (for example, the new North American Industrial Classification System uses a minimum of $200 million gross revenues (Chadwick, 2001)). Operationally, industries are defined in terms of their primary product. Thus, while many hotels provide food and beverage services, laundry and dry cleaning services, and telecommunication services in addition to accommodation, it is the accommodation product that characterizes them because that is their core business – their primary source of revenue. For measurement purposes, industries are organized into a hierarchical system such as the Standard Industrial Classification (SIC) System. Industries at each level are assigned a numerical code, with from one to four or five digits. The more digits, the more narrowly defined the industry. Box 7.1 identifies Canada's tourism industries at two-digit ("major group") and four-digit ("industry class") levels and aggregates these into the five sectors used in this chapter: transportation, accommodation, food and beverage service, recreation and entertainment, and travel trade.

Data for this chapter are obtained from Statistics Canada's Business Register, a repository of statistics reflecting the Canadian business population, and from a special tabulation of Canada Customs and Revenue Agency's (CCRA) account files. Data in the Business Register are based on CCRA account files as well as individual business censuses. The Register represents the universe of Canadian businesses that meet at least one of the following criteria:

(1) An employee workforce for which they submit payroll remittances to CCRA (e.g. income tax deductions); or
(2) a minimum of $30,000 in annual sales revenues; or
(3) incorporated under a provincial or federal act and have filed a federal income tax form within the past three years.

The public access Business Register provides counts by employment ranges for businesses that meet at least one of these three criteria. Employment sizes are based on the annual maximum number of employees aggregated to a full-time equivalent basis. Thus, a measure of 10 employees may represent 10 full-time employees, 20 half-time, or some other combination. Revenue data were obtained by a special tabulation through the National Accounts and Environment Division of Statistics Canada. These data are pre-tax revenues and, like employment, are reported in broad ranges. If the number of firms in any range is fewer than five, no count is released in order to protect the confidentiality of individual businesses.

The Business Register also provides counts of "indeterminate" establishments – businesses that do not meet any of the three criteria. A couple renting one or two rooms of their home to visitors for additional income, but who are not registered as a business nor have paid employees, would be an example of an indeterminate tourism establishment.

Box 7.1 Two-digit and four-digit Canadian SIC codes for tourism industries

45   Transportation Industries
4511   Scheduled Air Transport Industry
4512   Non-scheduled Air Transport, Chartered, Industry
4531   Railway Transport Industry
4541   Freight and Passenger Water Transport Industry
4542   Ferry Industry
4549   Other Water Transport Industries
4571   Urban Transit Systems Industry
4572   Inter-urban and Rural Transit Systems Industry
4574   Charter and Sightseeing Bus Services Industry
4575   Limousine Service to Airports and Stations Industry
4581   Taxicab Industry

85   Education Service Industries
8551   Museums and Archives

91   Accommodation Service Industries
9111   Hotels and Motor Hotels
9112   Motels
9113   Tourist Courts and Cabins
9114   Guest Houses and Tourist Homes
9131   Camping Grounds and Travel Trailer Parks
9141   Outfitters (hunting and fishing camps)
9149   Other Recreation and Vacation Camps

92   Food and Beverage Service Industries
9211   Restaurants, Licensed
9212   Restaurants, Unlicensed (including drive-ins)
9213   Take-out Food Services
9221   Taverns, Bars, and Night Clubs

96 Amusement and Recreation Service Industries

9621 Regular Motion Picture Theatres
9622 Outdoor Motion Picture Theatres
9629 Other Motion Picture Exhibition
9631 Entertainment Production Companies and Artists
9639 Other Theatrical and Staged Entertainment Services
9641 Professional Sports Clubs
9643 Horse Race Tracks
9644 Other Race Tracks
9651 Golf Courses
9652 Curling Clubs
9653 Skiing Facilities
9654 Boat Rentals and Marinas
9661 Gambling Operations
9691 Bowling Alleys and Billiard Parlours
9692 Amusement Parks, Carnival and Circus Operations
9694 Coin-operated Amusement Services
9695 Roller Skating Facilities
9696 Botanical and Zoological Gardens
9699 Other Amusement and Recreational Services n.e.c.

99 Other Service Industries

9921 Automobile and Truck Rental and Leasing Services
9961 Ticket and Travel Agencies
9962 Tour Wholesalers and Operators

Definition of sectors used in this chapter

SIC code ranges	Sector name
4511–4581, 9921	Transportation
9111–9149	Accommodation
9211–9221	Food and beverage
8551, 9621–9699	Recreation and entertainment
9951, 9962	Travel trade

Industry data in the Business Register is based on a unit of analysis known as a "statistical establishment". A statistical establishment is a business establishment that:

(1) produces a homogeneous set of goods or services;
(2) does not cross provincial boundaries; and
(3) provides data on the value of output together with the cost of principal intermediate inputs used along with the cost and quantity of labour resources used to produce the output.

In simplified terms, the analysis in this chapter can be described as based on businesses distinguished by certain accounting characteristics. If a business owner has a firm with two or more locations that combine their accounting, those locations will be counted as a single establishment. On the other hand, if the accounting is reported separately (for example, large hotel chains), each operation will be counted separately. For the purposes of this chapter, the analysis will be done at the four-digit level. Results are presented for each research question. All data are for 1999 except where noted.

Before turning to the results, it may be useful to highlight a limitation previously noted in the data. Establishments are classified according to their core business. Many tourism establishments may actually provide several different services that a customer may perceive as distinct businesses but that are still classified under one establishment. Thus, an operator may provide accommodation, food service, attractions, and tour operations – but will still be classified as a single enterprise according to the primary source of income. This is a particular problem for public sector attractions. Museums, galleries, historic sites, entertainment facilities, and other tourism operations provided by a municipal, regional, or provincial government will not be tabulated as belonging to any tourism sector – because the core business of the "operator" is "government". The counts shown, therefore, are conservatively biased in the sense that not all tourism services are captured. Given this restriction, it is still possible to assess the general geographic structure of Canadian tourism.

Results

What proportion of tourism establishments can be classified as small or medium-sized, by sector and by province/territory?

First, the concept of a small or medium-sized establishment needs to be operationally defined. Statistics Canada uses two measures: number of employees and revenues. In terms of numbers of employees, the following qualitative divisions are normally used: (1) a micro establishment is one with fewer than five employees, (2) a small establishment has 5 to 19 employees, and (3) a medium establishment has between 20 and 99 employees. At an aggregate or national level, more than 30% of the 140,000 tourism establishments in Canada are indeterminate; nearly another 30% are micro (Table 7.1). In other words, about 6 out of 10 Canadian tourism businesses have fewer than five employees. Over 85% are micro or small and over 98% have fewer than 100 employees – that is, 98 out of 100 of the nearly 150,000 tourism firms in Canada are SMEs.

Table 7.1 also shows there are some notable regional differences in the distribution of establishment sizes. Indeterminate establishments are concentrated in the two most populous provinces, Quebec and Ontario. Micro firms (1–4 employees) are over-represented in Atlantic Canada (Newfoundland, Prince Edward Island, Nova Scotia, and New Brunswick). Quebec and the prairie province of Saskatchewan also have concentrations of these micro firms greater than the national average. Atlantic Canada also has a slightly above-average concentration of firms in the 5–19 employee range as do the northern territories (Yukon, Northwest Territories, and Nunavut).

Medium-sized firms (20–99 employees) show relatively little regional variation. This is, in part, a function of the relatively limited number of firms in this size category. Eight of the 13 provinces and territories have between 13% and 15% of tourism establishments in this size range. An even lower variance was observed for the even fewer number of large firms (100+ employees). Eight provinces or territories had between 1% and 2% of their tourism and large firms in this size range.

The last row in Table 7.1 shows the distribution of all establishments in Canada by employment category. These data do put the notion of the dominance of small and medium-sized enterprises in tourism in a slightly different light. While just over 30% of all tourism establishments are indeterminate, nearly 45% (almost 50% more than in tourism) of all Canadian businesses are indeterminate. Almost one-third of all businesses are in the micro category, compare to slightly less than 30% for tourism. On the other hand, tourism firms are over-represented in the 5–19 (small) and 20–99 (medium) categories. They are also slightly over-represented in the 100+ (large) category, although the percentages for both tourism and all businesses is quite small. In sum: tourism has fewer indeterminate and micro firms than the economy as a whole. However, tourism has a higher share of small and medium-sized enterprises and is approximately equal to the overall economy in terms of the percentage

Table 7.1 Distribution of tourism establishments by employment category within province/territory (% in italics): 1999

Province	Indeterminate	1–4	5–19	20–99	100+	Total
Newfoundland	395	1,009	598	200	21	2,223
	17.8	*45.4*	*26.9*	*9.0*	*0.9*	*100.0*
Prince Edward Island	137	280	254	113	11	795
	17.2	*35.2*	*31.9*	*14.2*	*1.4*	*100.0*
Nova Scotia	787	1,235	1125	522	40	3,709
	21.2	*33.3*	*30.2*	*14.1*	*1.1*	*100.0*
New Brunswick	850	1,117	831	420	26	3,144
	27.0	*35.5*	*26.4*	*13.3*	*0.8*	*100.0*
Quebec	12,254	12,039	8,138	3,643	872	36,946
	33.2	*32.6*	*22.0*	*9.9*	*2.4*	*100.0*
Ontario	16,402	12,890	11,463	6,428	694	47,877
	34.3	*26.9*	*23.9*	*13.4*	*1.4*	*100.0*
Manitoba	1,302	1,416	1,188	791	62	4,759
	27.4	*29.8*	*25.0*	*11.6*	*1.3*	*100.0*
Saskatchewan	1,259	1,506	1,173	660	63	4,661
	27.0	*32.2*	*25.2*	*14.2*	*1.4*	*100.0*
Alberta	4,244	3,554	3,698	2,383	228	14,107
	30.1	*25.2*	*26.2*	*16.9*	*1.6*	*100.0*
British Columbia	6,076	6,821	5,823	3,154	303	22,177
	27.4	*30.8*	*26.7*	*14.2*	*1.4*	*100.0*
Yukon	68	95	128	48	2	341
	19.9	*27.9*	*37.5*	*14.1*	*0.6*	*100.0*
Northwest Territories	55	66	106	35	3	265
	20.8	*24.9*	*40.0*	*13.2*	*1.1*	*100.0*
Nunavut	10	19	32	8	0	69
	14.5	*27.5*	*46.4*	*11.6*	*0.0*	*100.0*
All Tourism Establishments	43,839	42,047	34,557	18,405	2,325	141,173
	31.1	*29.8*	*24.5*	*13.0*	*1.6*	*100.0*
All Canadian Establishments	818,785	602,996	285,828	106,506	18,890	1,833,005
	44.7	*32.9*	*15.6*	*5.8*	*1.0*	*100.0*

of large firms. The notion that tourism is dominated by SMEs is not incorrect, although the suggestion that, in this, it is dramatically different than the total economy is incorrect.

Table 7.2 presents the information in Table 7.1 in a slightly different format. Here firms are divided into "unincorporated" (i.e. indeterminate) and "incorporated" (all others). The provincial distribution of all establishments in both absolute numbers and percentages is shown in the first two data columns. For those familiar with the relative populations of Canada's provinces and territories, a rough correlation between population size and the number of establishments is immediately obvious. The same, too, is true of the distribution of incorporated establishments. However, a closer examination reveals certain differences. If the percentage of all incorporated establishments located in each province or territory is divided by the national percentage of all tourism establishments in that province or territory, one obtains an index summarizing the relative concentration of incorporated (and, conversely, indeterminate) establishments by each province/territory. These smallest, unincorporated establishments are most frequently found in the two largest provincial economies – Ontario and Quebec.

Table 7.3 provides a different perspective on the size distribution of tourism establishments – the numbers and percentages of firms by sector and revenue ranges. These data are for the year 2000 and, because they are drawn from a different year as well as different files than the public release Business Register, the establishment counts are slightly different by sector and province/territory. These differences are not important for the purposes of this chapter; rather, the focus is on the sectoral and geographic distributions, which are consistent among the various data sources.

Statistics Canada considers "small" enterprises to be those earning less that $10 million per year. Medium-sized enterprises are those earning from $10 million to $49.9 million. Large firms are those with revenues of at least $50 million. On the basis of these revenue criteria, over 99% of tourism firms are small enterprises.

Transportation firms have the highest concentration in the lowest income range of all sectors, with nearly two-thirds of all transportation firms report earning under $100,000 per year. This is due to the relatively large number of individual operators who own and operate their own taxi service. Small auto rental and leasing services also contribute significantly to this pattern. Transportation firms with the largest revenues are scheduled air transport firms and, to a lesser degree, rail transport firms.

Table 7.2 Distribution of tourism establishments by province and territory: 1999

Jurisdiction	Tourism establishments (N)	Tourism establishments (% of all Canada)	Unincorporated tourism establishments (N)	Incorporated tourism establishments (% of all Canada)	Index (% Incorp./% All)
Newfoundland	2,223	1.57	1,828	1.87	1.19
Prince Edward Island	795	0.56	658	0.67	1.19
Nova Scotia	3,709	2.62	2,922	2.99	1.14
New Brunswick	3,144	2.22	2,394	2.45	1.10
Quebec	36,946	26.11	24,692	25.26	0.97
Ontario	47,877	33.84	31,475	32.20	0.95
Manitoba	4,759	3.36	3,457	3.54	1.05
Saskatchewan	4,661	3.29	3,402	3.48	1.06
Alberta	14,107	9.97	9,863	10.09	1.01
British Columbia	22,177	15.68	16,101	16.47	1.05
Yukon	741	0.52	673	0.69	1.33
Northwest Territories	265	0.19	210	0.21	1.10
Nunavut	69	0.05	59	0.06	1.20
Canada	141,473	100.00	97,734	100.00	1.00

Table 7.3 Distribution of tourism establishments by sector and revenue ranges (% in italics): 2000

Sector	0–99K	100–249K	250–499K	500–999K	1M–1.9M	2M–4.9M	5M–9.9M	10M–19.9M	20M–49.9M	>50M	Total
Transportation	10,734 *0.65*	2,260 *0.14*	1078 *0.07*	853 *0.05*	684 *0.04*	374 *0.03*	187 *0.01*	103 *<0.01*	52 *<0.01*	65 *<0.01*	16,540 *1.00*
Accommodation	4,609 *0.32*	4,803 *0.33*	2,108 *0.15*	1,112 *0.08*	969 *0.07*	606 *0.04*	189 *0.01*	62 *<0.01*	29 *<0.01*	5 *<0.01*	14,519 *1.00*
Food service	28,348 *0.35*	23,045 *0.28*	13,942 *0.17*	8,854 *0.11*	5,317 *0.07*	1,599 *0.02*	132 *<0.01*	43 *<0.01*	–* *<0.01*	– *<0.01*	81,296 *1.00*
Recreation and entertainment	15,646 *0.53*	7,246 *0.25*	3,044 *0.10*	1,643 *0.06*	1,199 *0.04*	455 *0.02*	122 *<0.01*	57 *<0.01*	18 *<0.01*	18 *<0.01*	29,563 *1.00*
Travel trade	2,214 *0.31*	1,368 *0.19*	857 *0.12*	683 *0.10*	944 *0.13*	695 *0.10*	169 *0.02*	570 *0.01*	27 *<0.01*	16 *<0.01*	7,029 *1.00*
Total	61,551 *0.41*	38,722 *0.26*	21,029 *0.14*	13,145 *0.09*	9,113 *0.06*	3,729 *0.03*	799 *0.01*	322 *<0.01*	126 *<0.01*	104 *<0.01*	148,947 *1.00*

Source: Special tabulations by National Accounts and Environment Division, Statistics Canada

Note: * Data suppressed to avoid identification of establishments

Recreation and entertainment businesses also tend to have modest revenues, even by tourism business standards. A large number of individual performers, small-scale production companies, and small attractions are major contributors to this profile. The largest revenue-earners in the recreation and entertainment sector are international-calibre museums, professional sports clubs (e.g. National Hockey League teams), and casinos.

The food service, accommodation, and travel trade sectors each have about one-third of establishments earning less than $100,000, which is proportionately less than that for tourism establishments generally. Accommodation properties are over-represented in the $100,000–249,000 range, compared to the entire set of tourism establishments. The proportion of accommodation firms tends to mirror the distribution of tourism firms generally in revenue ranges $250,000 and higher. The smallest operators, not surprisingly, include tourist courts and cabins, guest houses, and campgrounds. The highest revenue earners are the large hotel chains. Virtually all motel operations have revenues under $10 million.

Food service operations – licensed and unlicensed restaurants, and take-out food services – may be found in virtually all revenue ranges. They are, however, under-represented in the under $100,000 category and over-represented in the $100,000–1 million range. Taverns, bars, and night clubs tend to have lower total revenues than the other food service categories.

Travel agencies and tour operators may be found in every revenue category. Compared to the national average, travel trade establishments are over-represented in revenue categories from $1 million upwards. This is particularly true for tour operators, which generally are larger operations than travel agencies both in numbers of employees and revenues.

While these aggregate figures are noteworthy, additional insights can be obtained by looking at the variations in the distribution by sector and geographic location (Table 7.4). This topic is considered as the next question.

How do the total numbers and percentages of establishments in each sector vary by province/territory?

Even a superficial glance at the numbers of firms by sector and province/territory in Table 7.4 suggests that the number of tourism establishments is a function of the population of the province. The most populous provinces, Ontario, Quebec, and British Columbia, tend to have the

Table 7.4 Distribution of firms by province and sector (% of provinces' total tourism establishments in italics): 1999

Province /Territory	*Transport*	*Accommodation*	*Food*	*Recreation*	*Trade*	*All*
Newfoundland	254	415	1,197	313	44	2,223
	0.11	*0.19*	*0.54*	*0.14*	*0.02*	*1.00*
Prince Edward Island	48	196	358	174	19	795
	0.06	*0.25*	*0.45*	*0.22*	*0.02*	*1.00*
Nova Scotia	306	641	2,019	650	93	3,709
	0.08	*0.17*	*0.54*	*0.18*	*0.03*	*1.00*
New Brunswick	285	500	1,710	606	43	3,144
	0.09	*0.16*	*0.54*	*0.19*	*0.01*	*1.00*
Quebec	2,902	3,908	22,475	6,127	1,543	36,946
	0.08	*0.11*	*0.61*	*0.17*	*0.04*	*1.00*
Ontario	5,141	5,359	25,027	9,445	2,905	47,877
	0.11	*0.11*	*0.52*	*0.20*	*0.06*	*1.00*
Manitoba	669	722	2,357	830	181	4,759
	0.14	*0.15*	*0.50*	*0.17*	*0.04*	*1.00*
Saskatchewan	468	920	2,355	800	118	4,661
	0.10	*0.20*	*0.51*	*0.17*	*0.03*	*1.00*
Alberta	1,360	1,608	7,797	2,583	759	14,107
	0.10	*0.11*	*0.55*	*0.18*	*0.05*	*1.00*
British Columbia	2,643	2,933	11,314	3,987	1,300	22,177
	0.12	*0.13*	*0.51*	*0.18*	*0.06*	*1.00*
Yukon	126	311	126	140	43	741
	0.17	*0.42*	*0.17*	*0.19*	*0.06*	*1.00*
Northwest Territories	80	66	74	29	16	265
	0.30	*0.25*	*0.28*	*0.11*	*0.06*	*1.00*
Nunavut	18	34	8	4	5	69
	0.25	*0.49*	*0.13*	*0.05*	*0.07*	*1.00*
Canada	14,240	17,613	76,817	25,688	7,060	141,473
	0.10	*0.12*	*0.55*	*0.18*	*0.05*	*1.00*

largest number of firms in each sector. The sparsely populated territories and tiny Prince Edward Island have the fewest firms. A simple bivariate correlation between numbers of firms by sector and provincial/territorial population (Table 7.5) confirms the link, with an r^2 larger than 0.95 for each sector. Table 7.5 also notes which province(s) were over-predicted or under-predicted by the regression model. Quebec has fewer transportation and travel trade firms than would be expected on the basis of population alone. Ontario has fewer accommodation and food service firms than predicted. The number of tourism firms in British Columbia is greater than predicted for every sector except food service firms.

To obtain better insight into forces affecting the provincial and territorial distribution of firms by sector, one can look at the percentage distributions reported in Table 7.4. Here the percentages represent the percentage of all tourism firms within any province/territory associated with any given sector. These percentages thus add to 100% for each province. If one considers the bottom row in Table 7.4, one can see that food services is the largest sector, accounting for 55% of all tourism firms in Canada. Recreation and entertainment firms are a distant second, with 18% of all tourism firms. These are followed by accommodation at 12%, transportation at 10%, and travel trade at 5%.

It is important to remember the definition of a tourism industry – one whose characteristic commodity receives a substantial demand from persons engaged in tourism. This does not mean that all establishments in any industry are patronized exclusively or even primarily by visitors. In fact, only about 20% of all Canadian food and beverage revenues are attributable to tourism. The level of data aggregation used in this chapter does not permit one to separate out those establishments in any industry that derive most of their revenues from visitors from those that do not.

Even with that limitation, certain regional patterns emerge. Canada's territories have a much higher percentage of tourism firms in the transportation and accommodation sectors than the rest of the country. On the other hand, the territories have a much lower percentage of food and beverage firms. The physically smaller provinces, especially Prince Edward Island, have a relatively low percentage of transportation firms. Quebec has a somewhat higher percentage of food and beverage firms than one would expect. Nunavut has a very small proportion of its tourism firms in the recreation and entertainment industry, while Prince Edward Island has a relatively high percentage. Atlantic Canada overall has a higher-than-expected percentage of accommodation and a lower-than-expected share of travel trade firms.

Table 7.5 Regression results: Numbers of firms by sector versus population

	# trans. firms	# accomm. firms	# food firms	# rec. firms	# travel trade firms	Total # of firms
R-square	0.964	0.972	0.969	0.993	0.968	0.986
Constant	62.119	229.891	147.193	7.930	-46.553	400.04
Coefficient (unstd)	0.467	0.507	2.594	7.930	0.265	4.720
Beta	0.982	0.986	0.984	0.997	0.984	0.993
Significance (Beta)	0.000	0.000	0.000	0.000	0.000	0.000
Over-predicted > 1 std	Quebec	Ontario	Ontario		Quebec	Quebec,
Ontario						
Under-predicted > 1 std	British Columbia	British Columbia	Quebec	British Columbia	British Columbia	British Columbia

What demographic or economic variables appear to contribute to the variations in the size and mix of tourism establishments by province/territory?

To supplement the superficial observations provided in response to the previous question, a series of stepwise regression analyses was run. The percentage of firms in each sector was regressed against a number of demographic and economic variables: area of province, total population, population density, percentage of population living in urban areas, provincial GDP, provincial GDP per capita, percentage of GDP generated by the goods-producing sector, and population growth rate (1991–1996).

As can be seen in Table 7.6, the percentage of a province's tourism businesses belonging to the transportation sector is significantly and inversely correlated with population density. This is consistent with the previous observation that the territories had a substantially higher percentage of firms in the transportation sector than did the provinces (indeed, all three territories had high residuals in the regression analysis, reflecting the very high percentage of firms in the transportation sector). Such a finding may be intuitively logical. Those regions of Canada with the lowest population densities (and, coincidentally, the least developed highway networks) have the greatest need for alternatives to private vehicles. The Yukon, Northwest Territories, and Nunavut support, in particular, a relatively large number of bush pilots who provide charter services for individuals wishing to travel around the territories.

The percentage of tourism firms belonging to the accommodation sector is significantly and inversely correlated with percentage of the population that is urban (i.e. lives in communities of 10,000 or more). Although the R^2 is relatively strong (>0.7), the causal logic is not immediately clear. Or to state the question more directly – why do less urban provinces and territories have a higher proportion of accommodation establishments?

The explanation may be found, in part at least, in the liquor legislation in the Yukon. In an effort to control both the availability of alcoholic beverages as well as to insure the safety of anyone over-imbibing in the harsh climate of Canada's far north, any Yukon establishment providing a bar also had to provide food service and, under most circumstances, accommodation. Thus, the relatively high percentage of accommodation firms is balanced by a relatively low percentage of firms in the food and beverage sector. The percentage of territorial food and beverage sector firms is half or less that of the national average. This legislation is not

Table 7.6 Regression results for distribution by sector

Dependent variable	Independent variables	R² change	R²	Unstd co-efficients	Beta	Sig.	Residuals Over-predicted >3 SD	Under-predicted >3 SD
% of firms in transportation	(Constant)			0.117		0.000		
	Population density	0.552	0.552	−0.002	−0.743	0.014		Yukon, NWT, Nunavut
% of firms in accommodation	(Constant)			0.336		0.000		
	% of population that is urban	0.723	0.723	0.003	−0.850	0.002		Yukon, Nunavut
% of firms in food and beverage	none significant							
% of firms in recreation and entertainment	(Constant)			0.102		0.002	NWT	
	Population density	0.631		0.003	0.962	0.001		
	Per capita GDP	0.208	0.839	0.000	−0.485	0.020		
% of firms in travel trade	(Constant)			−0.57		0.001		Yukon, NWT, Nunavut
	% of population that is urban	0.863		0.001	1.117	0.000		
	Population density	0.073	0.936	0.000	0.328	0.026		

present in the Northwest Territories or Nunavut, so some other force is responsible for the high proportion of food service establishments. The explanation for the patterns in these two territories is likely due to the very high proportion of tourism in the Northwest Territories and Nunavut being government and business travel. This supports substantial accommodation development but fewer attractions and travel trade establishments. Accommodation establishments also provide food services, thus making it more difficult for free-standing restaurants to compete in the very small economies of both territories.

The percentage of firms in recreation and entertainment is most strongly and positively correlated with population density, reflecting, in part, the importance of a large population base to support professional sports teams, performing arts companies, museums, and galleries. The percentage of firms in this sector is also significantly correlated with per capita GDP, albeit inversely. This may be a result of the importance of regional theatre and musical groups in Atlantic Canada – a region of Canada that traditionally has lower per capita GDPs than central or western Canada. Small-scale (as opposed to the large corporate structures of central and western Canada) performing arts companies, especially musical and regional theatre groups, are an important part of Atlantic Canada's culture as well as tourism product. The Northwest Territories was over-predicted, perhaps reflecting the dominance of nature-based tourism products in that region – the providers of which perhaps are classified under accommodations (as lodge operations) or travel trade (as guides and tour operators).

The concentration of firms in the travel trade is strongly and positively associated with the percentage of the population that is urban and, to a lesser degree, with population density. Indeed, common experience suggests the number and availability of travel agencies and tour operators tends to be closely tied to the size of the resident population market. It is worth noting that the three northern territories again emerged as having large residuals. Each had more travel trade firms than one would expect given their degree of urbanness and population density – suggesting that either the remoteness of the three territories may create a demand for travel agencies and outbound operators for the resident population, or that the strong nature-based tourism produce of the territories creates an unusually large potential for receptive tour operators and guides. Further research is needed to assess the validity of these two hypotheses.

Of the five sectors examined, only the provincial distribution of food and beverage firms did not have any significant correlation with the set of independent variables. This may be due, in part, to the lack of systematic variance in the percentage of firms in the food service sector in the 10 provinces. Indeed, as can be seen in Table 7.4 (p. 165), the percentage of food service businesses generally ranged between 50 and 55% for the provinces (the percentages for the three territories was markedly lower, but these may not have been sufficient to yield significant correlations).

Table 7.7 summarizes the distribution of firms by employment category and sector. The transportation, and recreation and entertainment sectors have substantially more indeterminate firms than the other sectors. As noted in connection with the discussion of revenue ranges and sectors, independent taxi and limousine drivers account for a relatively substantial portion of the number of transportation firms – and many of these fall in the indeterminate category. The same is true of individual performers and artists in the recreation and entertainment sector.

The travel trade sector has a disproportionately high number of firms employing 1–4 people. These firms tend to be small travel agencies, although a few very small tour operations may also be found in this

Table 7.7 Distribution of tourism establishments by sector and employment category (% in italics): 1999

Sector	*Indeterminate*	*1–4*	*5–19*	*20–99*	*100+*	*Total*
Transportation	6,906	4,793	1,551	707	283	14,240
	0.49	*0.34*	*0.11*	*0.05*	*0.02*	*1.00*
Accommodation	4,883	5,928	4,010	2,267	525	17,613
	0.28	*0.34*	*0.23*	*0.13*	*0.03*	*1.00*
Food service	15,363	21,508	24,580	13,827	1,536	76,817
	0.20	*0.28*	*0.32*	*0.18*	*0.02*	*1.00*
Recreation and entertainment	10,266	8,645	4,313	1,955	509	25,688
	0.40	*0.34*	*0.17*	*0.08*	*0.02*	*1.00*
Travel trade	1,836	3,107	2,765	282	70	7,060
	0.26	*0.44*	*0.25*	*0.04*	*0.01*	*1.00*
Total	43,839	42,007	34,557	18,405	2,325	141,473
	0.31	*0.30*	*0.25*	*0.13*	*0.02*	*1.00*

category. The food service sector – the largest sector of the five in terms of total numbers of firms as well as total numbers of employees – is over-represented in the traditional small and medium-sized categories (5–19 and 20–99 employees). In fact, fully half of all food service firms are in these categories, compared to only one-quarter for recreation and entertainment and about one-eighth for transportation.

Only about 2% of all tourism firms employ 100 or more workers. There is little variation in this percentage across the five sectors.

Finally, one can consider variables affecting the regional variation in the relative concentration of establishments of various sizes. Table 7.8 provides regression results between each size category (using province/ territory as the unit of analysis). The percentage of a province's or territory's firms that is indeterminate is strongly correlated with the degree of urbanization in that jurisdiction. The more urban the population, the higher the percentage of firms in the indeterminate category. This finding is not unexpected given the earlier observation that indeterminate firms were most heavily concentrated in the two most populous provinces, Ontario and Quebec.

The relative concentration of micro firms is significantly and inversely correlated with per capita GDP. The higher the per capita GDP, the smaller the proportion of firms with 1–4 employees, or, to put this the other way around, relatively poorer provinces and territories (i.e. relatively low GDPs adjusted for population) will tend to have a higher percentage of micro firms. The percentage of small firms (5–20 employees) by province is also correlated with population measures, but in a somewhat more complicated way: positively with population density and negatively with total population. Based on the regression results, Nunavut has substantially more micro firms than one would expect. All three northern territories have more small (5–19 employees) establishments than predicted by the regression model.

No significant correlations were observed between the independent variables and the two largest employment categories. This is probably due to the small number and lack of variation in the provincial and territorial percentages of businesses found in these two categories.

Conclusions

Canadian tourism represents a substantial portion of the Canadian economy, with 7.7% of all firms belonging to a tourism industry. Subtracting indeterminate firms (those with very low revenues and without paid employees from the count of establishments), there were about 97,000 tourism firms or about 9.6% of the 1.01 million firms (excluding indeterminate establishments) in Canada.

The distribution of these firms displays substantial regional variations in both the number and proportions of different types of tourism establishments on a provincial/territorial basis. Some of the variations are readily explained. For example, the territories, with their widely dispersed population and poor road network, support a high percentage of transportation businesses. The most populous and urban provinces tend to have a disproportionate share of commercial attractions, including performing art venues, large museums and galleries, and professional sports teams. However, other patterns require further research, such as the high proportion of tourism businesses in the Northwest Territories and Nunavut in accommodation and a low percentage in food services.

Tourism, while usually characterized as being dominated by small and medium-sized enterprises actually has fewer very small firms than the Canadian economy as a whole. Conversely, it has a slightly higher percentage of large firms than the overall business sector – although it should be noted that the total percentage of large firms in both the tourism and the overall business sector is quite small. Nearly 30% of tourism establishments are indeterminate, compared to nearly 45% for the total economy. These smallest establishments are concentrated in the two largest provincial economies, Quebec and Ontario.

In sum, the geographic and size distribution of tourism establishments, by sector, has been shown to be fairly complex, subject to a variety of demographic and economic variables. Tourism is dominated by SMEs but not as much as the total Canadian economy is. The size of the various tourism sectors differs substantially, with food services accounting for over half of all tourism firms.

References

Chadwick, R. (2001) The North American Product Classification System: Travel Arrangement and Reservation Services Industry Group (5615). Working paper prepared for Canadian Tourism Commission, Ottawa, Canada.

World Tourism Organization (WTO) (1999) *Tourism Satellite Account: The Conceptual Framework*. Madrid: WTO.

World Travel and Tourism Council (WTTC) (2001a) *Building Human Capital*. London: WTTC.

World Travel and Tourism Council (WTTC) (2001b) *Competitiveness Monitor*. London: WTTC.

Chapter 8

The Impact of Tour Operators on Tourism Development: A Sequence of Events

NEVENKA ČAVLEK

Introduction

Not much has been said or written up to now on the role and signifi-cance of tour operators on the development of tourism, particularly inter-national tourism. Although research in this field is expanding, tour operators in their relatively short history have not been studied nearly enough. However, their significance in the development of international tourism flows over the last 50 years has grown to such an extent that we can now say that they have become economic entities that have had a large influence on the development of international tourism in many tourism destinations in the world. Because of their key role in changing the previ-ous forms of the tourism phenomenon, tour operators have become a syn-onym for mass tourism. Tourism is often regarded as a "controversial sector" (Wahab, 2000: 104), and so also are the tour operators.

The business of tour operators was created and has developed mostly in Europe. According to the World Tourism Organization (WTO), tour operators contribute annually over 25% of all international tourism travel, and European tour operators share about 50% of the total worldwide flows of package holidays (Čavlek, 1998). When it comes to international tourist overnights, the relative contribution of tour operators to inter-national tourism flows is much higher. In order to understand the whole issue of the involvement of tour operators on the world market, and their significant impact on tourism development, it is necessary to observe their development within the framework of certain specific phases, using a holistic perspective by combining criteria that include different elements relevant to such a process of development. This is not an easy task because official data on the movement of the world package-holiday market are not complete. In most cases they are based on different forms of assessment and there is no consistent methodology either. This chapter will not cover all possible issues and approaches therefore, but will present a more practical application of some key ideas and findings.

For the purpose of this study the analyses of the influence of tour operators on international flows will be illustrated by examples of the largest European tourism generating markets, the German and the British markets.

The History of Tour Operators

The business of tour operators on a large scale can be linked to the phase of modern tourism – that after 1950. Many theoreticians support this statement. Van Doren and Lollar (1985: 469) point out that social, political, economic, technological and environmental changes after the Second World War have resulted in the "consequences" that now shape the present travel industry. Vukonić (1991: 30) stresses that:

> this is the period in which developing countries became aware of their tourism potential, and developed countries – as generators of mass tourism demand – became aware of the attractiveness of these regions and of the possibility for expanding tourism flows in these directions.

Such a situation was favourable for the development of new economic entities – tour operators. They sensed an opportunity to make profit from supplying package holidays, which, for a great number of potential consumers, comprised the organisation of travel and accommodation at tourism destinations. The opinion of those theoreticians of tourism who connect the appearance of tour operators with the possibility of using charter-flight transport in organising tourist travel is generally regarded as the most acceptable view point (Burkart and Medlik, 1974; Cooper *et al.*, 1998; Holloway, 1998; McIntosh and Goeldner, 1986; Mundt, 1993). The British travel firm, Horizon Holidays, is recognised as the first tour operator, who, in 1950, organised the first inclusive tourist tour – to Calvi (Corsica) – following a pre-arranged package based on a charter flight.

The phases of development of tour operators

Since 1950 world tourism has undergone significant changes, in terms of both its quantity and quality. The speedy development of tourism stimulated by tour operators has resulted in such changes, both in the economic as well as in the social and ecological spheres of the countries to which large tourism flows have been directed. Technology and the modern way of living make changes happen in our society in a shorter period of time than before. The significant changes that have occurred within the last phase of tourism development, which, according to most authors, began at the end of the Second World War and has continued until the present day, probably justify and make necessary the division of this last phase. The appearance of tour operators on the international tourism scene is certainly one of the reasons for a reassessment of the phase of tourism development since the Second World War.

Theoreticians of tourism who have attempted to divide the development of tourism into periods have dealt mainly with problems of economic and/or regional development, using various models of development (and growth), usually by applying only one of the possible criteria for such a division, and have, therefore, seldom given a holistic solution to this problem. In this way, Miossec (1976, 1977) defined the five phases of development through which tourism has passed until now, but Pearce (1987) has already discarded this model as unrealistic because it does not respect the component of space. There are also models by Hills and Lundgren (1977), Butler (1980) and Gormsen (1980), but none of them is based on the time division of these phases of development. Tourism theoreticians who have followed the principle of applying the dimension of time in determining the phases of the development of tourism differ in placing the beginning and the end of particular phases, which is natural, since they approach the problem by using different criteria. This suits Friedman's (1980) belief that every development has its own structure and that everyone dealing with it has his/her own ideas on how to develop this structure. Naturally, when we talk of development, we always understand a process or a complex of changes which is logical, or which shows certain rules of development, or is at least regular enough to enable us to come to reasonable or generally valid conclusions.

Most theoreticians who use a time division in determining the process of tourism development share the view that its development from the end of the Second World War until today is a single phase within which they do not find elements to justify an additional division. For example, Burkart and Medlik (1974) talk about three periods in the development of tourism: the first beginning with the appearance of the railway and ending in 1840; the second lasting from 1840 to 1914;

and the third, which the authors call the period of the modern world, beginning in 1920. Sessa (1983) also views the expansion of "modern tourism" in three phases: the first beginning in the early 19th century and ending at the beginning of the First World War; the second representing the period between the two world wars; and the third beginning after the end of the Second World War and still present today. We can find a similar division in Freyer (1998): the first Beginning Phase (die Anfangphase) from 1850 to 1914; the second Developmental Phase (die Entwicklungsphase) from 1914 to 1945; and the third High Phase (die Hochphase) from 1945 until today.

Among Croatian authors, Antunac (1985) uses the most sophisticated categorisation based on the development of tourism. The author differentiates four phases: the first starting around the end of the 19th century; the second beginning just after the dawn of the 20th century and ending after the First World War; the third taking place between the two world wars; and the final phase lasting from the Second World War until today.

If we start from the belief that, globally speaking, it is possible to view the development of an event from five basic standpoints, or through five basic fields – development as economic growth, as modernisation, as distributive justice, as a socio-economic transformation and as spatial reorganisation (Pearce, 1989) – it is clear that, in using each of these fields as a criterion for contemplating this issue, there will be different periodic categorisations and, consequently, different interpretations.

Paraphrasing Rostow (1960), who observes economic development through five consecutive stages of economic growth – the traditional stage, the transitional stage, the take-off stage, the maturity stage and the stage of mass consumption – when we define the stages of the development of tour operators, the same classification can be used. It is also worth noting Thurot's (1973) attempt to divide the development of tourism; Thurot explains the development of international tourism in the Caribbean by applying "the class criteria". Another interesting model is one by Fayos-Sola (1994) who, in defining the developmental stages of tourism, took into consideration several important elements, such as technological innovations and the social and economic environment.

By applying the above principles and criteria, and by including the principles of development in a market economy, it is possible to establish the following stages of the development of tour operators: the introduction of tour operators into the tourism system, the take-off stage, the maturity stage and the future stage of mass-consumption.

The introduction of tour operators into the tourism system

The socio-economic transformation of modern societies, propelled by many social and economic factors immediately after the end of the Second World War, brought a huge increase in leisure time spent outside the place of permanent residence. A new entrepreneurial spirit appeared first on the market of Great Britain around 1950, with the already mentioned tour operator, "Horizon Holidays". This year is taken as the beginning of the stage of the introduction of tour operators into the tourism system, which lasted until the end of the 1960s.

Horizon started with only 300 clients in its first year of operation and for four years had the market to itself (Bray and Raitz, 2001). In the 1950s, according to World Tourism Organization data (WTO, 1992a), the 10 leading receiving countries absorbed about 88% of all international tourist arrivals. Ten years later the situation was completely different. The 1960s were years of enormous growth in package holiday sales. In spite of the restrictions imposed on tour operators regarding the use of private charter airlines, some 630,000 tourists travelled from Britain on charter packages to European tourism destinations in 1963, while in 1965 there were over one million, or twice the number of those who travelled individually on holiday by plane (Burkart and Medlik, 1974). By the end of the 1960s, the British market was already dominated by tour operators who could be seen as being equal to the great tour operators of today with respect to the size of their chartered airline capacities.

The German package holiday market also developed very quickly. In 1962, Scharnow organised the first package holidays by air-charter transport to Majorca, the Costa del Sol and Tunisia. In Scharnow's first year of operation, 6139 German tourists spent their holidays at the mentioned destinations. Only 10 years later, this number had risen to 250,000, and, in 1973, to 636,000 tourists (Vellas and Becherel, 1995).

In these years of the introduction of tour operators into the tourism system, the first air-charter companies were established, for example Condor in Germany (1956) and Britannia Airways in Great Britain (1962). Condor transported 5000 passengers in 1956, 320,000 in 1965 and, by 1970, almost a million (internal company data).

In the period from 1950 until the end of the 1960s the tour operators' business expanded through the industrially developed countries of Europe. It was in this period that many tour companies were founded, which today represent the largest and most influential tour operators in the world. The most significant to appear in this period and which still operate on the markets where they have obtained an enviable reputation include: Club Méditerrané, founded in France in 1950; Tjaereborg, founded a little later in Denmark; Hotelplan, Switzerland, which organised its first air-charter holiday in 1950/1951; the Saga Group, UK, which has been operating on the market since 1951; Alpitour, Italy, which started its tour operating business in 1960; and Neckermann, founded in Germany in 1963. In 1965, Lord Thomson (a Canadian businessman) bought Universal Sky Tours, Britannia Airways and Riviera Holidays, thus establishing the foundations for the leading tour operator on the British market today, Thomson Travel Group, and, in 1968, TUI, Germany.

In the 1960s, the world's gross national product (GNP) grew by approximately 5–6% a year, international trade by around 7–8%, transport by around 10% and international tourism by approximately 11% (Behrens, 1977). Much of the growth in international tourism can be attributed to the proliferation of air-charter traffic developed by tour operators who offered package holidays based on air transport for destinations situated in the Mediterranean basin, which became the most significant. They already had a moderately developed tourism infrastructure and, later, with growing demand, built appropriate accommodation facilities.

In this introductory stage, tour operators in the leading tourism-generating markets of the world started to merge, developing into larger tourism concerns. They integrated with either airlines or hotels in destinations, with some tour operators building their own hotels in destinations to accommodate their increasing numbers of clients. However, some tour operators were satisfied with only horizontal mergers, either with other tour operators or with travel agencies. In the 1960s, this stage was primarily characterised by a typically "sales-oriented" tourism market, which meant that tour operators offered a limited product supply to the market. In this developmental stage, tour operators did not yet face a problem of selling their products, because, in most cases, demand was greater than supply. By 1970 tour operators had already been recognised as an essential part of the modern tourism system (Mill and Morrison, 1985), and became, in the later stages of their development, a dominant landmark in all the significant tourism-generating markets of the world (Čavlek, 2000).

The take-off stage

The second stage in the development of tour operators, designated as the take-off stage, starts with a new era in air transport with the introduction of the jumbo jet. In January 1970, Pan American World Airways transported 352 passengers from New York to London, using a new type of aircraft – the Boeing 747. This type of aircraft has played a very important role in the business of tour operating, because it not only increased transport capacities and at the same time lowered the costs per passenger/kilometre, but also its greater flying speed shortened the time needed to reach the chosen destination. In this stage, tour operators started to enter a phase of massive expansion in the main tourism-generating markets. In the period between 1950 and the beginning of the 1970s the trend of significant dispersion of tourism destinations can be observed and the market share of the top 10 destinations dropped to 65% (WTO, 1992a), which means that all other tourism destinations in the world absorbed the remaining 35% of world international tourist arrivals.

Other factors also influenced the significance of the role of tour operators in international tourism travel at this stage of development. First is the first energy crisis in the world, in 1973, followed by a second in 1979, both of which caused a drop in the rate of growth of international tourism flows (WTO, 1997), due to the limitations imposed on travelling. A second significant factor in the development of tour operators in tourism-generating markets was the deregulation of airline traffic, which began in the USA at the end of the 1970s. This later spread to Europe and, from there, gradually to the whole world, resulting in a general reduction in prices for domestic and international airline transport. Moreover, in the 1980s, as pointed out by Vellas and Becherel (1995), thanks to the development of tour operators, many charter airline companies became very influential and appeared as real competitors to the regular airlines, which were forced to change their tourism strategy. Already in 1970, air-charter companies in the UK transported a total of two million tourists on organised holidays out of a grand total of 5.75 million British people who travelled on holiday abroad that year (Burkart and Medlik, 1974). Regular airlines started to grant tour operators special tariffs and reductions, which in turn enabled the tour operators to create a wide range of products at very attractive prices; in the same way, airlines ensured additional clients for their aeroplanes.

The mass nature of travelling abroad on package holidays can be considered the main feature of the British tourism market from the 1970s until today (Lavery, 1993). In 1970, British people took a total of 40.25 million holiday trips longer than four days outside their place of permanent residence, but only 5.75 million of them, or 14%, were spent abroad (Burkart and Medlik 1974). However, 10 years later, in 1980, 25% of holidays taken by Britons were holidays abroad, that is, 12 million holidays, and by the end of 1980s this rate increased to 60% (UKCSO, various years), which means that the interest and ability of the British to take a holiday abroad has increased constantly. The dynamics of the development of this market can best be seen in Figure 8.1.

In 1970, 2.8 million Germans travelled on all types of package holidays (Behrens, 1977). The number of holiday departures outside the place of permanent residence has constantly grown. In 1970, the number of such trips lasting longer than four days amounted to 18.5 million, whereas by 1990 this number had more than doubled to 43.2 million (RA, 1991). At the same time, the total number of trips Germans made in that period also grew, as can be seen in Figure 8.2.

By analysing the development of the package holiday market in Germany, we can conclude that, with the increasing influence of tour operators and with the strengthening of their role in creating package holidays, the share of organised travel of the total number of holiday trips longer than four days has recorded constant growth. While the number of individual trips has decreased, the number of package holidays has grown (Čavlek, 2000: 327). For instance, in 1972 a total of 4.3 million Germans travelled on package holidays for longer than four days, while in 1989, according to data provided by DRV (1993), a total of 13.8 million package holidays abroad were sold, which means that 59% of all tourism travel abroad was realised through the organisation of tour operators.

This is the stage where supply started to grow faster than demand and where the names of new tour operators were constantly appearing on the market. At the same time, however, the first bankruptcies occurred. Competition grew fiercer than ever, and vertical and horizontal concentrations were very dynamic.

The maturity stage

The stage of maturity in the development of tour operators started with the emergence of the enormous political and economic changes in 1989 and 1990 in Eastern Europe and the Soviet Union on the one hand, and in China, Cambodia, Laos, Mongolia, Vietnam and some other countries on the other, which, in an economic sense, marked the beginning of the transformation of the socialist centrally planned economy into a decentralised, market economy, thus causing turmoil in the global economy, which was to have consequences for tourism. The opening of the borders of these formerly closed countries created the basic conditions for the free movement of goods and services and for undisturbed travel. The

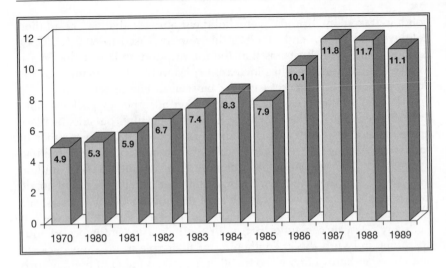

Figure 8.1 Air packages from the UK, 1970–1989 (in millions)
Source: Thomson Holidays, 1990

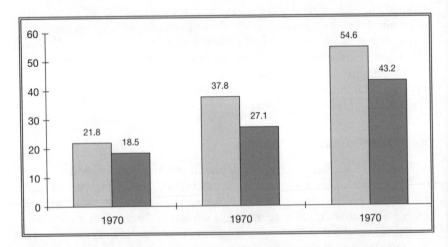

Figure 8.2 Development of the German travel market: Number of holiday trips in comparison to total travel, 1970–1990 (in millions)
Source: DRV, 1993

foundations were also set for the redistribution and spatial reorganisation of world tourism flows. Naturally, in the beginning, the intensity of the development of tourism in the countries above was much greater. These kinds of tourism movements can lead to a rise in standards of living and slowly bring about a better balance between receiving and generating tourism movements. This will mark the beginning of a new stage in the development of tour operators – the stage of mass-consumption.

China is often mentioned as the most striking example of the positive influence of these changes on the development of tourism. By opening its borders to the world in 1992, China's economic links with East Asia strengthened and GNP rose by 12% compared with 1991. Exports grew by approximately 18% and imports by 26%, whereas, at the same time, foreign direct investment, primarily in the tertiary sector, doubled to a record level of $11 billion (World Bank, 1993). What consequences these changes have had on China's tourism is confirmed by the fact that, in 1990, China recorded 10.48 million international tourist arrivals (WTO, 1996), and, in 1998, 24 million (WTO, 1999). Simultaneously, the increase of foreign currency inflow from tourism rose from $2.21 billion to $12.50 billion.

In the stage of maturity, tour operators in the largest generating markets in the world have not yet reached the phase of saturation. Each year they are increasing their tourism flow thanks to new programmes which are constantly being adapted to the fluctuating demands of tourists, as the examples of the British and German market prove. Despite the increase in the independent sector, sales of inclusive summer holidays are still on the increase (Cope, 2000) (see Figure 8.3).

Although there are no precise data on the size of the German package holiday market, as these specific items of data have not been collected, some research has been carried out which can at least approximately depict the size and strength of this market. In 2000, this package holiday market was estimated to comprise approximately 34 million organised trips. To put this into context, 53 of the most significant German tour operators in that year realised a total of almost 29 million organised trips, covering some 84% of the entire market (FVW, 2000).

However, even if, in the next few years, tour operators reach the saturation phase on particular markets within Europe, they would still be able to count on the yet barely exploited tourism-generating potential of the regions of Eastern and Central Europe, whose population, due to many years of restrictions, is very eager to travel. Since the living standards of this population are growing, this market could become a major

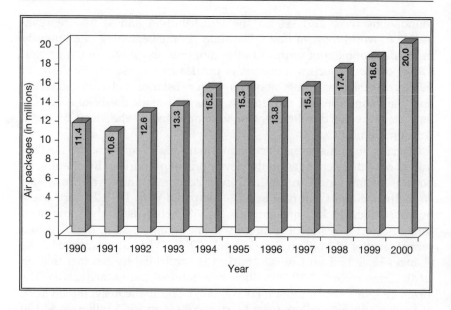

Figure 8.3 Air packages from the UK, 1990–2000 (in millions)

Source: Based on data from Cope, 2000; UK Central Statistical Office, various years

sector for tour operators. The growing interest of the leading European tour operators in expanding their business to this market confirms this. This part of Europe (Poland, the Czech Republic, Slovakia, Hungary, Bulgaria, Romania, Ukraine, Belarus and Russia) has the same-sized population as the major tourism-generating countries in Europe (Germany, the UK, Italy, France, the Netherlands, Austria, Belgium, Switzerland and the Scandinavian countries), that is, over 300 million inhabitants. Furthermore, the growing trend of tourism travel to long-haul destinations imposes a greater need to use travel organisers. Market analyses carried out on the largest tourism-generating markets of Europe and the USA (RA, European Travel Monitor, How the British Will Travel 2005, How Germans Will Travel 2005, How the Americans Will Travel 2007), show that long-haul tours are the fastest-growing segment of tourism demand. Practice confirms that, as the distance between receiving and generating tourism markets increases, the share of organised tourism travel grows in relation to the total amount of travel.

The stage of maturity can also be characterised as having an intensive effect on the concentration of capital in tourism. From the second half of 1998 until today the biggest concentration processes in the history of tourism can be recorded. Globalisation has also become a mega-trend in world development and is increasingly reflected in the business of tour operators. According to Keller and Smeral (1997), globalisation means the increasing interdependence of markets and production in different countries through trade in goods and services, cross-border flows of capital, international strategic alliances, mergers, exchange of technology, and other forms of co-operation. To survive in the very competitive tourism market today, it is almost a must for enterprises to link up strategically with companies that deliver different parts of the integral tourism product. The consequences of such concentration and integration processes are most noticeable in those tourism companies which try to create the most efficient forms of business organisation.

Tourism has become big business, and it is nowadays more and more controlled by big business! Although it has been estimated that the tourism business worldwide is dominated by small businesses (90%), with most sectors having more than 50% of the businesses classified as small (Gartner & Lime, 2000: 6), the airline industry and, more lately, tour operators are exceptions to this rule. The consolidation processes noted earlier are significantly changing the picture of the European leisure travel market. The results of their actions can be illustrated. As a consequence of the integration processes in the European market, four mega-travel concerns dominate this market today. Mother company, TUI AG, which owns, among others, TUI (the biggest tour operator on the European market) and Thomson Travel Group (No. 1 in the British market), and is also market leader in the Netherlands, Austria, Finland, Ireland and Poland (Mintel International, 2002), claims to control 70% of the total European package-holiday market. After the second largest German travel group, C&N (Condor and Neckermann) merged at the end of 2000 with Thomas Cook under the British name, Thomas Cook became the second largest European travel concern and thus pushed the British tour operator, Airtours (now known as My Travel Group) to third place among the largest travel concerns in Europe. Fourth place remained in the hands of another German travel group, Rewe Touristic, which consists of several tour operators. These data confirm that the concentration processes in the tourism markets have created powerful vertically, horizontally and diagonally integrated travel concerns with an expanding network of tour operators in many non-domestic markets, along with a growing network of travel agencies, very influential charter airlines and others. Because the tourism concerns are usually owners or major shareholders of accommodation facilities in the main destinations, they can easily control, or even dictate, the prices of these services, and can make rules in their favour. It means that the competition created in tourism-generating markets is moving into the tourism-receiving markets, too. One can strongly support the statement of Gartner and Lime (2000: 7), that "in the long run this [consolidation process] has serious implications for the condition of the physical plant which may not receive enough revenue to maintain the facility".

Tourism development influenced by tour operators has certainly resulted in not only positive consequences, but also negative ones for the development of tourism-receiving countries. Spain, which was the first to be targeted by tour operators, still has the most visible proof of the uncontrolled construction of accommodation facilities and the "laissez-faire expansion with little consideration given to planning and control" (Fletcher & Wanhill, 2000: 284). A total of 78% of all the accommodation facilities of the whole coastal belt of Spain is concentrated on the Mediterranean part of the Spanish coast alone. The leading British and German tour operators ensured occupancy for the newly built establishments, and the growing demand for newly developed tourism destinations encouraged foreign investors to construct hotels and tourism complexes at great speed. As a result of these developments, Spain was the leading European tourism-receiving destination at the beginning of the 1970s, in terms of foreign currency inflow from international tourism, and second in the world, behind the USA, leaving behind traditional tourism countries like Italy and France (WTO, 1992b). The following facts show clearly the rapid growth of foreign visits there: in 1930, 200,000 foreign tourists visited Spain; in 1960, nearly 6 million; in 1974, Spain recorded approximately 33 million international arrivals (Prahl & Steinecke, 1979); and, in 2000, according to WTO's data (2001), there were over 48 million international tourist arrivals, which placed this country in third position in the world's list of the most popular tourism destinations in the world (directly behind France and the USA).

A similar destiny in tourism development is shared by many other tourism destinations in the Mediterranean region which, thanks to tour operators, have been extensively developed. For example, Turkey recorded some 2.2 million international tourist arrivals in 1985 (WTO, 1995), 4.8 million in 1990 (WTO, 1998) and 11.5 million in 2001 (WTO, 2002). According to WTO data (1995, 1998, 2002) Greece registered 6.6 million international tourist arrivals in 1985, 8.9 million in 1990 and 13.1 million in 2000. The share of inclusive holidays from the UK to Turkey reached over 80% in 1998, and to Greece almost 79% (Cope, 2000: 30). Table 8.1 summarises the conclusions in a schematic way.

Conclusion

This short analysis of the development of tour operators in the tourism market has illustrated the significant impact that these economic entities have had on global tourism development. Thanks to package holidays created by tour operators, the number of those who have been able to realise their dream of spending a holiday for the first time outside their place of permanent residence has increased year by year. What is more, travelling away on holiday has become a part of a style of living. At the same time, the number of destinations which tour operators have included in their travel and holiday programmes has also increased. The range of tourism destinations attractive to tour operators has widened. Although some 20 years ago, in some tourism circles, opinions were expressed that medium- and low-quality supply would swiftly disappear from the market and with it cheap package holidays (Bemextours, 1992), this has not come about; on the contrary, the influence of tour operators has grown stronger from year to year, and with the strengthening of their role in creating package holidays that those with lower purchasing power can afford, the package-holiday market has expanded.

On the other hand, there has been increasing interest in tourism destinations which have recently started battling for a position in the market in order that tour operators would include them in their programmes. In all forecasts, several significant factors which have kept tour operators' package holidays at the centre of international tourism demand appear to have been overlooked. These are:

- low prices compared with individually organised holidays and travel;
- tour operators adapting to diversified tourism demand and the introduction of new products and activities in travel and holiday programmes;
- the introduction of flexible package holidays to respect more fully the wishes of clients;
- tailor-made travel and holiday programmes;
- all-inclusive programmes;
- the negotiating and purchasing power of tour operators today, which is so great that the most powerful dictate business terms to their destination partners.

It is difficult to believe that, having achieved such a strong position on the market, tour operators would allow the size of their business and their influence to decrease. The intensity of their development in the

Table 8.1 A schematic representation of the main characteristics of the stages of development of tour operators

Stage of development	Main characteristics	Environment	Leading tour operators
Introductory (1950–1970)	*Typical sales-oriented market* Limited number of tour operators on the market. Flourishing of charter air companies. Beginnings of integration of tourism concerns.	*Fast socio-economic transformation of society* High GNP growth. Increase in the number of days of paid holiday. Post-war modernisation and motorisation.	Horizon Clarksons Cosmos Touropa Scharnow Dr Tigges Club Méditerrané
Take-Off (1970–end of 80s)	*Transfer from a sales-oriented to a consumer-oriented market* Increase of supply faster that that of demand. First tour operator bankruptcies. A large number of new names among tour operators. "Apex" tariffs. Continuation of the process of integration. Sudden growth of the tour operators' offer of new tourism destinations.	*New era of air transport* Introduction of jumbo jets. Two energy crises. Deregulation of air-traffic.	Thomson Intasun, ILG Horizon TUI Neckermann Kuoni Club Méditerrané American Express Thomas Cook
Maturity (from the	*Restrained consumption – package holidays take on the characteristics of*	*Huge political and economic changes* Transformation of socialist	TUI Neckermann

beginning of the 90s)	*consumer goods* Consumer sensitivity to prices. Prominent trend in last-minute bookings. Change in the structure of supply with tour operators. Substitution of "standard packages" for "individualised packages". Diversification of the market of demand. Increasing number of specialist tour operators. Large investments in CRSs. Tour operators outgrowing their own markets.	economies into market economies. Opening of borders of countries behind the Iron Curtain. Free flow of goods and services. World recession. War in the Gulf. Creation of a single European market. Signing of the GATTS Agreement. Changes in the system of values of the population in the leading tourism generating markets.	LTU Amexo Thomson Airtours Club Méditerrané Nouvelles Frontières Kuoni DER First Choice
Mass consumption	*Globalisation of the tourism product* Prominent segmentation of tourism supply and demand. A few tour operators dictate conditions in the tourism market throughout the world.	*A significant growth in living standards in so-called Third World countries; changes in the system of values of the population living in those countries* Further shortening of the working week (increase of free time). Two dominant orientations of values: one towards material opulence and hedonism and the second towards non-material, alternative values and quality of life.	TUI Thomas Cook American Express

Source: Čavlek, 2000

world so far shows that they are actors who can adapt to changes and to new trends in the tourism market relatively quickly and successfully. Day by day they are becoming a more significant part of the overall tourism system and must be researched further.

References

Antunac, I. (1985) *Turizam i ekonomska teorija*. Zagreb: Institut za istraživanje turizma.

Behrens, K.Ch. (1977) *Handbuch der Marktforschung*. Wiesbaden: Betriebswirtschaftlicher Verlag Dr. Th. Gabler.

Bemextours (1992) Konjunkturne informacije. *UT Revija za ugostiteljstvo i turizam* 49 (12), I–XVI.

Bray, R. and V. Raitz (2001) *Flight to the Sun: The Story of the Holiday Revolution*. London and New York: Continuum.

Burkart, A.J. and Medlik, S. (1974) *Tourism: Present, Past, and Future*. London: Heinemann.

Butler, R.W. (1980) The concept of a tourist area cycle of evolution: Implications for management of resources. *Canadian Geographer* 24 (1), 5–12.

Čavlek, N. (1998) *Turoperatori i svjetski turizam*. Zagreb: Golden Marketing.

Čavlek, N. (2000) The role of tour operators in the travel distribution system. In W.C. Gartner and D.W. Lime (eds) *Trends in Outdoor Recreation, Leisure and Tourism* (pp. 325–334). Oxford and New York: CAB International.

Cooper, C., Fletcher, J., Gilbert, D., Wanhill, S. and Shepherd, R. (1998) *Tourism: Principles and Practice*. Harlow: Longman.

Cope, R. (2000) Outbound markets: UK outbound. *Travel and Tourism Analyst* 1, 19–40.

DRV (1993) *Fakten und Zahlen zum deutschen Reisemarkt*. Berlin: Deutscher Reisebüro und Reiseverastalter Verband.

Fayos-Sola, E. (1994) *WTO News, No. 3*. Madrid: WTO.

Fletcher, J. and Wanhill, S. (2000) Development economics. In W.C. Gartner and D.W. Lime (eds) *Trends in Outdoor Recreation, Leisure and Tourism* (pp. 277–285). Oxford and New York: CAB International.

Freyer, W. (1998) *Tourismus: Einführung in die Fremdenverkehrsökonomie*. Munich and Vienna: R. Oldenburg Verlag.

Friedman, J. (1980) An alternative development, and communalistic society: Some principles for a possible future. In J. Friedman, E. Wheelwright and J. Connell (eds) *Development Strategies in the Eighties: Development Studies Colloquium, Monograph No. 1* (pp. 12–42). Sydney: University of Sydney.

FVW International (2000) *Deutsche Veranstalter in Zahlen: Beilage zur FVW International No. 32*. Hamburg: FVW.

Gartner, W.C. and Lime, D.W. (2000) *Trends in Outdoor Recreation, Leisure and Tourism*. Oxford and New York: CAB International.

Gormsen, R.W. (1980) The spatio-empirical development of international tourism: Attempt at a centre–periphery model. In *La Consommation d'Espace par le Tourisme et sa preservation* (pp. 150–170). Aix-en-Provençe: CHET.

Hills, T.L. and Lundgren, J. (1977) The impact of tourism in the Caribbean: A methodological study. *Annals of Tourism Research* 4 (5), 248–267.

Holloway, J.C. (1998) *The Business of Tourism*. Harlow and New York: Longman.

Keller, P. and Smeral, E. (1997) Increased international competition: New challenges for tourism policies in European countries. Paper presented at the WTO, WTO/CEU-ETC Joint Seminar, Salzburg.

Lavery, P. (1993) Outbound Markets: UK Outbound. *Travel and Tourism Analyst* 3, 20–35.

McIntosh, R.W. and Goeldner, C., (1986) *Tourism: Principles, Practices, Philosophies*. New York: John Wiley & Sons.

Mill, R.C. and Morrison, A.M. (1985) *The Tourism System*. Englewood Cliffs, NJ: Prentice Hall.

Mintel International (2002) European Leisure Groups. *Travel and Tourism Analyst* 4, 1–20.

Miossec, J.M. (1976) *Elements pour une Théorie de l'Espace touristique*, C-36. Aix-en-Provençe: CHET.

Miossec, J.M. (1977) Un modèle de l'espace touristique. *L'Espace Géographique* 6 (1), 41–48.

Mundt, J.W. (1993) *Reiseveranstaltung*. Munich and Vienna: R. Oldenburg Verlag.

Pearce, D.G. (1987) Spatial patterns of package tourism in Europe. *Annals of Tourism Research* 14 (2), 183–201.

Pearce, D.G. (1989) *Tourist Development* (2nd edn). Harlow: Longman; New York: Wiley.

Prahl, H.W. and Steinecke, A. (1979) *Der Millionen Urlaub, von Bildungsreise zur totalen Freizeit*. Darmstadt and Neuwied: Luchterhand.

RA (1991) *Reiseanalyse*. Starnberg: Studienkreis für Tourismus.

RA (1993–1999) *Reiseanalyse*. Hamburg: FUR.

Rostow, W.W. (1960) *The Stages of Economic Growth*. Cambridge: Cambridge University Press.

Sessa, A. (1983) *Elements of Tourism Economics*. Rome: Catal.

Thomson Holidays (1990) *Annual Report*. Thomson Holidays.

Thurot, J.M. (1973) Le tourisme tropical balneaire: Le modèle caraibe et ses extensions. Doctoral thesis, CET, Aix-en-Provençe.

UK Central Statistical Office (various years) *Business Monitor: Overseas Travel and Tourism, MQ6*. London: UK Central Statistical Office.

Van Doren, C.S. and Lollar, S.A. (1985) The consequences of forty years of tourism growth. *Annals of Tourism Research* 12 (3), 467–489.

Vellas, F. and Becherel, L. (1995) *International Tourism*. London: Macmillan.

Vukonić, B. (1991) *Turizam u susret budućnosti*. Zagreb: Mikrorad.

Wahab, S.E.A. (2000) Trends and implications of tourism policy in developing countries. In W.C. Gartner and D.W. Lime (eds) *Trends in Outdoor Recreation, Leisure and Tourism* (pp. 103–109). Oxford and New York: CAB International.

World Bank (1993) *Annual Report*. Washington, DC: World Bank.

WTO (World Tourism Organization) (1992a) *Top Tourism Destinations*. Madrid: WTO (microfiche).

WTO (World Tourism Organization) (1992b) *World's Top Tourism Earners*. Madrid: WTO (microfiche).

WTO (World Tourism Organization) (1995) *World Tourism 1970–1994*. Madrid: WTO.

WTO (World Tourism Organization) (1996) *WTO's 1995 International Tourism Overview*. Madrid: WTO.

WTO (World Tourism Organization) (1997) *Yearbook of Tourism Statistics* (Vol. 1) (49th edn). Madrid: WTO.

WTO (World Tourism Organization) (1998) *Tourism Highlights 1997*. Madrid: WTO.

WTO (World Tourism Organization) (1999) *Tourism Highlights 1998*. Madrid: WTO.

WTO (World Tourism Organization) (2000) *Tourism Highlights 1999*. Madrid: WTO.

WTO (World Tourism Organization) (2001) *Tourism Highlights 2000*. Madrid: WTO.

WTO (World Tourism Organization) (2002) *Tourism Highlights 2001*. Madrid: WTO.

Chapter 9
The Impact of the Creation of Two Nation-states (Slovenia and Croatia) on Tourism in Istria

ANTON GOSAR

Introduction

Thomas Mann, the 1929 literature Nobel Prize winner, described in his novel, *Death in Venice*, the main character's turn of the century (19th into the 20th) pleasure-journey from Trieste, along Istria's coast, to the islands of Brioni, Pola and further on to Venice:

> And one day between the middle and the end of May he took the evening train for Trieste, where he stopped only twenty-four hours, embarking for Pola the next morning. ... What he sought was a fresh scene, without associations, which should yet be not too out-of-the-way; and accordingly he chose an island in the Adriatic, not far off the Istrian coast. It had been well known some years, for its splendidly rugged cliff formations on the side next the open sea, and its population, clad in a bright flutter of rags and speaking an outlandish tongue. But there was rain and heavy air; the society at the hotel was provincial Austrian, and limited; besides, it annoyed him not to be able to get at the sea – he missed the close and soothing contact which only a gentle sandy slope affords. ... He made all haste to correct it, announcing his departure at once. Ten days after his arrival on the island a swift motor-boat bore him and his luggage in the misty dawning back across the water to the naval station of Pola, where he landed only to pass over the landing-stage and on to the decks of a ship lying there with steam up for the passage to Venice.

Thomas Mann's and other descriptions, written at almost the same time by Lord Byron, Rainer Maria Rilke and biologist Robert Koch, have recognized the area of the northern Adriatic, and in particular the Istrian peninsula, as a region worthwhile to visit.

The History of Partition in the Northern Adriatic

Istria is a 4725 km^2 large Mediterranean peninsula, located between the Bay of Trieste and the Kvarner Bay. It has a rough, predominantly karstic landscape, with close to 500 km of coastline. The area has a rich history represented by the Roman amphitheater in Pulj–Pola and by several post-Roman and Venetian works of art in Poreč–Parenzo, Piran–Pirano, Koper–Capodistria and elsewhere. The multi-cultural Habsburg Empire (beginning of the 19th century) replaced the Venetian Republic in Istria until Austria's defeat in WW1. Due to Italy's contribution to the defeat, Istria was incorporated into the Italian Kingdom. The peninsula's division into the Italian (498 km^2), Slovenian (1055 km^2) and Croatian (3172 km^2) part is of recent history. After WW2, the winning powers decided that Trieste, the major regional center, should remain within the Republic of Italy and that the remaining area should become a part of Yugoslavia. The break-up of Yugoslavia, in 1991, has split up this part into the Slovenian and Croatian Istria, along the lines of the previous, internal administrative border of the multi-national Yugoslavian state. As a result of the past, the region of Istria in all three states continues to be multi-cultural, with a Croatian, Slovenian, Italian, Serbian, Jewish and German population. In this chapter tourism in the Slovenian (21%) and Croatian (68%) parts of the Istrian peninsula is discussed. In both nation-states, independent since 1991, the area discussed makes close to 5.5% of their territory.

The Italo-Slovene border in Istria (58 km on land, 29 km on sea) is a result of the post-WW2 negotiations. In most of its parts it does not coincide with the ethnic delineation or common cultural space, it does not recognize functional areas, it is not a physiographic border and nor is it a geometric boundary. It denies all the commonly known principles of border settings. The border is an outcome of negotiations between the post-WW2 superpowers. The Italo-Slovene border, as an outer border of the European Union is, in addition, unique as it has a modified regime. The implementation of the Schengen agreements (tight border controls) is enforced just to a certain degree due to the fact that a bilateral agreement is granting special privileges to Slovene and European Union citizens and travelers. Border posts on the Italo-Slovene border in Istria handled 16.8 million passengers in 2000. The border crossings of Sežana/Fernetti/Opicina (1.6 million tons of goods, 4.4 million passengers) and Škofije/Muggia (0.2 million tons of goods, 3.3 million passengers) are the busiest ones. For Slovenes and Italians Istria has become a playground – a recreation site of prime importance.

Despite earlier plans for a customs union, the former "socialist republics" (administrative divisions of provinces in former Yugoslavia) of Slovenia and Croatia agreed upon the creation of an international border. Its length in Istria is 101 km, along which five major border crossings on land have been designated. On both sides of the border national exit/entry posts were constructed. A joint boundary commission was formed in 1992 to precisely delimit and demarcate the borderline. The task to define the Croato-Slovene border was, it seemed, easy, as most of the border was designated as such since the Middle Ages (13th and 14th centuries); the only exception was the border in Istria, due to the facts described above. As the process of defining, determining, designating and demarcating the Croato-Slovene border continued, problems have arisen. They are grounded in legal theory, geography, history and politics. In 2001 the bilateral commission produced an agreement which seemed to have been acceptable for both sides. Heads of both governments sealed the agreement with a paraph, but civic organizations and politicians of all colors, in particular in Croatia, started campaigning against it. The parliamentary ratification of the agreement is still pending. Due to development of tourism, border delimitation in Istria has become a high priority for both states.

The Croato-Slovene land border reaches the Adriatic Sea in the small Bay of Piran. There never was a maritime boundary between Croatia and Slovenia. Ex-Yugoslavia declared the Bay of Piran as part of its straight baseline claim of 1965. The consequence of this action was to give the Bay the status of internal (Yugoslav) waters. Thus, the land-based Croato-Slovene republican boundary was not extended offshore and the bay remained administratively undivided. Today, Croatia prefers a maritime boundary based on equidistance. Article 15 of the 1982 Sea Convention states that the median line is to be adopted unless parties agree to the contrary. Each point of the median line is to be equidistant from the nearest points on the baseline from which the breadth of the maritime zone of each state is measured (Blake, 1994). Slovenia would like to invoke Article 12 of the 1958 Convention on Territorial Waters, stating that "an outlet to the open sea (international waters) is essential for a country". Along with it, the median line in the Bay of Piran would hinder the Slovene state's economy (fishing, tourism) and would enable a free passage towards the sole Slovenian maritime port of Koper–Capodistria.

The land-based delineation was under heavy pressure from Croatian and Slovenian claims. In negotiations, the above-named commission of experts has agreed to eliminate outspoken nationalistic claims and has decided to consider exclusively claims based on common law and international principles.

Slovenian party leaders have presented a dozen proposals based merely on historically relevant principles. The Slovene National Party envisions the border on the river Mirna, about 20 km to the south of the provisional demarcation line, as this was the only border in Istria (of the Free Territory of Trieste) ever to be internationally recognized (1945–1947). The Social Democrats of Slovenia claim the overall Savudrian peninsula, arguing that the autochthonous population, at the beginning of the 20th century (and by the time Yugoslavia became a state), was almost completely Slovene. Croatia claims the "de facto" boundary on the (old) Dragonja river. Initially, Croatian scientists and politicians expressed occasionally diverse views on this "River Case" (Klemenčić & Schofield, 1995). Slovenes could regard this as a threat as long as Croatia's claims could be understood to include and take away almost 5 km² of the land, including the airport of Portorož–Portorose.

For centuries, the bay and its shores were Piran's (a Venetian town from the 13th to the 18th century) main economic source. Continuing the tradition under Yugoslavia, the Slovenian side controlled the integral bay, whereas the Croats were in charge of the land to the south of the Dragonja river. It should be stated that, during the negotiations, Croatia's representatives expressed willingness to accept a line within the Bay of Piran which would be more favorable to Slovenia. It would divide the bay roughly in proportion 2:1 in favor of Slovenia. The Slovenian side has still not been persuaded. Even now, as the agreement on the border has not yet been ratified by the parliaments of Slovenia and Croatia, ships passing through Croatian territorial waters en route to the Slovenian commercial port of Koper (to the north of the Bay of Piran) enjoy the right of "innocent passage". There is also unhindered, lively tourist "trans-boundary" activity within the bay during summer. The data on official border crossings between Slovenia and Croatia in the region of Istria are impressive. In summer more than two out of three crossings are due to tourism (Table 9.1).

The History of Tourism in Istria

Tourism in Istria has a long tradition. Development-wise Istria can be compared with the Ligurian or French Riviera, but regarding recent

Table 9.1 Motives of motorists crossing the Croato-Slovene border at international border crossing posts in Istria (July 31, 2001, from 8:00 until 14:00)

Border crossings	Motives				
	Work (%)	Business (%)	Tourism (%)	Other (%)	Total
1. Jelšane	1.2	7.2	73.4	17.5	4,069
2. Starod	1.0	13.6	40.7	44.7	2,061
3. Sočerga	4.5	11.3	67.6	16.6	2,261
4. Dragonja	5.1	6.2	69.3	19.4	5,589
5. Sečovlje	3.7	8.4	63.3	24.6	8,076
Total	2.9	9.3	67.4	20.3	22,056

Note: Border crossings were made on the following routes: 1 = Ljubljana–Rijeka; 2 = Koper/Trieste–Rijeka; 3 = Ljubljana–Poreč/Pula; 4 and 5 = Koper/Trieste–Poreč/Pula

trends and visits a comparison with the Costa Brava in Spain would be more appropriate. As early as 1845 the most prominent modern-day Istrian tourist resort of Poreč–Parenzo offered a well-organized guide service; by 1883 Opatija (Abbazia) had become, among 195 Austrian resorts, the second most visited. Only the casino and spa resort of Karlovy Vary (Carlsbad) reported more visitors. In the year 1912, as Thomas Mann visited Istria, 114,162 visitors were registered in 19 Istrian tourist resorts. In 1938, the then Italian region of Istria had 129,838 foreign visitors (Blažević, 1987). Before the collapse of the Yugoslav multi-ethnic federation, Istria (within the administrative regions of Slovenia and Croatia) was visited by four million tourists, mostly German nationals (40%), followed by Italians, Austrians and Britons. In the mid-1980s Istria had on average 30 million bed-nights a year, therefore becoming, together with the coasts of Spain, the most popular sun, sea and sand destination in the Mediterranean.

Leisure in Istria was, at first, most popular among the nobility. In Opatija – Abbazia in Austrian times – visits by the Habsburgs, particularly by the Kaiser Franz Joseph and his family, pre-dated leisure stays by the Romanian King Karol, the German Kaiser Wilhelm II, the Swedish King Oscar and many others. The aristocratic trendsetters initiated a way of life, which was to become popular among intellectuals and the newly rich. As mentioned in the introduction, Rainer Maria Rilke (Duino–Devin), Lord Byron (Opatija), Thomas Mann and Robert Koch (Brioni) appreciated the not-too-distant, but still exotic, shores of Istria. In terms of the turn-of-the-century societal laws, winter and spring visits were more appreciated than the contemporary summer visits to the Mediterranean.

Tourism, as we know it today, was introduced by the railways – at first, as a year-round leisure-time activity, sought and experienced by German citizens of Austrian towns like Graz, Vienna, Maribor (Marburg) and Trieste. Due to the construction of the railway lines in the second half of the 19th century, the eastern, central and western parts of the Istrian peninsula became linked to the rest of Europe by easy and inexpensive communication. The central Istrian railway line to Pula (Pola) was, due to military installations there, mostly of strategic importance, whereas railways in the east and west served tourists as well. The owner of the track from Vienna to Trieste, known as the "Südbahn", constructed a side-line from Pivka (St Peter im Karst) to the harbor of Rijeka, thereby serving the interests of tourists keen on visiting Opatija on the eastern shores of Istria. The railways invested in hotel construction there, too. The most famous and luxurious turn-of-the-century hotel in Opatija, the hotel Kvarner, was the Südbahn's property. Along the western coast of the penninsula, the Trieste–Parenzo line was constructed. It brought investments by the Austrian state (Hotel Palace in Portorož–Portorose) and by the travel and insurance companies, like the Lloyd Triestino (Hotel Riviera, Poreč–Parenzo) (Blažević, 1996).

After WW1 investment into tourism and tourism growth contracted, given the competition of some Italian regions. Equally, a steeply declining trend could be observed in the first 20 years after WW2. The communist regime (of Yugoslavia) looked upon tourism as a remnant of the bourgeois pre-war period and hindered attempts by local communities in Istria to make a profit out of it. Instead, industrial development and mining were heavily subsidized. Many hotels became welfare housing units, enabling inland worker families to spend a week or two at the Adriatic coast at almost no cost to them. As General Franco's Spain, Yugoslavia, under Josip Broz-Tito, became in the 1960s the initiator of several developments in tourism. Being a leading member of the non-aligned movement, Yugoslavia gained almost unrestricted UN (United Nations) support as she declared the intention to go on with plans for (re)constructing the tourism industry. The UN know-how was used in several development projects ("The Upper Adriatic"; "The Southern Adriatic") and the World Bank provided financial arrangements (Jordan,

1997). The change affected Istria greatly and the contemporary image of Istria as a sun, sea and sand Mediterranean destination was completed in 1975. The major results of the construction era of the 1960s and 1970s are mega-hotels and resorts in Portorož–Portorose (Bernardin), in Poreč–Parenzo (Plava laguna, Zelena laguna), in Umag (Polynesia), in Pula (Veruda), in Vrsar (Anita) and in Rabac. The construction has mostly affected the western shores of the Istrian peninsula. Opatija, once the leading tourist destination in Istria, has fallen far behind in investments and visits. Poreč–Parenzo, with close to nine million bed-nights a year, became in 1985 the top dog in the Istrian resorts pack. On the other hand, Opatija's 2.5 million a year bed-nights placed the once-leading resort well below the Istrian and Mediterranean average.

Contemporary National Tourism Strategies in Istria

Within Yugoslavia, until 1991, the tourism strategy for the Istrian peninsula treated it as a single, interdependent area. The co-operation between Slovenia's tour operators, travel enterprises and the Croatian accommodation amenities in Istria was on the highest level. Excellent relationships and a good interdependent working environment could also be achieved due to the fact that the region as a whole had a common history and was, in part, inspired by regionalistic tendencies. In regions on the periphery of states such attitudes are common. Two Slovenian travel agencies, Kompas Jugoslavija and Globtour, dominated the tourist market of Istria, offering excursions and acting as middle-men between hotel/accommodation businesses and tour operators (for example) in Austria, Germany and the UK. The transfers from and to the Croatian airports of Pula, Rijeka and Ljubljana were often operated by the third Slovenian player – the travel and bus enterprise, Slavnik Koper. The major charter airline of former Yugoslavia, the Slovenian Adria Airways, handled close to 75% of arriving and departing passengers from the above airports. Yugoslavia, with its Mediterranean tourist resorts on the shorelines and islands of Istria, Dalmatia and Montenegro was, in the mid-1980s among the five leading European inbound tourist destinations (Gosar, 1999).

As of June 25, 1991, both Slovenia and Croatia declared independence and sealed their territorries with a (yet undefined) border. Co-operation in tourism ended almost overnight. The new laws of each of the two young nation-states had to be obeyed. Several travel agencies and bus companies, in particular in Slovenia, had to reduce their business or close not only some of their offices in the neighboring state, but also, due to lack

Table 9.2 Istria: Tourist accommodation in relation to the national level

Region	Beds (in 000)							
	2000		1997		1995		1985	
	All	In hotels	All	In hotels	All	In hotels	All	In hotels
Coast and the Karst*	**22**	**12**	**22**	**11**	**22**	**10**	**27**	**8**
Other Slovenia	57	24	58	23	51	19	56	22
Slovenia	*79*	*36*	*80*	*34*	*73*	*29*	*83*	*30*
Province of Istria**	**230**	**88**	**215**	**73**	**215**	**74**	**235**	**92**
Coastal provinces+	218	119	204	111	170	115	320	161
Other Croatia	243	18	227	17	224	17	265	38
Croatia	*691*	*225*	*646*	*201*	*609*	*206*	*820*	*291*

Notes:

* The tourist region, Obala in Kras (Coast and the Karst), includes the municipalities Piran–Pirano, Izola–Isola, Koper–Capodistria, Herpelje–Kozina, Divača, Sežana and Komen.

** All municipalities of the Istrian peninsula in Croatia (21), except Opatija.

+ Provinces (*županije*) of the Adriatic Coast in Croatia: Primorsko-goranska, Ličko-senjska, Zadarsko-kninska, Šibeniška, Splitsko-dalmatinska, Dubrovačko-neretvanska, except municipalities in Istria.

Table 9.3 Istria: Tourists in Istria in relation to the national level

Region	Tourists (in 000)							
	2000		1997		1995		1985	
	All	*Internat.*	*All*	*Internat.*	*All*	*Internat.*	*All*	*Internat.*
Coast and the Karst*	**516**	**271**	**504**	**274**	**405**	**188**	**537**	**294**
Other Slovenia	1,441	818	1,319	700	1,171	544	2,216	762
Slovenia	1,957	1,089	1,823	974	1,576	732	2,753	1,056
Province of Istria**	**2,162**	**2,016**	**1,391**	**1,217**	**893**	**685**	**2,325**	**1,464**
Coastal provinces+	3,937	3,268	1,905	1,160	1,061	466	5,587	3,283
Other Croatia	1,037	547	603	272	484	173	2,213	812
Croatia	7,136	5,831	3,899	2,649	2,438	1,324	10,125	5,556

Notes:

* The tourist region, Obala in Kras (Coast and the Karst), includes the municipalities Piran–Pirano, Izola–Isola, Koper–Capodistria, Herpelje-Kozina, Divača, Sežana and Komen.

** All municipalities of the Istrian penninsula in Croatia (21), except Opatija.

+ Provinces (*županije*) of the Adriatic Coast in Croatia: Primorsko-goranska, Ličko-senjska, Zadarsko-kninska, Šibeniška, Splitsko-dalmatinska, Dubrovačko-neretvanska, except municipalities in Istria.

of business, their own headquarters. In hotels in Slovenian and Croatian Istria a lack of "all-inclusive" tourists (who would normally come by plane and use all the amenities of the hotel) was evident. For several years hotels had to count on individual guests only. Adria Airways had to sell eight of their 14 mid-range jets and turbo-prop aicrafts.

Between 1992 and 1996 tourist enterprises in Slovenia and Croatia had to adapt to new geopolitical as well as economic realities. Not only did the break-up of Yugoslavia produce five independent states, it also generated violence for several years in the region (1991–1995; 1999), and, at the same time, changed the mainframe of the economy: from socialist central planning and the so-called soft communism economy (self-management) to a market economy (capitalism) and democracy. Independent national economic strategies, based on market economy, flourished. Often international experts helped to produce them. Slovenia's strategic plan was designed in 1992 under the leadership of Slovenian experts (Sirše *et al.*, 1992). The Croatian tourism strategy had to wait for several years, due to the instability and constant war-like conditions in the tourist region of Dalmatia, and was only published in 1996.

The Slovenian *Development Strategy for the Economic Sector of Tourism* almost forgot to put up strategies for Istria and the 47 km of Slovenian coastline. Instead, traditional spa and other inland thermal resorts gained priority in development. With 25 major spa resorts, Slovenia has right-fully claimed the name, the "Watering Place of Central Europe". Istria's Mediterranean coast in Slovenia was no longer seen as a source for sun, sea and sand tourism; instead, a great opportunity was sought in the geopolitical fact of being the closest neighbor to the gaming and gambling population of the Italian state. In the pre- and post-independence period, Slovenian entrepreneurs opened five Las Vegas-style casino establish-ments along the Italo-Slovene border (10 altogether in the young nation-state of Slovenia). The tourism strategic plan supported this trend. For Istria and the tourist area, Coast and the Karst, the strategy suggested, in addition, the development of event tourism enterprises (Sirše & Mihalič, 1999). Soon, near to Mediterranean beaches, as an addition to existing hotels, indoor tropical landscapes and aquaparks opened their doors. Hotels also increased their visits through the year-long continued organization of conferences and meetings.

The Croatian development strategy remained more conservative. With the exception of the capital of Zagreb, the pilgrimage town of Marija Bistrica, the Castle of Trakoščan and three traditional spa resorts (Krapinske toplice, Tuheljske toplice, Stubičke toplice), 85 remaining "major tourist resorts" (group A) are located on the Adriatic Sea. The following 14 tourist resorts of Istria are included: Opatija, Ičiči, Lovran, Medveja, Moščenička Draga, Rabac, Medulin, Pula, Rovinj, Vrsar, Funtana, Poreč, Novigrad and Umag (Narodne novine, 1994). Despite its traditional view of tourism, the Croatian development plan foresaw several man-made attractions, which would supplement the abundance of Mediterranean nature. Water-oriented sports like sailing, motor cruising, surfing and snorkeling are already booming in Croatian Adriatic resorts. Other sports, such as tennis, horseback riding and golf, have made way into traditional fishermen's villages, too. In the sub-coastal, hilly inland of Istria wine-routes and rural tourism have gained ground (Bošković, 2000; Jordan & Schappelwein, 2000).

Istrian tourism has a similar status in the economies of both countries. Slovenian Istria has 28% of the overall number of guest beds of the state; in Croatian Istria the number of guest beds is 33% of the Croatian total. The number of guest beds has not changed dramatically. In fact, in several tourist resorts it has fallen due to the reconstruction of hotels and the enlargement of rooms. New accommodation amenities are rare, as many potential investors hesitate to invest in regions where political instability was present during the last decade of the 20th century. Reconstruction of hotels, in particular in Slovenia, is therefore more common. But, if we compare the number of guest amenities in Croatian Istria with the same in the Slovenian part of the region (Table 9.4), a ratio of 1:10 is evident (90.4% in Croatian Istria and 9.6% in Slovenian Istria). Slovenes are relatively better at providing guest beds in hotels (41.7% in Slovenian Istria as against 38.4% in Croatian Istria).

The contemporary offer of amenities bears no relation to actual tourist visits to the region. Guest beds in Croatian Istria are predominantly of a seasonal character (April–September), whereas most Slovenian hotels do not close their doors during Fall and Winter. The Slovenian tourist region, Coast and the Karst, accommodates almost one-quarter of all visitors to Istria (23.9%). Nevertheless, due to the long-lasting instability in other tourist regions of Croatia, the importance of Istrian tourism business within the overall tourism economy has grown. In the peak years of Croatian/Yugoslavian tourism (1980–1986) the relation of guest visits was 23:77 in favor of other Croatian tourist regions. In the year 2000 Istria registered close to one-third of all visitors to Croatia (30.3%), becoming thereby the most profitable tourist region of the state. The same can be said for Slovenia: in the year 1985 just 19.5% of all visitors to Slovenia ended up on vacation in Istria, while in the year 2000 such visits amounted to 26.5%. Citizens of the neighboring EU countries, such as Austrians and Italians (24%), consider Istria as a playground in their own backyard and

Table 9.4 Istria: Accommodation amenities in leading tourist resorts

Resorts	Beds (000s)					
	2000		1995		1985	
	All	Hotels	All	Hotels	All	Hotels
Portorož–Portorose	9.5	5.1	8.9	4.5	12.2	4.5
Piran–Pirano	1.4	0.3	1.1	0.3	1.8	0.3
Strunjan–Strugnano	1.5	0.8	1.4	0.7	1.8	0.0
Izola–Isola	3.1	1.1	2.9	1.1	3.1	0.6
Koper–Capodistria	0.9	0.5	1.2	0.4	1.0	0.4
Ankaran–Ancarano	3.1	0.7	3.6	0.7	3.2	0.6
Slovenian Istria*	**21.8**	**9.1**	**22.1**	**10.6**	**23.1**	**7.5**
Umag–Umago	29.6	12.1	27.7	11.3	46.2	18.8
Novigrad–Cittanova	9.1	1.8	8.5	1.7	10.4	2.1
Poreč–Parenzo	50.6	23.9	47.3	22.3	49.3	23.2
Vrsar	37.8	4.0	35.3	3.7	38.7	4.1
Rovinj–Rovigno	33.7	12.2	31.5	11.4	32.8	11.9
Pula–Medulin	17.9	10.1	16.7	9.4	45.7	25.7
Rabac–Labin	10.1	5.8	9.4	5.4	11.4	6.3
Croatian Istria**	**230.3**	**88.3**	**215.2**	**73.2**	**234.5**	**92.1**

Notes:
* The tourist region, Obala in Kras (Coast and the Karst)
** The Province of Istria (Istarska županija)

therefore make the most visits. Germans are not far behind (23%), due to the fact that Bavaria is just a four-hour drive away (Statistični 2001: 635).

Market Economy and Globalization

Tourism growth, according to data of bed-nights and visitors to Istrian resorts, reflects the political and economic changes of the last two decades. Istria reached its peak in the year 1986, at the end of the second phase of the construction boom – initiated by the state and supported by the international funds – and at the beginning of the disintegration processes of the Yugoslavian state. More than 30 million bed-nights were registered – almost 27 million of them in Croatian Istria! The 13 leading tourist resorts (Table 9.5) had 23.8 million bed-nights. The region was popular among foreigners, who made 58% of tourist visits to Slovenian Istria and 64% to Croatian Istria. The first violent demonstrations of Serbian nationalism in Croatia and the plans for independence by leading politicians of Croatia and Slovenia in the summer of 1989 reduced the already sinking tourism visits to a minimum. In the fourth year of independence, in 1995, as the violent conflict in Croatia neared its end, Croatian Istria had just 31.1% of visitors in relation to its peak year in tourism. In Slovenia, where the independence declaration on June 25, 2001 resulted (just) in 10 days of fierce fighting, Istrian tourism survived with a 28.6% reduction in visitors. Comparing tourism data with the

Table 9.5 Istria: Bed-nights in leading tourist resorts

Resorts	Bed-nights (000s)				
	2000		1997	1995	1985
	All	International	All	All	All
Portorož–Portorose	988	657	926	751	1,464
Piran–Pirano	77	41	70	64	149
Strunjan–Strugnano	169	37	162	161	161
Izola–Isola	338	99	313	297	329
Koper–Capodistria	38	20	68	68	111
Ankaran–Ancarano	202	42	238	260	179
Slovenian Istria*	**1,974**	**896**	**1,975**	**1,740**	**2,393**
Umag–Umago	1,528	1,449		915	4,272
Novigrad–Cittanova	543	532		216	1,002
Poreč–Parenzo	4,425	4,304		1,639	5,335
Vrsar	1,784	1,760		872	2,839
Rovinj–Rovigno	2,122	2,055		922	3,154
Pula–Medulin	2,251	2,177		479	3,587
Rabac–Labin	923	882		276	1,186
Croatian Istria**	**14,439**	**13,797**	**9,510**	**6,217**	**21,375**

Notes:
* The tourist region Obala in Kras (the Coast and the Karst).
** The Province of Istria (Istarska županija)

national level of tourist visits and bed-nights, Istria fares much better than the national average, primarily due to its distance from the wars on the Balkan peninsula, but also due to the fast transition from communism to a market economy. Tourist visits in 1995 amounted to 57% in Slovenia and 24% in Croatia, compared to data for the mid-1980s.

The structure of visits changed dramatically. Whereas in Slovenian Istria visits made by guests from abroad declined by 46%, international visits to Croatian Istria, in relation to domestic ones, increased by 77% (as compared to 54% for the whole nation-state of Croatia). There are several reasons for such developments. One definitely lies in the tourism statistics. Since 1991, "domestic tourists" have been Croatian citizens only, whereas visitors from other parts of ex-Yugoslavia, being classed as "domestic" until then, are now considered "international visitors", among them Slovenes visiting Croatia. Therefore, in the Croatian statistics, visits to one of the traditional playgrounds of Slovenes, the Istrian peninsula (where close to 10,000 second homes and other real estate belong to Slovenian citizens), are not registered as "domestic" (meaning Yugoslav), but as visits from abroad. On the other hand, the wars in Bosnia and Herzegovina, and in particular in the Croatian province of Dalmatia – another traditional Slovene summer holiday destination – kept Slovenes either in their own state or in the near vicinity. Croatian Istria is in the immediate vicinity, just a couple of hours' drive from Slovenian visitors' homes. The absolute increase of "domestic" Slovene tourists in Slovenian Istria; the absolute and relative increase of Slovene tourism (as "international visits") in Croatian Istria; and the general decline in the numbers of other international visitors, characterized the tourist statistics in both nation-states in the 1990s. In 2002, Slovenia and Croatia have not yet reached the same number of tourist visits to the region as in the peak years within former Yugoslavia. In Croatia they have attained close to 66% and in Slovenia close to 75% of the 1985 visits. In general, a positive trend has been observed. In Istria, in the year 2002, the following trends and structures were observed:

- In both parts of Istria guests from neighboring regions and states of Central Europe (Italians, Austrians, Hungarians, Czechs, Bavarian Germans and Slovenes) dominate, thereby making a difference to the pre-independence years, when German, UK, Dutch and other citizens of Western Europe made the bulk of visits.
- All-inclusive air–hotel arrangements are becoming rare, and instead individual bookings and half-pension hotel bookings for motorists, made by travel agencies, are most common. Also, out-of-season

visits by groups of older people, traveling by bus, have become most popular.

- In Croatian Istria 75% of visits are made during the peak summer season (June, July, August) as visitors prefer to stay one week or more (Poreč–Parenzo average: 6.8 days!). For Western European naturist clubs the well-known resort of Vrsar–Koversada (7.9 days) and Rovinj–Rovigno (7.4 days) are leading destinations.

- In Slovenian Istria tourist visits in the peak summer season equal the number of visits in the other nine months of the year. The average visit lasts just 3.6 days, bringing to the foreground the fact that event tourism (congresses, meetings) and all-year-round weekend tourism, in particular in gambling and aquapark environments, are the general motives behind tourist visits. Similar trends can be observed in the neighboring Croatian tourist resort of Umag–Umago (5.9 day average), where the casino and different sports facilities (tennis training camps, marina) have both shortened the average length of stays and prolonged the season.

The most complex part of the post-independence and post-socialist transition period in Croatia and Slovenia has been the take-over of the state-owned tourist infrastructure, such as hotels, restaurants and beach properties, by banks, international consortiums and private owners.

Such take-overs are typical for countries in transition and work as follows: the former state-owned mega-enterprises get subdivided into smaller units (hotels, restaurants, shops, playing areas, beaches), each of them having its own independent legal structure. Local politicians bless this development in the name of the market economy. However, at this point, the value of those small units is at a minimum, as economic problems, haunting them from the past, have not been solved yet. Local or state-owned banks do, for a short while, become owners of the "problematic" tourist infrastructure. Then they sell it to the best local bidder or to an international consortium often through a fictitious tender that puts those units into the hands of well-informed individuals, often former communists and other politicians. Later, they often pass them on to investment groups or to hotel and travel enterprises. In the case of Croatia the latter have shown a particularly strong interest, for example:

- The Spanish hotel enterprise, Sol Melia, bought up major resorts in and around two Istrian towns – Umag–Umago and Rovinj–Rovigno. The naturist camp and several hotels in Vrsar have new owners who come from the UK and German travel agency management sector. Hotels in and around Pula–Pola are in the hands of the Italian finance and investment institution, Marconi (Šuligoj, 2000a). Istria's largest tourist resort, Plava laguna (The Blue Lagoon) was bought up by a Croatian émigré and owner of copper mines in Chile. The enterprise is managed by an American management institution (Oddelek, 1999).

- Just recently, in 2002, another tourist resort on the peninsula, Savudrija–Savudria, opposite to the Slovenian Mediterranean resort of Portorož–Portorose, has opened its doors. The construction of the resort was financed by an investment group consisting of the Hypo-Adria Bank, which is an Austrian, Italian and German financial institution, and several small-stock owners and private investors who have joined forces with an Italian finance institution, the CEIT of Padova (Šuligoj, 2000b).

In Slovenian Istria the transition period in which central planning was replaced by a market economy had similar "rules and regulations" as described above. But the interest of foreign investors in investing in Slovenian tourist infrastructure was far lower, though. Slovenian regulations for foreign investment were not as inviting as those in Croatia. Instead, reputable domestic firms, most often in the second part of the last decade, have consecutively shown interest in becoming owners of the existing tourist infrastructure. The profit they have gained in the first years of the market economy has been invested into hotels, marinas, aquaparks and other businesses related to the tourist industry:

- The spa resort of Terme Čatež, also owner of a castle and a golf course, invested in the hotel infrastructure of Koper–Capodistria, the capital of Slovenian Istria. The in-town hotel has become a congress center, while another hotel on the outskirts of the town has built several indoor and outdoor freshwater and saltwater pools – a swimming delight in a fake tropical environment. The investment was made possible due to the fact that the spa resort had tremendous numbers of visits during the unsettled situation in the Balkans. Between 1990 and 1996 Slovenes found their "continental sea" in several thermal and mineral water resorts, among which those of Terme Čatež are the biggest (Popit, 2000).
- The pharmaceutical firm of Krka, which already owned two spa resorts (Dolenjske toplice, Šmarješke toplice) in the vicinity of its production facility in Novo Mesto, bought up the coastal hotel complex of Savudrija and rearranged it to meet the standards of the spa resorts, offering several wellness programs (Popit, 2000).

- The petrol and gas distributor, ÖMV-Istra benz, has shown interest in Portorož–Portorose, the largest tourist resort on the Slovenian Riviera. At the time of writing, the firm has a major say in the Portorož Marina and controls two major hotel enterprises (Morje, Palace) in town (Popit, 2000).
- A questionable association of local politicians, tourist entrepreneurs and decision makers with the Australian/Singaporean firm, Ton-City, has proven to be a flop. The promises of this international consortium to reconstruct the century-old hotel, Palace, have come to nothing. The park and the uninhabited hotel, constructed by the Austrian Monarchy in 1906, are almost a ruin and a disgrace for the tourist resort, the City of Roses (Šuligoj, 2000b).

The questionnaire TOMAS (Tourism Marketing Study), distributed among several thousand tourists in Croatian and Slovenian Istria in 1994, 1997 and 2000, has shown that the environment, the sea, the sun, and the unspoiled karstic and mountainous hinterland, are topmost priorities for the tourists deciding to visit both Istrias. The observations made by tourists point to the shortage of games and events, in particular presentations of local ethnography (dances and songs), and other offerings (sports) that would get the adrenalin flowing. According to TOMAS, Istria is a region preferred by tourists with a mid-sized budget, families with children and those aged between 20 and 40 years. The most probable origin of the ideal tourist in Istria is a nation-state in West- or East-Central Europe (see also Marušić, 1997; Mikačić, 1994; Škafar *et al.*, 1998).

In 1999, students of Turistica – the College of Tourism at Portorož–Portorose – conducted a qualitative survey among owners and managers of tourist enterprises in four major tourist resorts of Istria: Portorož–Portorose, Umag–Umago, Poreč–Parenzo and Opatija. Summing up the results of the inquiries made, the following remarks regarding problems in the tourist industry have been stressed (see also Gosar, 2001):

- The history of "central planning" during communism hinders smooth sailing through the laws of the new market economy, in particular the so-called "denationalization" (transfer of state property to new owners) and "re-privatization" (property returned to known private owners).
- The independence and sovereignty of Croatia and Slovenia, including their international border, has separated both economies and therefore cut off the previous interdependence of the tourism industry. This hindrance does not affect tourism business as such, but tourists have to wait at several borders and have to have

different visas in their passports, etc. In order to meet all the formal-
ities, a Russian tourist, taking a holiday in Croatian Umag–Umago,
and booking a one-day bus excursion to the Italian Trieste (Castle
Miramare) and Venice, needs three visas (Croatian for re-entry;
Slovenian for transit; plus the European "Schengen" visa), costing
almost half of the one-week all-inclusive hotel arrangement.

- The instability in the Balkans has had long-lasting effects, despite
  the fact that both Slovenian and Croatian Istria never experienced
  political tensions. The placement of refugees from the war-torn
  areas of Croatia (and Bosnia-Herzegovina) into amenities, close to
  operating tourist businesses, has proven to be a great mistake by
  the Croatian government. Tourists at their leisure and refugees who
  have lost all their property and home do not have much in common.

Table 9.6 Istria: Bed-nights according to citizenship, 2000

	Slovenian Istria		Croatian Istria		Istria	
Citizenship of visitors	Bed-nights (000s)	Bed-nights (%)	Bed-nights (000s)	Bed-nights (%)	Bed-nights (000s)	Bed-nights (%)
Croatia	13.2	0.7	643.2	4.5	656.4	3.6
Slovenia	946.4	47.9	2,165.4	15.0	3,111.6	16.9
Austria	143.0	7.2	1,696.5	11.7	1,839.5	10.0
Italy	183.7	9.3	2,165.8	15.0	2,349.5	12.8
Hungary	20.8	1.1	411.3	2.8	432.1	2.4
Czech Rep.	13.8	0.7	1,217.4	8.4	1,231.2	6.7
Slovakia	4.3	0.2	285.5	2.0	289.8	1.6
Poland	9.9	0.5	495.9	3.4	505.8	2.8
Russia	44.9	2.3	101.3	0.7	146.2	0.8
Germany	275.5	14.0	4,013.1	27.8	4,288.6	23.3
France	6.3	0.3	22.3	0.1	28.6	0.2
Netherlands	11.9	0.6	664.9	4.6	676.8	3.7
UK	5.6	0.3	96.8	0.7	102.4	0.6
Other	294.7	14.9	459.6	3.2	754.3	4.1
Total	1,974.0	100	14,439.0	100	18,387.0	100

Table 9.7 Slovenia/Croatia: Bed-nights according to citizenship, 1985, 1995, 2000

Citizenship of visitors	1985		1995	2000		Growth
	Bed-nights (000s)	Bed-nights (%)	Bed-nights (000s)	Bed-nights (000s)	Bed-nights (%)	Index (2000/ 1985)
Slovenia						
Croatia	726	8.5	212	251	3.7	35
Slovenia	2,670	31.4	3,448	3,315	49.3	124
Austria	389	4.6	441	527	7.8	135
Italy	632	7.4	388	650	9.7	103
Hungary	33	0.4	58	86	1.3	261
Czech Rep. and Slovakia	47	0.6	56	74	1.1	157
Germany	913	10.7	572	773	11.5	85
France	69	0.8	39	53	0.8	77
Netherlands	368	4.3	83	125	1.9	34
UK	612	7.2	66	153	2.3	25
Other	2,051	24.1	520	712	10.6	35
Total	8,510	100	5,883	6,719	100	79
Croatia						
Croatia	8,790	13.0	4,370	5,138	13.1	58
Slovenia	6,321	9.3	2,060	5,015	12.8	79
Austria	4,718	7.0	1,255	3,358	8.6	71
Italy	4,215	6.2	798	4,526	11.6	107
Hungary	674	1.0	217	1,418	3.6	210
Czech Rep.	3,054*	4.5*	889	4,734	12.1	196**
Slovakia	3,054*	4.5*	200	1,249	3.2	196**
Germany	16,818	24.9	1,915	7,804	19.9	46
France	1,203	1.8	76	181	0.5	15
Netherlands	2,249	0.4	234	901	2.3	40
UK	3,874	5.7	108	410	1.0	11
Other	15,749	23.3	763	4,449	11.4	28
Total	67,665	100	12,885	39,183	100	58

Notes:
* Czechoslovakia ** in relation to data of Czechoslovakia

Conclusion

The Mediterranean tourist destination Istria of former Yugoslavia, now shared by the independent nation-states of Slovenia and Croatia, has recently experienced an untypical tourism cycle, described above. Major reasons include:

- the ethnic disputes, conflicts and wars in other, relatively distant, areas of the Balkans;
- the transition from a socialist central planning economy to a market economy;
- the global change in the behavior of tourists and the travel industry; and
- the division of Yugoslavia into several sovereign nation-states, including Croatia and Slovenia, separated by international borders.

The above has had an enormous effect on tourism in both Croatian and Slovenian Istria, where rules of law, tourism strategies and applied economics differ from the times when the region as a whole was part of a politically and economically unified state (Gosar, 1998). The record numbers of visitors reached in the 1980s have not been recouped yet. The Slovenian part has come closer to the goal, but one must take into account that Croatian Istria has 10 times as many accommodation amenities and therefore sets the pace for the tourism industry in the region.

Many questions have not yet found the answers and solutions that politicians and other decision makers in the region and states should be offering after the disintegration of former Yugoslavia:

- to promote the states' recognition as independent states (not the war-torn Yugoslavia!) and as two tourist destinations: Croatia and Slovenia;
- to define and delineate the border between Slovenia and Croatia;
- to solve the problem of Croatian refugees from the war-torn parts of former Yugoslavia;
- to define the rules regarding several thousand leisure and tourism properties owned by (now) foreign citizens and firms whose lawful residence officially is (now) in another sovereign state; and
- to produce plans for cross-border co-operation and revitalize the once excellent regional partnership.

The persistence of these problems could not eliminate tourism in the region or hinder its steady growth since 2000, but it could slow up the very promising growth in the numbers of tourists that industries of

Croatia and Slovenia have registered in the last couple of years. In addition, the events of September 11, 2001, when the US was attacked by terrorists who used passenger jets to destroy parts of the infrastructure of New York City and Washington DC, caused definite uncertainty in the matter. But, if general trends in tourism should come to the foreground again, tourist destinations that can be reached by motorists, as is the case of Istria, should not fear.

In Croatia and Slovenia new peaks in tourism can be achieved only if global partners would co-operate and if foreign and domestic investors would promote and/or produce more and newer attractions. Investors have shown interest in the tourism industry of Istria, but there is a fear that many of them are keen just to make short-term profits. This attitude does not benefit the region or its peoples.

References

Blake, G.H. (1994): Croatia's Maritime Boundaries, pp. 38–46; IN: Croatia – A New Euripean State, University of Zagreb, Zagreb.

Blažević, I. (1996) *Turistička geografija Hrvatske* (2. izdanje). Pula: Sveučilište u Rijeci/Pedagoški fakultet u Puli.

Blažević, I. (1987) *Povijest turizma Istre i Kvarnera*. Opatija: Otokar Keršovani.

Bošković, D. (2000) Restrukturiranje i prilagođavanje turističke ponude Hrvatske Europskim in svijetskim trendovima. *Turizam [Tourism]* 48 (2), 153–166. Zagreb: Institut za turizam.

Državni zavod za statistiku Republike Hrvatske (2000) *Turizam: kumulativni podaci 1998–1999*. Priobčenje br. 4.4.2/11 (V. Mikačić, ed.). Zagreb: Državni zavod za statistiku RH.

Gosar, A. (1998) Probleme der Grenzziehung zwischen Kroatien und Slowenien: Grenzen und Grenzregionen in Südosteuropa (Frank-Dieter Grimm, ed.). *Südosteuropa Aktuell* 28, 33–50.

Gosar, A. (1999) Reconsidering tourism strategy as a consequence of the disintegration of Yugoslavia: The case of Slovenia. *Turizam [Tourism]* 47 (1), 67–73. Zagreb: Institut za turizam.

Gosar, A. (2001) Učinki slovensko-hrvaške meje in osamosvojitve na turizem v hrvaški in slovenski Istri [Sociogeographic problems of border regions along the Slovenian–Croatian border] (=Dela 16), 135–165. Ljubljana: Oddlek za geografijo, Filozofska faculteta, Univerza v Ljubljiani.

Jordan, P. (1997) *Beitraege zur Fremdenverkehrsgeographie der noerdlichen kroatischen Kueste*. Klagenfurter geographische Schriften, No. 15. Klagenfurt. Zagreb: In stitut za turizam.

Jordan, P. (2000) Hrvatski turizam pred izazovima globalizacije. *Turizam [Tourism]* 48 (2), 195–203. Zagreb: Institut za turizam.

Jordan, P. and Schappelwein, K. (2000) International tourism attractions in Central and Southeastern Europe 1999. In *Atlas Ost- und Südosteuropa*. Wien: Österreichiches Ost- und Südosteuropa Institut (map and text).

Klemenčić, M. and Schofield, C.H. (1995): Croatia and Slovenia: The Four Hamlets Case, Boundary and Security Bulletin 2/4, pp. 65–77, University of Durham: International Boundaries Research Unit, Durham.

Mann, Thomas (1957) *Death in Venice*. Penguin Books Ltd. Harmondsworth, Middlesex, pp. 20.

Marušič, Z. (1997) *Stavovi i potrošnja turista u Hrvatskoj – TOMAS '97: Osnovni izveštaj*. Zagreb: Institut za turizam.

Mikačič, V. (1994) *Stavovi i potrošnja turista u Hrvatskoj – TOMAS '94: osnovni izveštaj*. Zagreb: Institut za turizam.

Narodne novine (1994) Zakon o krajevima sa turističkim potencialima. Narodne novine br. 75. Zagreb.

Sirše, J. and Mihalič, T. (1999) Slovenian tourism and tourism policy: A case study. *Revue de Tourisme* [*The Tourist Review; Zeitschrift für Fremdenverkehr*] 3, 34–47. Zurich: AIEST–Internationale Vereinigung wissenschaftlicher Fremdenverkehrsexperten.

Sirše J., Stroj-Vrtačnik I. and Pobega N. (1992) *Strategija razvoja slovenskega turizma*. Ljubljana: Inštitut za ekonomska raziskovanja.

Škafar, A., Božič, A., Zaletel, M. and Arnež, M. (1998) Anketa o tujih turistih v Republiki Sloveniji v poletni sezoni 1997. *Rezultati raziskovanj 704*, 43–47. Ljubljana.

Statistični urad Republike Slovenije (1999) Letni pregled turizma 1997. Rezultati raziskovanj 736, Ljubljana.

Statistični urad Republike Slovenije (2001) Gostinstvo in turizem 2000. *Statistični Letopis*, 441–456, 603–605, 635, Ljubljana.

Zavod SRS za statistiko/Kšela, J. (ur.) (1989) *Letni pregled turizma 1985–1987*, 467: 120–129. Ljubljana.

Zavod za statistiku Republike Hrvatske/Mikačič, Škafar, A. (ed.) (2001) Turizam 2000: Istarska županija. Zagreb.

Chapter 10

The Foot-and-Mouth Outbreak of 2001: Impacts on and Implications for Tourism in the United Kingdom

R. BUTLER AND D. AIREY

Introduction

The outbreak of foot-and-mouth disease (FMD) in the UK which began in February, 2001, has had significant impacts on many aspects of rural life, particularly agriculture and tourism. The ramifications of the outbreak for tourism at least are still manifesting themselves and likely to be doing so for a considerable time to come. It has become clear in the period since the disease was first diagnosed that the impacts on tourism are likely to be the most serious from an economic viewpoint, although the social effects, as well as economic ones on agriculture may, in fact, be more permanent.

This chapter focuses on the effects and implications of the outbreak on tourism in and to the UK. Because of the absence of reliable and verifiable statistics on such a recent event, this chapter can provide only a review of currently available information and what is essentially speculation on future events and developments. The chapter begins with an introduction to the disease and the current outbreak. It then reviews the scale and nature of tourism in the UK by way of context to the subsequent discussion. Attention then shifts to the effects of the outbreak on tourism demand in and to the UK, on the image of the UK as a tourist destination, on public awareness and policy responses to the outbreak, and finally to impacts on tourism supply within the UK. There is then discussion on four specific themes: the vulnerability of tourism, the importance of image and perception, the awareness and response to

215

crises, and the level of accuracy of knowledge. The last section concludes the chapter with a discussion of potential implications of the outbreak in the short and long term.

Foot-and-Mouth Disease (FMD)

FMD disease is a viral disease endemic in several continents, and is highly contagious among vulnerable species such as cattle, pigs, sheep and goats (DEFRA, 2001). While horses are resistant, other species, such as deer, foxes and hedgehogs, and rodents such as rats, are also affected, as are many other animals not indigenous to the UK, but often found in zoos and wildlife parks. Although it cannot be cured, the disease is rarely fatal, and most adult stock recover within two to three weeks, although they may carry the virus for up to two years. The seven strains of the virus are distinct and exposure to one does not give immunity to the others. The incubation period is generally short, 3–5 days, although 2–21 days have been recorded. FMD is spread by direct and indirect contact with infected animals, particularly within the first few days of infection, and can be transmitted by air, by mechanical means, e.g. on vehicles and people, and also from uncooked swill and frozen food. The virulent nature of the disease, the speed of incubation and the variety of methods of infection make containment of an outbreak difficult, and this situation is complicated by modern farming methods, in particular the frequent and considerable movement of animals around the country.

Contrary to confused public opinion, there are no implications for the human food chain, and restrictions imposed on the sale of meat and dairy products is primarily for reasons of animal health, not human safety, although there is little doubt public confidence in related food products has been shaken (particularly in Europe, following the outbreak of BSE some years earlier). There has been only one recorded instance of a human contracting foot-and-mouth in the UK, in 1967, and the human form is short-lived and very mild.

FMD is not as rare in Europe as appears to have been believed. In the UK there was a major outbreak in 1967, and other outbreaks in 1922, 1923–1924 and 1953. There were only two years between that last date and 1967 in which at least one case was not recorded. Following the 1967 outbreak and the introduction of more stringent elimination measures, only one case, caused by windborne virus from France in 1981, has been recorded in the UK (in the Isle of Wight). The last significant outbreak in Europe was in 2000 in Greece. The recommended procedures for eradicating outbreaks includes the immediate slaughter of infected animals and those animals in contact with them, rendering (destroying) of carcasses, prohibiting movement of animals, establishing quarantine zones for animals and people, disinfecting premises and equipment, and burning articles which cannot be decontaminated. Because of the virulence of the disease, rapid commencement of such actions is essential to contain an outbreak. This means that rapid confirmation of cases is also crucial, as the virus is produced most rapidly in the first few days of infection.

At this point the cause of the 2001 outbreak is still not certain, although the site of the first outbreak was confirmed within a few days as a pig farm at Heddon-on-the-Wall in Northumbria. It is thought that the infection came from pigswill. The disease was confirmed on 20 February, having been reported the previous day. By that time seven other farms had already been infected, and sheep from infected farms had been sent to market in Hexham and subsequently to Cumbria. Within a further four days sheep had also gone to Carlisle, Devon, Dumfries and Cheshire, all before the first outbreak had been confirmed. Subsequent evidence of an anecdotal nature has suggested that many of the movements of sheep are unrecorded "around the edges of the various livestock markets" (DEFRA, 2001: 1) which makes tracing dispersal of flocks extremely difficult.

The 2001 outbreak was much larger and much more widespread than the last major one in 1967 and involved a much greater number of animals being slaughtered. The 1967 outbreak was spatially limited to west central England, with no cases in Scotland, Ireland or the south of England, whereas the 2001 outbreak involved the majority of the counties in England and Wales and the Scottish Borders, with only parts of eastern and southern England still remaining clear. Essex and Kent were outliers in the southeast. Four cases were recorded in Northern Ireland, and very few outside the UK. Major concentrations occurred in Cumbria/Dumfries and Galloway, Devon, and, most recently, Yorkshire. By July 2001, over 1800 cases had been recorded and over 3 million animals destroyed, compared to just over 1400 cases in total in 1967, and the Appendix on p. 236 lists overall costs and animals destroyed (DEFRA, 2001).

UK Tourism

UK tourism has been marked by four key trends over the past two decades. First, there has been a rapid and consistent growth in numbers of UK residents travelling abroad. As shown in Table 10.1, this sector of tourism has grown from 17.5 million visits in 1980 to 53.8 million in 1999,

Table 10.1 UK tourism

Million visits	1980	1985	1990	1995	1999
Domestic (holidays 4 plus nights)	36.5	37.0	32.5	na	27.0 (1)
Domestic (total)	146.0	144.0	110.0 (2)	121.0	146.1
Incoming	12.5	14.4	18.0	23.5	25.4
Outgoing	17.5	21.6	31.1	41.3	53.8

Sources: International Passenger Survey; British National Travel Survey; UK Tourism Survey; British Home Tourism Survey
Notes:
(1) 1998
(2) estimated

a growth of more than 200%. A key factor behind this has been the development of attractive and affordable offerings by the international tourist industry, especially the large tour operators, to destinations offering sun, sea and sand. The second trend has been the more steady growth in international visitors to the UK, which has more than doubled over the period but which has had weaker growth in the last few years. Here the attractions of the UK in the form of cultural and city destinations, as well as shopping, English language and the countryside, are meeting competition from a range of other destinations in an increasingly global tourism marketplace. Third, demand for UK domestic holidays of four or more nights has been in a long-term decline, with international competition taking the trade from the traditional British tourist destinations, typically at the seaside. Finally, domestic short holidays, visits to friends and relatives, as well as business travel, have been generally buoyant, although, when combined with domestic long holidays, the overall picture for domestic tourism is effectively static.

This brief outline provides an important context for some of the key issues facing UK tourism prior to the arrival of FMD. In brief there have been fairly long-standing elements of concern about the overall competitiveness of the tourism sector in the UK in an increasingly global world. As an indicator of this the UK Government has launched a number of studies and initiatives designed to meet the challenges of competition (see for example DNH, 1995; DCMS, 1999). The unease about the overall position of UK tourism was particularly compounded during Autumn 2000 and Spring 2001. The strength of the pound sterling against the European currencies played a part in this but, perhaps more importantly, a number of events which were reported internationally were anticipated to have a particularly negative effect on tourism. These included a major accident on the rail network, a short-lived but severe fuel crisis, torrential rain and flooding and ongoing concern about BSE or mad cow disease. Against this background the emergence of FMD, and the associated publicity of the actions designed to control and eradicate it, can be seen as the latest problem for a sector that was already experiencing difficulties.

Impacts of Foot-and-Mouth Disease

Impacts on demand

It is always difficult to disentangle the effects of any individual event on tourism demand, even more so when the event is recent. As already explained, the 2001 outbreak of FMD arrived at a time when the UK tourism industry was already experiencing and anticipating problems. The difficulties of identifying effects are also compounded by the multi-sector nature of the tourist industry, by its regional distribution and the regional spread of the disease and by the fact that the disease has been operating over a period of time. As far as the multi-sector nature of the industry is concerned, it is clear that, while some sectors experienced problems, others have remained buoyant. The extremes of this are that most of the outgoing tourism businesses have been experiencing high or higher demand, which in turn is part of a long-term trend, while other sectors such as farm tourism have suffered a collapse of demand.

Similarly, some parts of the country were very badly affected, particularly Cumbria where the outbreak was very fierce, while in others the effects were very limited. For example, the coastal resorts of the south of England reported high demand from visitors, mainly domestic, over the 2001 Easter and spring holiday periods. Anecdotal evidence is also provided of holiday visitors who bypassed Cumbria, to head for Scotland for the hill-walking, adding perhaps an additional 200 miles with associated expenditure to their journey. Over time, the movements in demand fell into two clear periods associated particularly with the reaction and response of the Government and the media to the problem. Initially, visitors were encouraged to avoid the countryside. This, as well as the media images of burning carcasses, served to depress both UK and international demand. Later, following the realisation that the collapse in demand for tourism was having an economic effect on the countryside just as great as that created by the FMD itself, the Government changed its approach and sought to encourage visitors back to rural areas. This was met with some success in many areas.

A few indicators can serve to illustrate the seriousness as well as the patchiness of the apparent influence on demand. In 2001, it was shown that:

- The effects of FMD on domestic tourism would reduce the annual expenditure of domestic tourists by £1.5bn and of same-day visitors by £3.6bn (Christel DeHaan Tourism and Travel Research Institute, 2001).
- FMD had reduced international tourist receipts by £2.3bn annually or by 19% from expected levels in 2001. Reductions were largest in the UK's largest source market, the United States, where visitor expenditures fell by 26% compared with the level that they would have reached without FMD (Christel DeHaan Tourism and Travel Research Institute, 2001).
- Total expenditures by tourists and day visitors in the UK would fall by £7.5bn (Christel DeHaan Tourism and Travel Research Institute, 2001).
- The damage to tourist firms would be highest in Cumbria, Scotland and Wales (Christel DeHaan Tourism and Travel Research Institute, 2001).
- In one of the worst affected regions, in the first month of the crisis, March, the Lake District suffered a 75% decline in bookings compared with the previous year (CMSC, 2001).

Impacts on the UK as a tourism destination

As shown by the figures above, the UK is a major tourist destination at the international level and has a very large domestic tourism market. In general the appeal of the UK to foreign tourists is tied closely to heritage, combined with ties to families and friends, urban short breaks and special events. London is the principal attraction and the major gateway for air arrivals. Thus the focus of much of the international tourism is urban, and visits to rural areas tend to be focused on specific attractions, such as Shakespearean heritage at Stratford, Stonehenge and literary heritage links in the Lake District and Yorkshire. Some rural areas such as the Cotswolds also attract significant numbers of foreign visitors, but widespread travel throughout the countryside, especially in England and Wales, by foreign visitors is small compared to the numbers remaining in urban centres. In contrast, domestic tourism and leisure-related trips focus very heavily on rural areas. More than 100 million trips are made to "the countryside" in the UK annually (Countryside Commission, 1998). Many of these are short-distance trips, mostly not involving an overnight stay, but still involving considerable expenditure on and use of rural tourism and recreation facilities and services. As noted elsewhere in the chapter, the effects of the outbreak were not identical on all aspects of tourism. However, with respect to the image of the UK as a tourism destination, the effects were consistent and entirely negative.

The attraction of urban areas noted above notwithstanding, much of the overall appeal and tourist image of the UK is related to rural imagery. The rural landscape of the UK, particularly the mixed farming landscape of England – the "green and pleasant land" of Shakespeare – has been immortalised in paintings by such as Constable, poetry by Wordsworth, literature by numerous contemporary and past authors, and by films and television series too numerous to list. The public tourist perception of the UK in part is of a rural idyll and anything which shakes that image has the potential to do great harm to the tourism industry, even if the image is not entirely correct, nor experienced by the majority of foreign visitors. It has been argued that "most significantly of all (influences) in terms of reinforcement or maintenance of rurality is tourism" (Butler and Hall, 1998: 116).

The negative scenarios were reinforced by regular items in the news media on the outbreak itself, and by related events that gained additional coverage. One example will suffice to illustrate this. As late as six months arter the outbreak was officially ended, airline passengers from the UK to several countries were still required to walk over a disinfected mat, ostensibly to disinfect footwear (in some cases ignoring footwear in baggage). This unfortunately continued to reinforce the negative image of the UK in the minds of potential visitors. When Prince Charles visited Canada in April 2001, there was global coverage of His Royal Highness descending from the plane at Ottawa and duly walking over a red carpet soaked in disinfectant. His itinerary was changed to avoid him visiting farms in western Canada, again dramatising that people coming from the UK were potential carriers and, by implication, that visiting the UK involved some risk, thus negatively affecting the UK as a tourist destination.

A number of overseas governments reacted to the outbreak by focusing attention and some restrictions on visitors from Britain. Publicity material was produced warning of the dangers of FMD to the home country, the importation of foodstuffs was banned or restricted and material not previously publicised began to appear (Hall, 2001), again drawing

attention directly to the outbreak and indirectly impacting on the attractiveness of the UK as a destination. Other governments sought to take
advantage of the situation by advertising the availability of their countries with no or minimal influence from FMD, thus increasing pressure
on the UK industry. The likely permanence of these developments is
discussed in the final section of the chapter.

Impacts and policy effects

As already suggested, the reaction of the Government to the outbreak
of FMD, as far as tourism is concerned, can be divided into two clear
stages. In the first, there was almost a "knee-jerk" reaction to control the
spread of FMD by discouraging all visits to the countryside. This was in
line with the policy of massively restricting movements of livestock.
Measures included advice to avoid contact with farms, to avoid walking
in areas where there were livestock and to avoid making unnecessary
visits to rural areas. Footpaths and other rights of way in the countryside
were closed in virtually all parts of the country and major land owners,
including the National Trust and the Forestry Commission, cut off
public access to much of their land. In other words, large parts of the
British countryside were put off limits to visitors. This by itself made
headline news around the world. As already noted, this action, coupled
with media images of slaughtered and incinerated animals, as well as the
Government's decision to delay elections, created an image of a country
and countryside in crisis, with dramatic effects on tourism demand.

In the second period, which started towards the end of March 2001,
and followed significant lobbying by the tourism interests as well as
other parts of the rural community, the policy response shifted fairly
radically, with measures to offset the problems for tourism in the country
at large. There was some confusion here in that restriction of access
remained fairly widespread in the countryside, while at the same time
visitors, especially from overseas, were being reassured that the UK was
still a good place to visit. The confusion became even more pronounced
later in the period when Government Ministers were personally encouraging domestic visitors to the countryside itself at the same time as many
of the restrictions were still in force.

The rough comparison between the relative economic importance of
tourism and agriculture in the UK given in Table 10.2 provides a source
for understanding the policy shift as well as the confusion. In brief,
tourism is too important economically, in comparison to agriculture, for
the Government to sacrifice it. Yet, at the same time, with its historical

Table 10.2 Comparison of agriculture with tourism in the UK

	Agriculture	*Tourism*
Contribution to employment	1.5%	7%
Foreign exchange earnings	£8.4bn	£12.5bn
Contribution to GDP	1%	4%
Contribution to tax revenues	£88m	£1.5bn
Revenue growth 1996–1999	–21%	+26%

Source: ETC, 2001a

importance and the long-standing link between land-ownership and political power, the agricultural lobby is particularly strong. Against this background it is understandable that the Government's initial reaction was to turn attention to agriculture but, when the economic realities became clear, to seek at least to mollify the tourism interests.

Sharpley and Craven (forthcoming) have identified three broad categories in the policy responses pursued by the Government in this second period. The first was to attract visitors to the UK in general as well as to the countryside, the second was to improve accessibility in the countryside, especially in relation to public footpaths, and the third was to support tourism businesses affected by the crisis.

On the face of it the summary of the measures provided in Box 10.1 suggests a fairly comprehensive package which was introduced relatively speedily. However, what this fails to highlight is the scale of this support compared with perceived needs or, perhaps more importantly, compared to that provided to the agriculture sector. Some indication of the perceived needs can be seen from the English Tourism Council's (ETC) request for £35.5m against the £3.8m provided. Against the agriculture sector, which was estimated to have received £898m (from DEFRA) from the public purse in compensation for slaughter alone, the support was relatively insignificant.

The public policy issues for tourism from this experience are both encouraging and discouraging. On the positive side, the British Government clearly, and fairly speedily, recognised the importance of tourism and, for some of the time, particularly in relation to the opening of footpaths, it was clear that tourism was gaining ground over the agriculture lobby. In part of course, this is because the agriculture lobby itself, with a proportion of its income dependent on farm stays and other

Box 10.1 Measures to support tourism

Attract visitors

- Additional funding for the British Tourist Authority (£14.2m) for overseas promotion and for the English Tourism Council (£3.8m) for support for domestic tourism. The Scottish Parliament voted £12.7m to visitscotland and the Wales Tourist Board received £1m. (BTA and ETC had bid for £22m and £35.5m respectively.)
- The Government launched a public information campaign involving overseas and domestic ministerial visits (including a visit by the Deputy Prime Minister) as well as a high profile "World Travel Leaders Summit" that involved a senior member of the Royal Family.
- Telephone hotlines and a website were established by the tourist boards.

Improve accessibility

- The Government worked with the national bodies to encourage the opening of footpaths in areas unaffected by the disease.

Support for business

- A moratorium was agreed on various tax payments (VAT, PAYE, NI and UBR), with deferment agreed on an individual basis and interest not charged on deferred payments.
- The Government funded 95% of UBR hardship relief for three months for affected businesses in Wales of up to £50,000 rateable value and in England and Scotland of up to £12,000 rateable value.
- Extended loans of up to £250,000 but at a premium of 1.5% interest through the Small Firms Loan Guarantee Scheme were granted.
- A £50m Rural Business Recovery Programme to enable Regional Development Agencies to assist small tourism and other businesses in England was established.
- A Rural Skills Action package, which gave advice to those temporarily or permanently laid off, with 10 Jobcentres acting as one-stop shops offering a single way into benefits, training and other services, was put together.

Sources: Sharpley and Craven, forthcoming; British Hospitality Association, 2001

forms of rural tourism, had some uncertainty as to the desirability of opening up the countryside. On the more gloomy side, it is clear that public thinking is still a long way from identifying tourism as a key activity in the same way as agriculture, or, to put it another way, the historical power base of agriculture, dating from a time when the country and its leaders depended on agriculture, is still very much in place. One interesting change in Government structures, announced following the General Election of early June 2001, was that Government responsibility for agriculture was to be moved from the Ministry of Agriculture, Fisheries and Food (MAFF) (which has now been abolished) to a new ministry, the Department for Environment, Food and Rural Affairs (DEFRA). This places agriculture into a wider Government context which may be less sharply protectionist of the commercial interests of farmers.

Impacts on tourism supply

The effects of the outbreak on the supply of tourism facilities and services is difficult to assess quantitatively. The most serious effect was through the closure of large parts of the countryside to visitation, through footpaths being formally closed to prevent the spread of the infection and through other facilities being closed and events being cancelled to avoid transference of the disease. Initially at least, very little of the accommodation supply was closed or unavailable, unless it was located within a quarantined area. As the disease spread, facilities such as youth hostels in rural areas were closed in increasing numbers. Most hotels, guest houses and bed and breakfast establishments remained open throughout the epidemic, although many received very little trade and had to reduce staff and some facilities. At the height of the epidemic the vast majority of nature reserves, gardens and historic properties in rural areas were closed. By mid-April 2001, some of the major zoos and wildlife parks were closed and others had some species removed from view, although a majority of privately run stately homes were open and the major theme parks remained open throughout the epidemic.

The cancellation of events, particularly where these were of international importance or of international newsworthiness (including the UK local elections) further publicised the outbreak and the limitations it imposed on activities and travel in the UK. Where these events were particularly rural in nature, such as fairs, equestrian events, festivals and country shows, the rural image was further denigrated. The Cheltenham Gold Cup racing event was cancelled, and the Republic of Ireland Government requested horse owners not to send racehorses to events in the UK, not because horses themselves are vulnerable to the disease but because of the risk of the disease being carried on a host. The TT motorcycle racing event on the Isle of Man (scheduled in late May/early June) was cancelled for the first time in peacetime in its 94-year history because of the disease-free status of the island and the risk of introduction of the disease. Crufts Dog Show was postponed from March to May 2001, with implications for a considerable number of European owners, particularly in view of recent changes made to quarantine laws in the UK which would have resulted in larger numbers of foreign entries than previously. A number of county agricultural shows and festivals were cancelled, although most other major horseracing events, such as the Grand National, the Epsom Derby and Royal Ascot were held. Even at these events there were media pictures of celebrities walking over disinfectant-soaked straw, continuing the negative coverage. Football games in general were not affected – major league, cup competitions and European participation continued unaffected – but the Six Nations Rugby Union competition was postponed until the autumn of 2001 for completion at the request of the Irish Rugby Union to avoid large numbers of spectators crossing to the Republic and to Northern Ireland (there being only one case in the Republic and four Northern Ireland).

Thus, while the reduction in supply was small in the overall context of what was available, the cancellation or postponement of some high-visibility events and the initial general impression that the countryside was closed undoubtedly created an image that much less was available than was actually the case. As discussed elsewhere, the changes in policy and guidance from the Government further confused the situation and uncertainty and lack of clarity of information still remained. Regional and local bodies made various efforts to convince potential visitors that it was appropriate and safe to visit much of the countryside, including newspaper advertisements, posters and television coverage, but the efforts often suffered from lack of co-ordination and even presented conflicting messages.

Themes

Fragility and vulnerability of tourism under exogenous forces

Much of the tourism literature is concerned with the impacts of tourism upon economies, environments and communities (Mathieson and Wall, 1982), rather than on the impact on tourism of exogenous forces. Increasing attention is being paid to the effect on tourism of negative events such as terrorism and natural disasters, although only limited literature has appeared in academic publications. There has been little exploration of the effects of something such as an outbreak of FMD on tourism and thus a conceptual framework or context for such a study is absent. It is not proposed to provide such a context here, but to note that there are similarities to other situations in the effect of the event, the treatment of the event in the media, and the response of various agencies to the event and its coverage.

In the UK context perhaps the closest comparison can be made with the impacts of oil spills on tourism, in particular the grounding and sinking of the "Braer" off the coast of Shetland in 1993, with the subsequent spillage of 85,000 tons of crude oil (more than in the Exxon Valdez incident in Alaska). The event drew immediate and excessive media coverage, over 500 media representatives arriving on scene within a week of the event and global coverage of storms, a wrecked ship, dead birds, oil slicks and depressed and affected individuals, along with forecasts of environmental and economic catastrophe (Butler, 1996). Central public sector response was vague, uncertain, contradictory and confusing, although in that case local authority response was generally hailed as exceptional and highly effective. In the event, the threatened catastrophe did not materialise, certainly because of natural events and not human actions. However, tourism to Shetland was affected, with immediate cancellations and an overall decline of some 10% in numbers over the previous year. Subsequently, however, tourism has recovered to pre-event levels (Mullay, 1994). This was accomplished because of promotion, almost all by the local sectors, and favourable, though very limited, media coverage.

Some clear messages emerge from this and other events in the context of tourism. First is that tourism is highly vulnerable to such exogenous forces and cannot be shielded effectively from their effects in most cases. Second, such effects are likely to be more serious for tourism where the environment is a key element in its attractiveness, as was the case in Shetland and is the case of the image of tourism in the UK. Third, central government cannot be relied on automatically to respond quickly, efficiently and appropriately, especially if the event is not national or not perceived as of national importance. There is no doubt that the speed and nature of the response to the FMD outbreak was conditioned by the importance given to agriculture and the influence of the former ministry (MAFF) and because it was anticipated that it could be a national problem. Fourth, and it remains to be seen if this is the case for the FMD outbreak, compensation for anticipated losses, e.g. tourist non-arrivals, is hard to obtain, compared to compensation for proven losses, e.g. slaughtered animals. Where intangible losses are involved, for example loss of image, the difficulty in obtaining compensation is even greater, both from the private (insurance) and public sector. Fifth, and perhaps most depressingly, there is often little which is or can be done to prevent a recurrence of the event in the future, with similar, if not even more severe effects.

Importance of image and perception

In exploring the relationship between tourism and FMD it is difficult to separate reality from image and perception. Clearly the slaughter and disposal of up to 3 million animals or up to 7% of the nation's livestock represented a fairly dramatic event and this had a number of "real" effects on tourism, both immediate and long-lasting. The reality of pyres for burning the slaughtered livestock in the Lake District and elsewhere obviously had a strong deterrent effect on visitors. In the same way, and possibly of far more importance in the long term, the potential changes in agriculture and associated land management practices may have had a real effect on the nature and attractiveness of the English landscape. In essence the English countryside, which is one of the country's key attractions, is a direct result of human intervention, primarily though agricultural practices developed over centuries. If these change as a result of a collapse in agriculture, then the landscape changes. In this sense Middleton (2001) has likened agriculture to the horse that is responsible for pulling the tourism cart. If the horse is weakened, then the cart cannot proceed. In a very real way this focuses on the crucial relationship between tourism and the countryside and in the end a long-term benefit of this crisis may be a better appreciation of this link.

Beyond this, many of the more immediate effects on tourism was more to do with the image and perception of the disease and its effects rather than the reality. In reality only a very small proportion of the country was seriously affected by the disease itself and for the overwhelming majority of the residents of the UK their only awareness of the disease was through the media and by the closing of country footpaths for a brief period. Yet, for all this, the images were very vivid and, as in so much of tourism, they became the reality, especially for those making decisions about where to take their vacations. At the most simple level the image of burning car-casses in the UK acted as a powerful message that this was not a country to visit in 2001. When this is linked with some of the other problems noted earlier of rail accidents, or BSE (which has no links with FMD), then the message becomes even more powerful and the need for effective news management becomes even more urgent. The reality of FMD is that it has been prevalent in many different parts of the world for a long time – Africa, Latin America and Southeast Asia. As the New Zealand Biosecurity Minister commented in May 2001: "Even when the foot-and-mouth outbreak is confirmed as eradicated in Britain it is still widespread in a lot of places a lot closer to New Zealand than Britain". Yet even this did not stop the US National Center for Infectious Diseases in its March 2001 update on FMD from focusing solely on the UK (CDC, 2001).

Of course some of the particular difficulties for the UK from FMD lie with the image and nature of the UK itself as a tourist destination. For many domestic and international visitors the attraction of the UK lies in its landscape and rural areas. Hence anything that detracts from this does damage to the tourist image as a whole. In other words the effects of FMD are magnified though the rural image of the destination and, clearly, for the international visitor, this appears to infect other types of tourism as well. The same outbreak in a destination that is noted for beach tourism would most likely make its impact felt in a very different and lesser way.

Awareness and response

The lack of awareness of the likely impacts on tourism and thus the appropriateness of the response to the outbreak were fairly apparent and have been noted earlier. Whether the nature of the response to the outbreak was appropriate will be debated for some time to come. The central government has argued that it had little choice but to follow a policy of immediate slaughter of infected animals and those within three kilometres of confirmed cases and create exclusion zones, and that vaccination was not a feasible option. From the tourism point of view, there is little doubt that mass vaccination and much more limited slaughter, perhaps of only confirmed cases, would have been likely to have had much more limited negative publicity and less serious effects. One can argue that, because tourism is worth more than agriculture in economic terms, prime consideration should have been given to determining what response would have had the least negative effects on tourism, rather than what was perceived best for the agricultural export market. Such arguments are irrelevant now, and run in the face of what was conventional politics and wisdom at the time of the outbreak: that agricultural interests were paramount with respect to agricultural issues and the outbreak was seen as an agricultural issue. Response was therefore left initially with the ministry responsible (MAFF) which had no mandate with respect to tourism and appears to have had little understanding of the role or importance of tourism in the rural economy. The Cabinet, through subsequent government policy appears to have accepted this situation initially.

Once it became clear that it may not have been the best response, and the scale of the impact on tourism and associated businesses was realised, counteracting measures were taken. While the basic policy for dealing with the disease was not changed (rightly or wrongly), senior Government Ministers, including the Prime Minister, who eventually took personal charge of the response, appeared in the media encouraging the public to visit the countryside, and doing so themselves. This response is continued, with the Prime Minister spending part of his summer holidays in the UK to set an example of appropriate behaviour and support for UK tourism. Despite these subsequent responses, the overall result was a classic case of the issue–response cycle in respect of media coverage and public and private sector behaviour. Immediate and extensive negative imagery set the tone and the nature of the event, and subsequent efforts, at least in the short term, proved ineffective in counteracting this situation.

One remains to be convinced that full and accurate awareness of the scale, the role and the integrated nature of tourism, both in rural and urban Britain has really been appreciated. It is highly likely that a similar response might be adopted if FMD should flare up again. It could be argued that, if tourism survives, as it almost certainly will in most areas, then it will again be treated as not needing specific attention, as, having survived such an impact, it will be able to survive anything. The newly created ministry with responsibility for rural affairs (DEFRA) did not gain the tourism mandate as some had argued in the media, and this was almost certainly an appropriate decision. As opposing views noted, tourism in the UK, particularly international tourism, is not only or even primarily a rural activity and placing it in a rural ministry would have been inappropriate. If there is a good side or positive feature of the outbreak for tourism, it can only be that it is now much better known and more appropriately appreciated than it was, but how permanent such a shift in awareness is remains to be seen.

Level and accuracy of knowledge

One of the starkest lessons from the 2001 outbreak of FMD is how poor is the level and accuracy of knowledge of events as and when they happen. At the macro level, speculation about the scale of the impact varied from the British Hotels Association's assertion that the hotel sector would lose £5bn of business that year to reports from a London-based consultancy company suggesting that during the first month of the crisis in March hotel occupancy had actually increased (*Travel Trade Gazette*, 2001). This weakness in information will certainly have contributed to the hesitant start made by the Government in March in its recognition of the significance of FMD for tourism. The picture has been further clouded by a simple lack of understanding on the part of consumers. For example, there is anecdotal evidence that some potential tourists were anxious that as a result of FMD the food in the UK was unsafe to eat, that FMD was a form of BSE or that the countryside was simply closed. Much of the official effort to address the crisis dealt with this type of misunderstanding, but even as late as mid-June 2001, when FMD appeared to be firmly under control, with only a handful of reported cases each day and much of the countryside returned to normal, many consumers still had very negative views of the situation. For example, in a survey of English Consumers (ETC, 2001a):

- 39% agreed that "you could not enjoy going to the countryside because you would see the destruction and disposal of animals because of Foot and Mouth".
- 45% agreed that "you cannot go for walks in the countryside because most of the footpaths are closed".
- 55% agreed that "people should keep out of the countryside to avoid spreading Foot and Mouth".

For an activity that rests on image for its success and survival the proper control and communication of image is crucial for tourism. The UK experience of FMD in 2001 is that control of the image was lost. With this in mind, one of the most important lessons from these events clearly is the need for speedy and accurate information. At this level this is a task for government as well as for industry.

Conclusions and Implications

One can never be sure what the full range of implications of such an event as the one discussed here will be, particularly when the event is not concluded. Two major implications emerged soon after the outbreak ended. The first is related to the impact of the outbreak on the image of, and hence demand for, Britain as a tourist destination.

We have raised the issue of image several times in this chapter. It is clear that, while the FMD outbreak had clear major implications for and impacts on agriculture in the UK, the impacts upon tourism, particularly international tourism, are much less direct and tied very specifically to questions of media coverage and the image produced and publicised. While there were some direct impacts on tourism, many of them, such as footpath closures, impacted much more on domestic rather than international visitors to the countryside, yet the major impacts in terms of demand seem to have been on international tourism. This has to be directly related to the image of the UK that has been disseminated abroad.

The importance of image to the development and maintenance of a tourist destination is well documented (Gartner, 1993, 1997; Gunn, 1988; Hunt, 1975), even if the process of image formation and the ways in which image influences destination choice are still unresolved. Buckley and Klemm (1993: 185) note that "a favourable image is an essential requirement for any tourist destination". Similarly it is clear that destinations which suffer from negative images will find it difficult to attract tourists given the variety of choice of destinations available now. Developing a positive image and overcoming a negative one can be both time-consuming and expensive, and is never guaranteed success. Gartner (1993) has identified several components in the image-formation process, including "autonomous" agents, such as news reports, articles and documentaries about places, which, because of their autonomy or lack of bias, are generally seen as credible and thus have major impacts on image development. He argues (1997) that, because of the high credibility and market penetration of such elements, they may be the only agents capable of changing an area's image in a short period of time.

In the case of the 2001 FMD outbreak, there was extensive national and international coverage of developments in the UK for over four months, much of it in this autonomous form – for example, news coverage on television and in newspapers, press releases and discussion pieces in magazines and journals. It would be astonishing if such coverage had not had negative effects upon the image of the UK and its countryside. Whether these effects are long term or were of a short duration remains to be seen. A television news report (ITN, 2001) indicated that overseas visitation to the UK in May 2001 was 11% down from the comparable figure for 2000, an improvement over the decline of 21% in the April figure. The lack of media attention to the outbreak, the decline in the slaughter of animals and in carcass disposal, and the lack of "pathos" or human interest stories all served to remove images from the daily media. Gartner (1997) suggests that, although the autonomous change agent may be significant in the short term, it may not change an image permanently over the long term, a point made earlier by Boulding (1956), who argued that negative images had to be constant and prolonged to lead to an entirely new image of a feature or place.

Ahmed (1991) discussed ways of improving a destination's negative image, including capitalising on the positive components, organising familiarisation tours and, where possible, taking advantage of negative features. The relevant authorities undertook the first two procedures, albeit possibly belatedly in the first case. The familiarisation tour of foreign dignitaries, involving the Prime Minister, the Duke of Edinburgh and the Royal Residence at Windsor seemed successful, although it was almost immediately undermined by a suspected case of human FMD two days afterwards. The third approach is more difficult to envisage, since there would be little that people might want to see related to the outbreak. Promoting quiet footpaths or lack of crowds, while effective in destinations normally selling such attributes, would be more likely to remind people of why such areas were quiet in a destination such as England.

It is almost inevitable that the only way to counteract the effects of negative publicity is through an increase in positive publicity and promotion. This is not as easy as may be thought, as one has to ensure that promotion does not serve to remind potential visitors of the negative event (a common problem following all forms of disaster – for example, transportation accidents). Government advertisements for the domestic market tackled the problem head on, i.e. by claiming boldly that "The Countryside is Open". Such an approach appeared to be reasonably effective in the short term and tourist numbers recovered reasonably well, given the other negative factors such as the continued negative effects of September 11 and a high pound sterling relative to other countries.

The second major implication for tourism in the UK relates to both the general level of awareness of the importance of tourism and, in particular, government appreciation of the role and scale of tourism in the UK and in rural areas especially. UK governments at most levels generally have not paid much attention to tourism over the past decades, never giving it full or sole ministerial status, and appearing to hold the viewpoint that, while it was valuable, it was an area for the private sector and tourists would always come to the UK. The grasp of its role in rural areas in particular seemed very weak – the previous Ministry of Agriculture, Fisheries and Food (MAFF) was very much the government decision maker for rural areas. In this context tourism was under the Department for Culture, Media and Sport, which was seen as the more junior partner. The report of that Department (CMSC, 2001: xv) commented that "public authorities failed initially to appreciate the severity of the crisis in tourism" and went on to note that even after several weeks the Government was still "not sure of what the effect was going to be on the tourism industry" (CMSC, 2001: xv). The about-turn in policies noted earlier is further evidence of the failure to realise at the beginning just how large and how important tourism was to both the rural economy and way of life, and to the UK economy and employment generally.

There is little doubt that this lesson has been learned to some extent, although at considerable cost and probably still with some unbelievers. As a columnist for *The Times* pointed out, the fact that the Treasury was unable or unwilling to provide 20 million pounds for tourism promotion, when MAFF was spending more than that amount in killing uninfected animals each week, suggested that the lesson and appropriate priorities had still not been learned (Jenkins, 2001: 19). It is doubtful that politicians yet fully appreciate the important role of tourism in the UK rural economy, despite this having been noted in a Rural White Paper of 2000 (ETC/CA 2001). The situation is compounded by the point made earlier: that it is domestic tourism (and leisure and recreation) that makes the greatest use of the UK countryside in a direct manner, but, to international visitors, the UK countryside is a key element in the attractiveness and image of the country as a whole. A decline in overseas visitors might not be felt as directly in rural areas as in urban settings, again highlighting the variable nature of the scale and direction of the effects of the outbreak.

These arguments are supported by statements, or lack of them, in two reports from that year. One by Hoskins (2001) on *Rural Recovery after Foot-and-Mouth Disease* made almost no mention of tourism. On page 6 it was noted: "The tourist trade after the dreadful experience of the spring and early summer, [has] benefited from a recovery in business during the past three months, *except of course for those in areas where visitor numbers are still restricted*" (emphasis added). The author appeared not to realise that tourism normally increases in the summer in the UK and that many of those areas which had restrictions on visitor numbers were major tourist destinations such as the Lake District and Devon. The only recommendations which this report called for with respect to tourism were equally vacuous: "The development of the tourist industry, putting a priority on quality rather than quantity, which will need the engagement of all rural stakeholders if it is to succeed" (Hoskins, 2001: 12); and "Support for upgrading the tourism proposition" (Hoskins, 2001: 14).

The then newly appointed Secretary of State (DEFRA), Margaret Beckett, addressing the Brussels conference on Control and Prevention of Foot-and-Mouth in December 2001, said nothing about tourism. The only reference in the proceedings of that conference was a comment from a Discussion Group of Farmers and Agribusiness, which produced the amazing statement that "Activities, other than those directly related to agriculture businesses e.g. [sic] forestry and tourism, may be seriously affected during a crisis" (European Commission, 2002: 18).

Any permanent change in agricultural and hence rural activities as a result of the outbreak could have real impacts upon both the appeal and direct use of the countryside for tourism. Further declines in mixed farming and particularly the disappearance of livestock could negatively affect the appearance and accessibility of the countryside for tourism and recreation. Over time, such changes may also affect the image of the UK countryside and thus the appeal to overseas visitors also. Farming in many parts of the UK was in dire straits before FMD and its recovery rightly needs to be a high priority. If tourism is not included in the recovery plans and its current and potential importance in maintaining the economic and social viability of rural communities not appreciated, agricultural recovery and rural stability is unlikely to be achieved. Thus there is much more to the second implication than simply the belated recognition of the importance of tourism and the need to assist its recovery and well-being.

Whether lessons will really be learned from the 2001 outbreak and whether there is a desire to determine the full details and appropriateness of actions taken is unclear. As late as early January 2002, the Government had still refused to hold a full public inquiry, although it commissioned several limited ones (Elliott, 2002a). One was a "lessons learned" inquiry, but with no legal powers to call witnesses; another was a scientific inquiry by the Royal Society; and there was a policy commission on the future of food and farming (but not tourism) (Elliott, 2002b). Some indication of public and special interest concerns can be judged by the collection of 126,000 signatures for a petition calling for a full-scale public inquiry. On 19 February 2002, the High Court received a legal challenge, mounted by a number of organisations, including the BBC, to the continued Government refusal to hold such an inquiry. However, on 15 March the High Court ruled that the decision to hold or not to hold such an inquiry was the right of the Government, thus rejecting the challenge. It seems likely that the search for answers and accurate statistics is likely to take longer than the epidemic took to run, although hopefully it will not cost the taxpayer as much.

The chapter has attempted to draw out some interpretations and conclusions from an event which was not seen at the start as having particular significance for tourism by many of the parties initially involved. That perception changed very rapidly as events unfolded and developments took place. It is almost certain that some predictions proved to be unfounded and developments occurred which were not foreseen – such is the nature of tourism and forecasting. One thing that does appear certain is that the FMD outbreak of 2001 will be regarded as a tourism disaster just as much or more so than an agricultural one.

Appendix

Key statistics of foot-and-mouth

Compensation for animals slaughtered	£1,047,321,000
Compensation for seized and destroyed items	£29,187,000
Cost of cleaning and disinfecting premises	£254,588,000
Cost of disposal and transportation of carcasses	£170,770,000
Veterinary costs	£15,152,000
Direct cost to taxpayer	£2,059,000,000
Total premises with animals slaughtered	9,996
Total animals slaughtered with FMD or on contiguous properties	4,080,001
Total slaughtered under welfare regulations or movement restrictions	2,573,317
Other animals slaughtered	c.2,000,000
Total animals slaughtered	8,653,318

Source: Figures supplied by DEFRA, 2002

References

Ahmed, Z.U. (1991) The influence of components of a state's tourist image on product positioning strategy. *Tourism Management* 12 (3), 331–340.

Boulding (1956) *The Image*. Doubleday: New York.

Buckley, P.J. and Klemm, M. (1993) The decline of tourism in Northern Ireland: The causes. *Tourism Management* 14 (2), 184–194.

Butler, R.W. (1996) Sustainable tourism: The case of the Shetland Islands. In L. Briguglio, R.W. Butler, D. Harrison and W. Filho (eds) *Sustainable Tourism in Islands and Small States: Case Studies*. London: Cassell.

Butler, R.W. and Hall, C.M. (1998) Image and reimaging of rural areas. In R.W. Butler, C.M. Hall and J. Jenkins (eds) *Tourism and Recreation in Rural Areas*. Chichester: Wiley.

British Hospitality Association (2001) *Annual Report 2000*. London: BHA.

CMSC (2001) *Tourism: The Hidden Giant. Culture Media and Sport Committee, Fourth Report* (Vol. 1). London: The Stationery Office. At http://www.publications.parliament.uk/pa/cm200001/cmselect/cmcumeds/430/43002.htm. Accessed 5 July 2001.

CDC (2001) *Travelers' Health*. At http://www.cdc.gov/travel/other/fmd-europe-mar2001.htm. Accessed 5 July 2001.

Christel DeHaan Tourism and Travel Research Institute (2001) *Quantifying the Economic Impact of Foot and Mouth Disease in the UK*. Nottingham: Nottingham University Business School.

Countryside Commission (1998) *Annual Report*. Cheltenham: CC.

Department of Culture, Media and Sport (DCMS) (1999) *Tomorrow's Tourism: A Growth Industry for the New Millennium*. London: DCMS.

Department for Environment, Food and Rural Affairs (DEFRA) (2001) At http://www.maff.gov.uk/animalh/diseases/fmd/disease/methods/slaughter/compensation/asp._Accessed 5 July 2001.

Department for Environment, Food and Rural Affairs (DEFRA) (2001) At http://www.defra.gov.uk. Accessed 30 January 2002.

Department of National Heritage (DNH) (1995) *Tourism: Competing With the Best*. London: DNH.

Elliott, V. (2002a) BBC fights Blair on inquiry. *The Times*, 12 January, 8.

Elliott, V. (2002b) Blair faces questions on handling of epidemic. *The Times*, 1 January, 6.

English Tourism Council (2001a) *Foot and Mouth Disease and Tourism: Impact on Tourism*. At http://www.englishtourism.org.uk/default.asp. Accessed 5 July 2001.

English Tourism Council (2001b) *Attitudes to Foot and Mouth in the Countryside of England*. At http://www.englishtourism.org.uk/default.asp. Accessed 5 July 2001.

European Commission (2001) Final Report of the International Conference on Control and Prevention of Foot and Mouth Disease, European Commission, Brussels, 12–13 December.

Gartner, W.C. (1993) The image formation process. *Journal of Travel and Tourism Marketing* 2 (2/3), 191–216.

Gartner, W.C. (1997) Image and sustainable tourism systems. In S. Wahab and J. Pigram (eds) *Tourism Development and Growth*. New York: Routledge.

Gunn, C.A. (1988) *Vacationscape: Designing Tourist Regions*. Houston, TX: University of Texas.

Hall, C.M. (2001) Personal communication, Otago, New Zealand.

Hoskins, C. (2001) *Rural Recovery after Foot-and-Mouth Disease*. London: DEFRA.

Jenkins, S. (2001) All sense sacrificed to the golden calf. *The Times*, 25 April, 20.

Mathieson, A. and Wall, G. (1982) *Tourism Impacts: Physical, Social Economic*. Harlow: Longman.

Middleton, V.T.C. (2001) Foot and mouth disease: Carry on killing the countryside. *Tourism Journal* (Summer), 10.

Mullay, H. (1994) Personal communication, Shetland Tourism, Lerwick.

Office International Des Epizooties (2002) *List of Foot and Mouth Disease Free Countries: Resolution No. XVII*. Rome: World Organization for Animal Health.

Sharpley, R. and Craven, B. (2002) The 2001 foot and mouth crisis: Rural economy and tourism policy implications – a comment. *Current Issues in Tourism* 4 (6), 527–537.

Travel Trade Gazette (2001) 28 May, 41.

Part 4: The Shape of the Future

Part 4 Introduction
The Shape of the Future

Does tourism have a future? This question is usually answered in two different ways. In the first mode, researchers explore the issue as trend spotters. Every other year there is a new fashionable way of doing tourism and plenty of products make the rounds of the market to accommodate the new peremptory need. Both the industry and the tourists seem in need of anticipating what will be fashionable and at the same time affordable. Researchers oblige in due course. The second mode looks at the fundamentals and, though it may be gloomier, it is definitely necessary. In spite of the optimistic and expansive scenarios favoured by WTO and WTTC for the foreseeable future, can there be some unanticipated threats that demand a less sanguine approach to international tourism development? After September 11 and the bomb attacks on tourists in Bali, Indonesia, and Mombasa, Kenya, it seems that global terrorism has become a genuine hazard for tourism as we know it. It may be too early to account for the complete impacts of this unexpected guest, but there are reasons to believe that he will resist leaving the party without turning it into a slugfest.

The chapters presented by Geoffrey Crouch and Myriam Jansen-Verbeke (Chapters 11 and 12) clearly belong in the trend-spotting category. Crouch's dwells on space tourism and its foreseeable future. On 28 April 2001 Dennis Tito became the world's first space tourist. Did this event mark a watershed in the development of a new tourist product? It may be too early to tell, but undoubtedly exploring space in leisure is a dream shared by many people. Space tourism already encompasses a sizeable amount of activities and attractions, from land-based or terrestrial space tourism to high-altitude and sub-orbital space tourism to the real thing – orbital space tourism itself. However, for the time being, the latter still looks like another exclusive club reserved for the well-heeled. This may change within a few years, though, reaching the stage where space tourism may become affordable for a sizeable market, which leads to the following issue – is there such a market? The different studies quoted by Crouch respond in the affirmative, reckoning with a total global demand that might vary between 170 passengers per year, if the price tag were US$1 million per tour, to 20 million passengers per year if it went down to US$1000. The rest of the chapter deals with the technological, legal and health issues that will have to shape consumer behaviour if this still visionary form of tourism is to actually take off.

Heritage tourism and the enjoyment of cultural attractions are quickly becoming a significant part of the global tourism market. In order to attract the attention of the operators and to become part of the tourist's evoked set, many destinations the world over are making big invest- ments to host and organize cultural events. Jansen-Verbeke suggests that, while the "event formula" is in vogue among local politicians and the media, its salutary effects for the local stakeholders cannot always be taken for granted. Accordingly, it has become urgent to develop gauges to measure the real impacts and effects of events such as the European Cultural Capital of the year. Basing her chapter on the Bruges, Belgium, experience in 2002, Jansen-Verbeke concludes that it is necessary to develop a monitoring system to track the real success of cultural events and to widely communicate its conclusions. All too often organizers of similar venues forget to take into consideration their long-term effects and learn the lessons of comparable examples.

Valene Smith (Chapter 13) tackles head-on the most puzzling issue con- fronting tourism nowadays – global terrorism. The attacks of September 11 on New York City and Washington DC bruised, among many other things, the tourist industry worldwide. Taking her cue from Barber's "Jihad vs. McWorld", Smith sees the conflict not as a clash of civilizations, but as the expression of the tensions created by the emergence of a single global civilization. When the traditional frames of reference are shattered, many people make up for their lost worlds in messianic movements or in fundamentalist terrorism. For the author, the "new war" will definitely affect tourism, although it is too early to visualize all of its eventual impacts. One of the first casualties has been the world airline industry, which was already experiencing an economic downturn before September 11, and now faces a "terrorism tax" in the form of increased airport secu- rity fees and renewed fear of flying on the part of the public. On the other hand, there will also be new forms of tourism (visiting Ground Zero or the caves of Tora Bora, Afghanistan; demand for destinations and activi- ties that enhance spirituality) and new encroachments on civil liberties. We are only just beginning to portray the future.

Chapter 11

After Tito, Where To From Here? Marketing Issues in the Development of Space Tourism

GEOFFREY I. CROUCH

Introduction

On April 28, 2001, Mr Dennis Tito became the world's first space tourist. Was this a one-off event, or the beginning of the commercialization of space for the general public that will see larger numbers of space tourists following in the vapor trail of Mr Tito?

Space tourism has been talked about for some time (Ashford, 1990), but, in the last decade or so, proponents of space tourism and space tourism entrepreneurs have escalated their efforts to make space tourism a reality in the 21st century. Mr Tito has helped space tourism overcome the so-called "giggle factor" recognized by proponents as a key impediment. Nevertheless, it is still too early to judge the path and pace of the development of space tourism.

It seems quite probable that, if another millionaire steps forward, the Russians may again be keen to accept payment for a journey into space. It is clear, however, that larger numbers of space tourists cannot be accommodated in this same fashion. The proponents of space tourism and the opening of space to the general public, including at least some in the scientific community, also argue that space tourism will benefit space science and exploration as the most likely and effective means of significantly reducing the cost of space transportation (Collins, 1999; Aldrin, 2001).

Before examining the various factors likely to shape the development of the space tourism market, this chapter briefly summarizes space tourism developments thus far. It also provides a brief overview of market research studies which have attempted to estimate the potential size and nature of the market for space tourism.

A Brief Summary of Space Tourism Developments

Although Tito was the world's first paying *orbital* space tourist, *terrestrial* space tourism has been underway for many years. In the last few years, *sub-orbital* space tourism has enabled aspiring space tourists to come even closer to achieving their dream. Numerous activities and endeavors have occurred or are currently underway to foster the development of space tourism. Some of these are summarized below. A more detailed exposition can be found in Smith (2000), but advances and developments in the field are occurring rapidly.

Terrestrial space tourism

Space-based science fiction probably began long before Jules Verne wrote *From the Earth to the Moon* in 1865. Humans have probably wondered what it would be like to travel beyond the confines of their terrestrial world for millennia. For the first time, however, the 20th century demonstrated that it was possible for humans to safely travel into space and return, and that significant numbers of ordinary people would probably do so within a lifetime of the first pioneering astronauts and cosmonauts.

But space tourism has its beginnings on Earth. Terrestrial space tourism probably began with the movement of astronomical observers to different locations in order to observe better certain astronomical phenomena such as eclipses and the movements of the planets. In the past, nautical expeditions such as those by the English seafarer, Captain James Cook, often included, among their principal aims, observation of heavenly bodies. Today, groups of professional and amateur astronomers take organized tours on cruise ships and by other means to favorable observing locations. The most recent example was the total solar eclipse on June 21, 2001, when optimal viewing in Africa was provided. Although small, the tourism industry already caters to this niche market.

When NASA began launching rockets, people flocked to Cape Canaveral to witness a launch. Twenty years and just over 100 shuttle flights after the first, tourists still turn up in huge numbers every time a space shuttle is launched. The Kennedy Space Center at Cape Canaveral hosts large numbers of visitors each year and sells limited numbers of launch tickets to the general public interested in seeing a launch up close. Titusville, Cocoa Beach, and adjoining towns experience steady numbers of visitors all year round. NASA's Johnston Space Center in Houston has also built a public facility to host significant numbers of terrestrial space tourists each year. The Russians also permit tourists to visit their Yuri Gagarin Cosmonaut Training Center at the Zhukovsky Air Base in Star City, Russia. There, limited numbers of presumably well-heeled tourists can tour the facilities and experience elements of the training program, such as underwater Zero G simulations.

The Smithsonian Air & Space Museum in Washington DC presents a large number of space exploration artifacts and experiences to the general public. The US Space and Rocket Center in Huntsville, Alabama, operates a space science museum and has been running "Space Camps" since 1982. The Space Camp concept now operates in several countries. Feasibility studies have been undertaken to assess the prospects for a ground-based "virtual" space theme park and suggest that such a project might get off the ground in the near future. One project involves sending a small vehicle to the moon equipped with a camera. This vehicle will be able to be remotely controlled from the Earth, where groups of virtual moon visitors will be able to sit on a simulation platform taking turns to control the moon vehicle while experiencing every turn, bump, and vista along the way.

Entrepreneurs have been quick to seize terrestrial space tourism market opportunities. One such company, *Space Adventures Ltd.* (www.spaceadventures.com), for example, offers or has offered the following terrestrial space tours:

- *Space Shuttle and Premier Launch Tour*: a three-day visit to witness a shuttle launch at the Kennedy Space Center hosted by an astronaut.
- *Capital Space Tour*: a four-day tour to various facilities in or near Washington DC, including the Air & Space Museum, the Space Systems Laboratory at the University of Maryland, and NASA's Goddard Space Flight Center.
- *Astronomy of the Ancients*: tours to Maya and Inca Indian sites whose cultures were guided by the patterns of stars and planets.
- *Mysteries of the Universe Tour*: includes the Keck observatory in Hawaii, the Meteor Crater in Arizona, the SETI (Search for Extraterrestrial Intelligence) exploration at the Very Large Array National Radio Astronomy Observatory in New Mexico, and the Arecibo Observatory in Puerto Rico.

- *Solar Eclipse Black Sea Cruise*: a recent 11-day tour combining visits to ancient sites, Istanbul, and a cruise to the path of a total solar eclipse.
- *Russian Space Tour*: a nine-day tour including visits to the Yuri Gagarin Cosmonaut Training Center and Mission Control Center near Moscow, and the Baikonur Cosmodrome, Russia's primary space port.
- *Skywatcher's Inn*: a high-altitude, dark-sky location in Arizona ideal for night-sky observing.
- *Mars Robotics Seminar*: a weekend, hands-on course involving participants in the design of the Mars Sample Return Rover.
- *Model Rocketry Weekend*: a course on the basic principles of rocket science and model rocketry.
- *Neutral Buoyancy Training*: a simulated underwater experience with former astronauts.

Terrestrial space tourism is likely to continue to grow in these directions, satisfying at least some of the dreams of the many people fascinated by space.

High-altitude and sub-orbital space tourism

In terms of taking people off the ground to enjoy some of the experiences previously only available to astronauts and test pilots, the Russians presently lead developments in this area. For example, it is currently possible to experience weightlessness aboard the cosmonaut training aircraft, an Ilyushin-76, designed to fly along a parabolic arch so that occupants experience "zero G" (http://www.spaceadventure.com/zerog/index.html). An American company is converting a Boeing 727 to offer similar flights in the US. The Russians also offer flights on board several MiG fighter jets, including the MiG-25 "Foxbat", which can ascend to an altitude of 80,000 feet traveling at more than twice the speed of sound. At that altitude, pilot and passenger are above 99% of the Earth's atmosphere, the sky above appears black, and the curvature of the Earth is clearly visible.

Several private ventures are also developing craft capable of conveying tourists into sub-orbit similar to the flight that sent the first American, Alan Shepard, into space. Such sub-orbital flights will travel briefly to an altitude of about 100 kilometers (62 miles). The US awards astronaut status to those who fly above 50 miles. Examples include the *Eclipse Astroliner* of Kelly Space & Technology; the *Roton* of the Rotary Rocket

Company, which has already undergone some test flights; the *Proteus* of Scaled Composites, Inc., founded by Burt Rutan, who flew the *Voyager* aircraft around the world non-stop some years ago; the *Pathfinder* of Pioneer Rocketplane Corporation; and the *Ascender* of Bristol Spaceplanes, Limited.

To stimulate ventures of this nature, the US$10 million X-Prize was established in 1996. The prize will be won by the first private team to launch a spaceship capable of carrying at least three adults to an altitude of at least 100 kilometers on a repeatable basis. The X-Prize was established by the St Louis business community to commemorate the achievement of Charles Lindbergh, who won the Orteig International Prize when he was the first person to fly non-stop from New York to Paris in 1927. Currently 22 teams have registered and are vying for this prize.

Orbital space tourism

Tito's week in space in April 2001 as a guest of the Russians on board the International Space Station (ISS) made headlines around the world. At a purported price of US$20 million, Mr Tito made news as much for the controversy and embarrassment he created for NASA, who were reluctant to allow Tito to spend time on board the ISS, as the fact that he became the first orbital space tourist.

News reports (David, 2001) suggest that the Russians may have additional individuals also willing to pay a high price to travel into space, including the movie producer and director, James Cameron. While the Russians may well seek to derive further revenue for their ailing space program in this fashion, the dispute with NASA over whether to permit space tourists to visit the ISS suggests that orbital space tourism is unlikely to prosper to the extent that it relies on the use of the ISS, which was designed as a scientific platform rather than a public accommodation facility.

However, one module of the ISS is potentially capable of accommodating space tourists on a commercial basis. The company, Spacehab, is completing a commercially developed and operated module, *Enterprise*, that is to become part of the Russian side of the ISS in 2003. Spacehab will provide customers with a service package that includes everything a user needs to conduct business in space, including:

- commercial access to the shuttle and station;
- planning and approvals needed to operate in space;

- assistance in locating needed equipment and coordinating payloads with other users;
- transportation of private payloads to and from orbit;
- the power, data management, environment, and human assistance to operate payloads; and
- delivery of data and return of payloads to their owner.

Spacehab reports (http://www.spacehab.com/welcome/welcome_index.htm) its customers as including educators and students, and "space enthusiasts worldwide".

The main interest in orbital space tourism, however, centers on taking larger numbers of tourists into space in order to generate sufficient economies of scale and learning effects, such that the cost per passenger will drop dramatically and as quickly as possible (Commercial Space Transportation Study Alliance, 1994). There are many varied ideas for achieving this, ranging from fanciful "spacecruiseship" concepts to floating hotels constructed from used shuttle external fuel tanks, "cyclers" that swing back and forth between the Earth and either the Moon or Mars, fueled by gravity alone, and passenger spacecraft designed to piggy-back existing rocket launch technology. An example of this latter approach is the concept of Starcraft Boosters, Inc. (Aldrin, 2001).

Orbital space tourism in larger numbers now appears potentially just a few years away. A joint NASA/Space Transportation Association (STA) study (O'Neil *et al.*, 1998: 3) "concluded that private, high priced 'adventure' trips to space with greater than today's commercial airline risk could become possible in the next few years. Much larger scale, lower priced, orbital operations, could commence in the decade thereafter." The Tito flight has proved the first part of this prediction accurate. The same report also observed:

> we now see the opportunity of opening up space to the general public – a "sea change" in our half-century sense that people in space would continue to be very few in number, would be limited to highly trained professionals who, at personal physical risk, would conduct mostly taxpayer supported scientific and technical activities there under government purview. (O'Neil *et al.*, 1998: 21)

The Space Tourism Market

Surveys of the space tourism market were reviewed by Crouch (2001). The NASA/STA study (O'Neil *et al.*, 1998), which surveyed a sample of 1500 US families in 1996, found that 34% of respondents "would be interested in taking a two-week vacation in the Space Shuttle in the future", and 42% were interested in the concept of space travel aboard a space cruise vessel offering accommodations and entertainment programs similar to an ocean-going cruise ship. To the question "what would you be willing to pay per person for such an experience?", 7.5% indicated US$100,000 or more.

The Commercial Space Transportation Study (1994) employed a "bottoms-up" method to estimate the market based primarily on income, wealth, age, and ticket price. The approach produced three demand curves based on low, medium, and high probabilities of occurrence. The estimated demand curves suggest worldwide annual passenger demand of the orders summarized in Table 11.1.

Studies in Japan (Collins *et al.*, 1994a, 1994b, 1995) on 3030 people found that 45% of those over 60 years of age, and nearly 80% of those under 60, would like to go into space. In addition, the most popular activities were found to be to "look at Earth" and "space walk", followed by "astronomical observation", "zero G sport", "zero G experiments", and "other". About 20% indicated a preparedness to spend a year's pay or more on space tourism, and most interest was in travel of several days' duration.

Collins *et al.* (1996) undertook an additional telephone survey in Japan. Seven of 500 respondents indicated that they would be prepared to pay between 5,010,000 yen and 10,000,000 yen (approximately US$40,000 to US$80,000) for a two-day stay in orbit. Although only 1.4% of respondents, this equates to 1.7 million potential Japanese customers.

A similar survey in the US and Canada (Collins *et al.*, 1995) found that 61% of the population were interested in space tourism, a little over 10% stated they were prepared to pay a year's salary or more for the privilege, and most were interested in stays of several days or longer requiring some form of orbital accommodation.

Abitzsch (1996) also estimated space tourism demand by Germans. Some 43% of Germans expressed an interest in participating in space

Table 11.1 Worldwide annual passenger demand for space tourism

Ticket price	Probability		
(US$)	Low	Medium	High
10,000	3,000,000	150,000	6,000
100,000	20,000	1,000	60
1,000,000	200	70	20

tourism, a lower proportion than the Japanese (70%) and Americans/Canadians (61%). Abitzsch produced a "global market" demand curve by consolidating the results from the various studies and arrived at the estimates in Table 11.2. These figures are significantly more optimistic than those in Table 11.1.

Barrett (1999) also replicated the Collins *et al.* (1995) survey in the United Kingdom on a much smaller sample of 72. Some 35% of respondents indicated an interest in taking a trip into space if it became a reality, and 12% expressed a preparedness to pay one year's salary on such a tour.

A spacecruiseship survey in 1999 of 2002 Americans sought to assess interest in, and demand for, a six-day journey from the Earth to the Moon and back on a luxurious spacecruiseship for the Bigelow Companies (Roper Starch Worldwide, 1999). To the question, "If you had the money, how interested would you be in taking this adventure?", 35% answered "interested" or "very interested". An astonishing 38% indicated a year's salary or more when asked, "If you could save up, how many years' income equivalent would you pay for such an experience?"

A recent assessment of market demand by Kelly Space & Technology, Inc. (undated) was based on market research by Harris Interactive polling services of 2022 respondents. Their estimate suggests an expectation of private citizen demand for space travel growing to about 7000 and 1800 passengers per year by 2030 for sub-orbital and orbital travel respectively. As the methodological basis for this study is not reported, no assessment of its reliability and validity is possible.

Space tourism development proponents acutely recognize the need for additional market research:

> Carrying out more detailed market research is highly desirable in order to understand the requirements and potential of this market better. (Collins & Isozaki, 1997)

Table 11.2 Global market demand

Price per ticket (1994 $)	Passengers per year
1,000	20 million
10,000	5 million
100,000	400,000
250,000	1,000
500,000	170

[T]here have been no rigorous scientific surveys . . . that can be "taken to the bank" by a space tourism company. . . . This is ironic and, to proponents of space development and particularly space tourism, frustrating, because such surveys would cost a pittance (<<1%), compared to current government programs, such as NASA's X-33, that are ostensibly aimed at reducing the cost of access to space. In addition, their value in promoting confidence in the market to poten-tial space tourism investors would be vast, in comparison to the technology studies toward which the majority of U.S. government funds are currently being deployed. (Simberg, 2000: 3)

These market research estimates cannot be considered reliable esti-mates of likely actual demand for space tourism, but may be indicative of the level of public interest in the prospects for space travel by the general public. More rigorous methodologies, such as discrete choice modeling, are required if demand is to be estimated with greater reliability and validity.

Market Development Issues

How, and in what direction, is the space tourism market likely to develop over the next several years and beyond? Any attempt to make predictions is fraught with a wide variety of uncertainties in light of the present embryonic stage of space tourism development, technolog-ical constraints and uncertainties, and limited public exposure to the possibilities. Nevertheless, it may be possible to identify the factors most likely to shape the development of this industry and thereby to gain a sense of the more likely directions. In doing so, some effort will be made to recognize technological factors, although the main focus of this chapter deals primarily with market development issues.

Technological considerations

The technology for transporting and hosting visitors in space already exists. However, it is currently very expensive and is not, at this stage, designed to serve the needs and interests of tourists. The present technology is also funded and controlled largely by governments which display varying interests in encouraging the development of space tourism. While the Russians have been first to exploit orbital space tourism and appear keen to continue to pursue supplementary funding for their space program, it would appear unlikely that they will be in a position to significantly develop the technology for sending tourists in larger numbers into space unless investors are prepared to fund a Russian space tourism program. This would seem to be unlikely as long as commercial western efforts to develop space tourism appear to be a safer avenue for investment.

Competition for the X-Prize may result in technological developments capable of taking tourists into space for short durations for sub-orbital or low-Earth-orbit flights. Teams competing for the X-Prize must be fully privately funded and there is no evidence at present to suggest that any of these teams have particularly deep pockets given the costs involved. It is likely that the majority of these teams will simply run out of money or their designs turn out to be inferior.

It is hard to imagine how space tourism could grow and flourish without the technological involvement of NASA. The participation of NASA would imply a level of safety and competence that would provide some encouragement to financial markets and investors, yet NASA presently displays conflicting attitudes towards space tourism. On the one hand, NASA has participated in studies of space tourism, recognizing the potential enormous advantages and economies to be derived from the development of space tourism that could also benefit future space science and exploration. On the other hand, NASA has also displayed some hostility towards this commercial activity (Riley, 2001), as though it were somehow less acceptable or appropriate than other commercial applications in space.

Technologically, the ideal would appear to be a partnership between NASA and private interests to develop transportation systems that will facilitate the development of space tourism while also serving other space transportation needs for space science, exploration, military applications, and other commercial opportunities.

Legal and regulatory considerations

Taking members of the general public into space raises many legal and regulatory issues. The question is a complex one because it is presently quite unclear how commercial space travel would be controlled, and laws tend to lag behind innovations (Wollersheim, 1999). Would the US Federal Aviation Administration have jurisdiction over space tourism, or would a new regulatory agency need to be established? How would/ could space tourism be regulated internationally? Would initial development flights be subject to any regulation? To what extent would regulation impede the development of space tourism?

The legal environment in the US might make it very difficult for US space tourism entrepreneurs to commence operations. For this reason, the legal environment in Russia might be more attractive to those wishing to develop space tourism services under less restrictive circumstances. "If passengers are to take space trips with current systems, novel approaches will have to be taken to allow them to legally do so" (Simberg, 2000: 8).

Medical considerations

Pressurized environments and gas compositions; acceleration forces on the body; pitching, rolling, and vibration; weightlessness; and radiation are the main medical considerations for space tourism (Mitarai, 1993). The space tourism industry will also need to contend with medical emergencies and rescue contingencies. Nausea and illness are common among astronauts as they adjust to a weightless environment, despite rigorous training methods. Such medical challenges will be more acute among space tourists and, while some people may be deterred from participating in space tourism for these reasons, many tourists may feel that these effects are a small price to pay for the experience.

Despite these medical considerations, the available evidence suggests that many older space tourists will be able to cope with space travel (Apel, 1999). Indeed, although surveys suggest a higher interest among the young to travel into space, the propensity to actually travel into space among older tourists may be higher as a result of accumulated wealth, a greater sense of mortality, and fewer years left in which to undertake such an experience.

Consumer behavior considerations

While price sensitivity and demand elasticity have attracted the principal interest in market research to date, other consumer behavior issues will also play a significant role in the direction and development of the space tourism market. The public perception of risk and safety can be expected to play a major role. The Challenger disaster in 1986 set back NASA's shuttle program considerably. Any similar incident in the development of space tourism is likely to have major ramifications that could cost commercial interests dearly, relying as they do on a revenue stream to remain in business.

Real and perceived living conditions aboard any spacecraft will also affect the degree of interest in space travel at the margin. Popular images of space tourists traveling in luxury and comfort aboard floating hotels and spacecruiseships are unlikely to be realized for some time. Although this may matter little to intrepid space tourists, it can be expected to influence the behavior of those who are less willing to put up with some hardship in getting to, and living in, space.

Space tourism operators will need to give careful consideration, in the design of their services, to important factors such as toilets, crews and employee hosts, and customer compatibility. Although most attention will be focussed on the design of the space travel experience itself, space tourism operators would be wise also to give careful consideration to the design of the pre- and post-travel stages that can play a major role in the overall perceived value of the experience.

Competitive dynamics

The market demand for space tourism will be significantly shaped by the competitive services and behavior of alternative space tourism operators. Studies have indicated that the cost of space tourism operations could potentially decrease dramatically in early years as operators benefit from economies of scale and "learning effects" (Collins & Ashford, 1988). Hence, there will be an advantage to those operators who can attract the greatest market share and therefore benefit most from declining costs. This, of course, is dependent on there being enough competition, or at least the threat of competition, that will drive operators to focus on cost reduction. In the absence of the threat of competition, strategies may focus instead on profit maximization in order to satisfy investors. Under this scenario, the space tourism market is likely to develop much more slowly.

Conclusion

Space tourism is poised to dramatically impact the travel and tourism industry this century. Many varied factors, however, are likely to shape the speed and direction taken as the space tourism market develops. While it is difficult at this early stage to forecast the most likely scenarios, some developments appear more likely than others, as follows:

- NASA's current ambivalence appears likely to continue for a while yet, impeding the US' ability to respond to this market.
- Russia appears unlikely to limit its interests in space tourism to Tito. Providing other wealthy customers step forward, it is likely

that the Russians, as an important participant, will transport others into space in the International Space Station, despite US objections.

- Investors are unlikely to fund space tourism enterprises until adequate market research studies are undertaken.
- Even with strong positive overall market research results, investors must pick the strategy and technology most likely to succeed, as there are sure to be a number of losers despite market success.
- Space transportation systems that can serve a range of uses in space, including space tourism but also satellite placements in orbit, space science and exploration missions, military applications, and other commercial uses, are more likely to be the eventual winners.
- Despite some reluctance by NASA and the European Space Agency, the eventual involvement of national space agencies seems inevitable.

Many challenges lie ahead for the development of a safe, viable, commercial space tourism industry. These include, among others, technical, regulatory and legal, economic and financial, medical, marketing and commercial, and environmental and sustainability issues. Although these challenges will be significant, it would appear that commercial forces and mankind's lust for space travel will eventually meet these challenges.

References

Abitzsch, Sven (1996) Prospects of space tourism. Paper presented at the 9th European Aerospace Congress: Visions and Limits of Long-term Aerospace Developments, Berlin, May 15.

Aldrin, Buzz (2001) Space tourism and the evolution of rocket science: A symbiotic partnership in the making. *Supplementary proceedings of the 32nd Annual Conference of the Travel and Tourism Research Association* (Fort Myers, Florida, June 10–13).

Apel, Uwe (1999) Human factors and health in space tourism. Paper presented at the 2nd International Symposium on Space Tourism, Bremen, April 21–23.

Ashford, D.M. (1990) Prospects for space tourism. *Tourism Management* 11 (2), 99–104.

Barrett, Olly (1999) An evaluation of the potential demand for space tourism within the United Kingdom. Unpublished paper. At http://www.spacefuture.com.

Collins, Patrick (1999) Space activities, space tourism and economic growth. Paper presented at the 2nd International Symposium on Space Tourism, Bremen, April 21–23.

Collins, Patrick and Ashford, D.M. (1988) Potential economic implications of the development of space tourism. *Ad Astronautica* 17 (4), 421–431.

Collins, Patrick and Isozaki, Kohki (1997) The JRS Space Tourism Study Program Phase 2. In *Proceedings of the 7th ISCOPS* (Nagasaki, Japan, July).

Collins, Patrick, Iwasaki, Yoichi, Kanayama, Hideki, and Okazaki, Misuzu (1994a) Potential demand for passenger travel to orbit: Engineering construction and operations in space IV. In *Proceedings of Space '94, American Society of Civil Engineers* 1, 578–586.

Collins, Patrick, Iwasaki, Yoichi, Kanayama, Hideki, and Ohnuki, Misuzu (1994b) Commercial implications of market research on space tourism. *Journal of Space Technology and Science* 10 (2), 3–11.

Collins, Patrick, Stockmans, Richard, and Maita, M. (1995) Demand for space tourism in America and Japan, and its implications for future space activities. Paper presented at the 6th International Space Conference of Pacific-Basin Societies, Marina del Rey, California. *Advances in the Astronautical Sciences* 91, 601–610.

Collins, Patrick, Maita, M., Stockmans, R., and Kobayahi, S. (1996) Recent efforts towards the new space era. Paper presented at the 7th American Institute of Aeronautics and Astronautics International Spaceplanes and Hypersonics Systems and Technology Conference, Norfolk, Virginia, November 18–22 (AIAA paper no. 96–4581).

Commercial Space Transportation Study Alliance (1994) *Commercial Space Transportation Study.* Place: CSTSA.

Crouch, Geoffrey I. (2001) Researching the space tourism market. In *Proceedings of the 32nd Annual Conference of the Travel and Tourism Research Association* (Fort Myers, Florida, June 10–13), 411–420.

David, Leonard (2001) *Beyond Tito: Space Travelers Wanted.* At http://www.space. com/businesstechnology/technology/tito_next_step_010501-1.html.

Kelly Space & Technology, Inc. (undated) *Space Transportation Market Demand, 2010–2030* (NRA8–27 final report). At http://www.kellyspace.com.

Mitarai, Genyo (1993) Space tourism and space medicine. *Journal of Space Technology and Science* 9 (1), 13–15.

O'Neil, Daniel, Bekey, Ivan, Mankins, John, Rogers, Thomas F., and Stallmer, Eric W. (1998) *General Public Space Travel and Tourism: Volume 1 Executive Summary.* Washington, DC: National Aeronautics and Space Administration and the Space Transportation Association.

Riley, Mark (2001) US foils space cowboy's $40m mission. *The Age* (Melbourne), 22 March, 10.

Roper Starch Worldwide (1999) Spacecruiseship study. Unpublished.

Simberg, Rand (2000) Near-term prospects for space tourism. Unpublished report prepared for The Sophron Foundation by Interglobal Space Lines, Inc.

Smith, Valene (2000) Space tourism: The 21st Century "Frontier". *Tourism Recreation Research* 25 (3), 5–15.

Verne, Jules (1865) *From the Earth to the Moon and a Trip Round It.* Stroud: Alan Sutton, 1995.

Wollersheim, Michael (1999) Considerations towards the legal framework of space tourism. In *Proceedings of the 2nd International Symposium on Space Tourism* (Bremen, Germany, April 21–23).

Chapter 12

Mutagenecity of Cultural Events in Urban Tourist Destinations

MYRIAM JANSEN-VERBEKE

Introduction

In the context of global competition, cities all over the world are now developing cultural resources into tourist attractions and promoting the unique, authentic and genuine "cultural experience". In order to capture the attention of tour operators in the market of city trips and to penetrate into the tourists' mental map, many urban tourist destinations are now investing heavily in cultural events and in the diversification of their cultural agenda (blockbuster exhibitions, themed activities, festivals and shows).

Apparently, the "event formula" is appreciated as a marketing strategy for tourist destinations and increasingly as an incentive to get local stakeholders involved with tourism. However, the actual balance of costs and benefits of events for the local community are rarely demonstrated with hard empirical data. The long-term impact of an event on the image of a tourist destination and on a local economy remains an area of speculation, so it is appropriate to question the mutagenecity of events. There definitely is a need to understand the capacity of events to induce sustainable changes in order to monitor the effects on the local economy and community. The challenge is to develop a monitoring system as a management tool. This has inspired many researchers, but so far most explorative studies have failed to transcend the conceptual exercises. Comparative case studies and more empirically underpinned analyses of the process of change are needed to support future management of cultural tourist destinations. This chapter reflects on the parameters of changes that are induced by events in the urban system.

257

Cultural Tourism and Urban Mutagenesis

The identification of the nature and the dynamics of mutations induced by tourism in the urban system represent a most challenging research topic. When looking at the city as an organic system it becomes obvious that relatively permanent changes in the hereditary material occur, involving both physical and social changes.

Mutagenesis, or the occurrence or induction of mutation, can be analyzed in a multidimensional way, in terms of mentifacts, sociofacts and artifacts, taking into account the characteristics of the site and the region. *Mutagenecity*, or the capacity to induce changes, lies in the interaction at local and regional scales, of social, cultural and physical agents (Jansen-Verbeke, 1998a). Therefore the analysis of the multidimensional process of change requires clear definitions of parameters in each of the dimensions, prior to the major exercise of applying integrated models of tourism impact assessment. Responsible planning for a tourism destination starts with an understanding of the complexity of the tourist system and the changes in demand. The multiple purpose trips of visitors to urban destinations tend to emphasize the demand for a multifunctional supply of facilities. Looking at tourism as an integrated function of the urban system may reduce the risks of imbalance between tourism, culture and other social functions.

This search for identifying and measuring changes in the urban system was carried out in several historical cities in Flanders, all of which are ambitious to become competitive destinations for cultural tourists (Jansen-Verbeke, 1998b). The analytical model for tourism mutations includes parameters referring to the physical environment (the hardware), the social and economic environment (the software) and the organizational context (the orgware).

Hardware

The physical structure of historic cities has a certain degree of inertia. Changes in the urban landscape take time and above all imply major investments, hereafter referred to as the *hardware* of the tourist product. Mutations induced by tourism can easily be traced in the urban morphology – in fact the urban landscape is a mirror of the dynamics in land-use patterns. Clearly tourism is an important, albeit not an exclusive, agent in this restructuring of historic cities (Ashworth & Tunbridge, 2002). For instance, the tourismification of the built heritage initiates the development of new patterns of space use. When the location of these magnets in the urban setting turns out to be favorable, they will function as the nucleus of new tourism clusters (Jansen-Verbeke & Lievois, 1999; Porter, 2000) A coherent tourist opportunity spectrum in a concentration area indeed has a high marker value for tourists. However, in some cities new building projects have erased the historical pattern and landmarks and links between heritage sites have been disrupted.

In order to integrate single artifacts or points of attraction into the tourist magnetic field, the concept of corridors has been introduced into urban planning. Clusters and corridors are structuring the tourist's space use. This concentration process of tourist activities in specific areas and along connecting corridors can be studied over time. The results of spatial analyses can be mapped, an exercise which allows the location and identification of the physical impact of tourism. Several software packages for spatial analysis can be applied to simulate these spatial dynamics. The number and location of tourist attractions, such as hotels, restaurants, pubs and souvenir shops, are useful parameters to delineate the expansion of tourist clusters. However, tourism impact studies rarely focus on the mutations in the hardware of cities, although these tend to be irreversible (Ashworth & Tunbridge, 2002; Jansen-Verbeke, 1997).

Software

Whereas tourism impact on the hardware may take years before the urban landscape is branded as a tourist destination, the software is much more flexible, responding in an alert and opportunistic way to market trends. The hybrid infiltration of tourism in the local economy and in social and cultural domains of community life depends on the success of a tourist destination (Faulkner & Tideswell, 1997; Wall, 1997).

A range of new economic activities demonstrates economic changes and development of an "economy of hospitality". As a consequence, the attitude and interests of the stakeholders in local tourism are affected. Some of these mutations can be deducted from the expansion in the hospitality sector, but also from the volume and nature of tourist flows and tourists' behavior and expenditure patterns. Longitudinal visitor surveys include parameters which allow the tracing of the evolution of visitor numbers, their motives and expenditures, and above all the re-imaging of the tourist destination. Also, email surveys among internetvisitors to the websites of tourist destinations open new perspectives to study changing images.

The social and cultural impacts of tourism are often referred to as a highly critical issue in the perspective of sustainable tourism. Parameters of social changes are the degree of community involvement and the attitude of locals. These can be studied by longitudinal opinion polls with residents and other users of the urban environment. The results of these allow the measurement of the social carrying capacity and can decode, in an early stage, any signal of irritation in the host–guest relationship (Lindberg & Johnson, 1997). The issue of tourist–resident interaction is a key issue in the study of tourism impact (Pearce, 1998; Bryon, 2002). So far, research on the parameters of social and cultural change in the urban context is mostly characterized as pragmatic case studies and rarely moves to the level of theory building. In addition there is a tendency to emphasize the antagonism between host and guests, although this interaction evolves over time when the mutations induced by tourism become an organic part of the urban system (Jurowki *et al.*, 1997).

Orgware

As tourism becomes an aspect of daily life in many cultural destinations, it can be assumed that the organizational capacities of the local community and the urban decision makers are progressing to a professional management structure. In practice the organization of tourism requires an integrated approach, since several sectors and agents are involved in planning for hospitality, culture and spatial management (land use, building and conservation, traffic). This implies a move from the traditional sectoral planning and policy system toward an integrated urban governance model. For many local governments this is a critical stepping stone (Russo, 2002). In order to understand and eventually advise on this learning process in site management, the "orgware" can be analyzed.

A forum of decision makers and stakeholders, both public and private, needs to discuss at regular intervals the impact of tourism on the local community and in particular the common interests and possible discrepancy between objectives and realizations. In an ideal situation this forum should include representatives of the different public sectors directly and indirectly involved in tourism, such as culture, conservation, planning and traffic (UNESCO Venice Office, 1999).

Eventually this form of urban governance guarantees a greater commitment of local agents. Several experiments with focus groups, with Delphi panels and with task forces, for an integrated quality management of the tourist destination, have been reported (WTO, 1993). The development of a management support system, using longitudinal databases, can be the first step in monitoring this urban mutagenesis. This increased attention to the orgware of tourism is a response to the process of scale enlargement – of growing competition between urban destinations – and is supported by the awareness that, if you cannot measure the evolution of tourism, you cannot manage it.

Mutagenecity of Cultural Events

The capacity of cultural events to induce mutations or to accelerate the process of tourismification is a challenging and interesting research issue. The temporary nature of events and "trial and error" characteristics are typical for the take-off stage of a new form of urban tourism. In fact the phenomenon of *panem et circenses* is as old as the city itself – the only new element is the way in which cultural events and community festivities are now managed and marketed as tourist products.

In a changing social and economic environment, the need to redefine "critical success factors" of events becomes evident. Success is usually measured in terms of additional visitor nights and expenditures, data that offer an easy and good selling argument to potential sponsors and fit well into the ambition of local politicians and tourism marketers to gain media coverage. Nowadays, the outlining of long-term objectives for events has become a critical success factor, including the implementation of effective management tools. Sustainable tourism management requires an assessment, in an objective and relevant way, of the actual added value of a cultural event. As a rule, this type of information is also requested to legitimize the public investment in events. In fact this recent awareness amongst decision makers opens the way for the development of an efficient management instrument. Local authorities and decision makers need to anticipate wanted and unwanted effects in order to manage and control impacts. Defining the parameters to measure the impacts of an event is a major challenge for policy researchers.

Multidimensional impact studies

Scanning the effect of temporary cultural injections in the tourism system is rarely performed in a comprehensive way. In many cases events are seen as therapeutic injections meant to revitalize and diversify urban tourism. Scanning, however, offers a framework for anchoring cultural events in a sustainable way into the urban system.

Clearly, future policies concerning events need to be based on an effective Tourism Information System (TIS) and on transparent communication of information to all stakeholders. The advantages of an efficient management tool cannot be denied, particularly when changes in community attitudes are taken into account. A critical evaluation of the local resources and community involvement is a first step in this procedure. For the organizers, planners, sponsors and marketers, this implies collaborative support to collect data in a multidimensional and longitudinal way, in order to measure the impact of the event. The dimensions in cultural tourism as indicated above prove to offer a useful reference framework to assess the impact of events.

Innovation and renovation of the hardware

The ambition of many event organizers is to develop new infrastructure or to revitalize that which already exists. Building projects for new theaters, conference centers, visitor centers, hotels and museums are often launched in the context of an event policy and intended to become landmarks for the tourist destination. In a way, this current practice can be appreciated as a long-term investment in the local Tourist Opportunity Spectrum. Particularly in historic cities, the organization of events holds incentives for the conservation of built heritage and the introduction of new uses for old forms.

If successful, these new magnets will gradually change tourist patterns in the city. Studying the actual use of space by event visitors and comparing this with the results of systematic and longitudinal analyses (using GIS) of urban space use in general, leads to a better understanding of the functional dynamics in a tourist destination. In addition, the space use data eventually can be a most effective tool for the development of visitor management, for traffic policies and for strategic land use planning.

Balance of economic costs and benefits

As a rule the economic dimension of the impact of an event catches the full attention of organizers, sponsors and local authorities. The success of an event tends to be expressed in terms of "return on investment". Direct economic benefits can be deducted from specific parameters which are measured in the occasion of an event, such as the number of tourist nights, the amount of tourist expenditures, the turnover in the local business and revenues from public facilities.

Indirect economic benefits can be estimated by the number of (temporary) employed, and by observing trends in sponsorship, prices and, not least, the share in the market of city trips. Long-term economic benefits, such as the image of the destination, the revaluation of historical buildings and the prospects for event businesses, can only be demonstrated some time after and, as a rule, are rarely taken into account.

Data on the cost of an event are less transparent. Full information of all the costs involved for the local community is seldom discussed publicly. Tracing the actual input to the local economy requires hard data, which in many places is a serious problem because of their non-availablity. However, with the current boom in the provision of events and the great success of some events and the failure of others, the question of return on investment has often become an important local political issue.

Catalyst for a cultural revival

To what extent are cultural events catalysts for a cultural revival? Cultural events are supposed to enhance the quality of cultural activities, the level of expertise in cultural economy, and the quality of cultural experiences by both visitors and residents, and to result in raising the image of a "cultural tourist destination".

Apart from the degree of participation and measurable changes in the image of a place, it is difficult to find relevant indicators. Parameters to measure cultural dynamism could include participation scores in cultural activities, increase or decrease in the diversification of cultural activities, opportunities for new initiatives by artists and small and medium-sized enterprises and, not least, political support for multicultural and community based activities.

In fact, signals of a cultural élan can be found in the number of initiatives in the public and private cultural sector, in the diversification of the cultural agenda (supply side) and, of course, in the participation of locals and visitors (demand side).

In order to evaluate if this cultural drive has a sustainable effect in terms of events on the local community, much more empirical evidence needs to be presented (Jansen-Verbeke, 2003). There are examples where local traditions and heritage resources are indeed rediscovered as the basis for the creation of (new) tourist products, but there are also multiple examples where the organization of events has eroded authentic cultural traditional values (Getz, 1998; Montanari, 2002). The debate on potential drawbacks of cultural innovation and commodification has only started recently.

Carrying capacity of the local community

So far, the issue of social benefits and costs of community involvement or irritation has not yet been placed on the checklist of many event organizers. However, the attitude and involvement of the local stakeholders toward cultural events are crucial factors in the long-term cost-benefit balance. The implications of events on the local community form a valid research question.

As well, the affinity of the local community with the theme of the "cultural event" is a critical point; traditional or grass-root themes can be easier in generating local support, whereas more specialized or imported themes may face a lack of local interest and support.

Cultural events, in order to generate a genuine interest within the local community, need to create opportunities for the local trades, crafts, gastronomy, shopkeepers, local pubs and restaurants. Some cultural themes are more inspiring to commercialize than others.

Social carrying capacity is also directly related to the perceived impact of an event on the quality of the residential environment. In the excitement of establishing the program for a cultural event, this issue seldom appears on the shortlist of event organizers. Nevertheless, it is crucial to the discussion on sustainable development of a tourist destination.

Taking into account the multiple linkages of events with many aspects of urban life and business, there is a need to define the inner and outer circle of actors involved. The inner circle includes actors directly engaged in the organization, the exploitation and the marketing of an event, in fact all the agents who play a role in the initiative (decision makers) and stakeholders. The outer circle includes all users of the city who are, in one way or another, affected by the additional tourist and cultural activity, including residents, commuters, shopkeepers and shoppers, visitors, students and public officers.

In order to measure the attitude of both groups, there is the option of a large-scale survey or a focused interview with opinion leaders. Measuring the attitudes of the local residents to an event, the degree of involvement in it and its acceptance and perceived benefits is clearly a major research challenge.

The need for an event monitoring system

To develop an effective monitoring system implies collecting data that allow longitudinal analyses, to register – in time and place – visits and visitor numbers (different places, different times), in order to follow the trends in tourist behavior. In order to serve as an efficient management tool, the monitoring system needs to include parameters for the different dimensions of change. Above all, the method for measuring needs to be realistically applicable in terms of cost and time investment, and must allow for the establishment of a longitudinal and comparative database.

The role of policy-supporting research is to develop such a system, based on an understanding of the urban system (selecting relevant parameters of change) and of the interactivity in the distinct processes of change. With reference to the efficiency of the management tool, some relevant questions were raised by WTO (1993):

- What types of data are available to measure the impact of an event (frequency, validity, representativity, continuity)?
- What is the level of tourism education, the skills in tourism data interpretation?
- What aspects of tourism development in the community, now and in the future, should be monitored?
- What are relevant indicators of the social and cultural context of an event, and of the effect of public awareness programs on tourism?
- How and when is relevant information on tourism and on an event communicated to the community?
- Which techniques and guidelines are being developed to improve the quality of tourist facilities and services?
- Last, but not least, is there a local forum to implement the principles of integrated quality management in the urban tourist destinations?

Each of the dimensions of an event's impact requires a specific research approach: these include spatial analysis and fieldwork, statistical analysis, surveys, interviews, focus groups, Delphi panels and website opinion polls. Obviously there need to be strong arguments to gain the support and collaboration of event organizers and local authorities for such an experiment which, in the preparatory stage, may appear to be purely academic. Although these data and insights would be an ideal starting point for a monitoring system, the benefits of this type of intellectual exercise are not easy to communicate.

Taking into account that cultural events do have social and financial implications for the local taxpayer and also that political awareness on this issue increases through the media coverage, among other factors, the chances of a host community introducing a monitoring system have become greater.

Milestones in the process of mutagenesis

Since the objective is to trace changes over time, a longitudinal approach is required. In the ideal research scenario, the implementation of a monitoring system should start at point zero, which is prior to the decision to organize a cultural event.

However, this generally proves to be an unrealistic option, since the cultural agenda of most urban tourist destinations offers a continuous series of events, small and large, local and international, so it is virtually impossible to isolate the impact of one particular event as the impacts are cumulative.

In the case of a major event (e.g. selection as Cultural Capital of Europe) one can assume a distinct difference between the impacts of tourism in the different stages (prior, during and after the event). Looking at the tourism impact of events as a process, an acceleration or accentuation of particular changes can be expected. In order to define the added value of a cultural event, these dynamics need to be analyzed systematically – synchronically and diachronically – in their different dimensions.

Stage 1: Prior to the event

The impact of an event starts in the preparatory stage of a community being a candidate to host and organize a mega-event. Once the decision has been taken, local authorities and the private sector (trendsetters first) anticipate the opportunities by developing strategic plans.

In an early stage these activities are hardly manifest, but in reality they do initiate a process of product development and affect the short-term planning priorities. Gradually, the external communication starts (formal, informal, via press and other media) and sets an image of expectations.

This process of planning and development can be traced by participatory observation and by selective interviews with the initiating agents and decision makers. This pre-event stage is, in many ways, a crucial one and includes the involvement of actors and local agents, image building and external communication, creating goodwill and community support, innovative product development and reconsidering the policy priorities.

In this stage, the objectives and procedures of organization and marketing strategies are outlined. It is then the moment to agree on the critical success factors and the ways to check – ad interim – the achievements, defining the parameters to follow the progress and the calls for interventions or corrective actions. The decision to introduce a control mechanism and to select relevant indicators implies the setting up of a well-organized steering committee with clear objectives and the ambition to manage the process in a transparent way. The idea of a monitoring system and hence external auditors rarely appeals to many decision makers. The practice rather is to limit this task to a post-fact evaluation.

Stage 2: During the event

Surveys and opinion polls during the event have become a ritual feature, although frequently all reference to a pre-event stage might be lacking, as well as the possibility to compare the results with those of other events (different places, different time). The questionnaires are often ad hoc, geared at collecting quantitative data and not always designed in a professional way. Consequently, the results are frequently of little use for understanding the added value of an event. These surveys function as a cover for so-called good management, rather than as an effective management tool or an instrument for developing views on long-term sustainable forms of tourism.

Examples of a science-based monitoring system are exceptional, because they are expensive and, above all, few are willing to pay to know what might go wrong – hardly the politicians, who are mainly concerned about short-term success and positive media coverage. The message, "if you cannot measure, you cannot manage", has been widely accepted in the business environment, but so far has had little positive response in the public sector.

Stage 3: Post-event evaluation

In order to define the "added value of an event", a post-fact evaluation only is hardly valid. There needs to be a reference point and a possibility to eliminate the effect of trends that are not directly induced by the event. As a rule, the evaluation reports on events tend to highlight an increased number of visitors, the direct economic results, the eye catching achievements (new infrastructure) and the international press coverage, but pay little or no attention to the social balance of costs/benefits, nor to the possible long-term effects on the destination.

While highbrow statements on cultural revival may inspire the objectives of many cultural events, there is little conceptualization of how to measure the actual changes induced by the event. In addition, analyzing the "morning-after effect" might not be the right way to assess the long-term impact of an event on the image of the place, on the growing involvement of the local community and on the hidden (as not measured) positive and negative effects.

Ambitious Events: Cultural Capital of Europe

This European initiative has in many ways been the start of a success story. There are now clear signals that the formula erodes in some way: by including second-rank cultural cities, by copying successful ingredients in other places and cultural contexts, by too-high expectations, by not learning from failures in other experiments, by lack of competence to manage and, not least, by increasing competition between cities.

A city of culture is supposed to be a focus of cultural life in the national or regional environment, with a tradition and grass-root expressions of culture. This definition slightly differs from the current profile of popular destinations for the cultural tourist. The latter model of "cultural" urban tourism has taken many forms and is becoming a booming market. The distinction lies in the way local authorities are setting out the lines of cultural and tourism policy, in an integrated or in a polarized management model. The polarization between culture and tourism at the local level can be demonstrated by analyzing the objectives and the emphasis that is put on the role of events:

- as an incentive for change in the urban management;
- as a strategy in the competition between urban centers;
- as an instrument for image building; and
- as a lever for projects and community involvement.

Many cities are now in a stage of "trial and error" in their ambition to harmonize cultural policies and tourism expansion and gradually discover that cultural events have a rather short half-life. The common challenge lies in managing the events so they become more than a temporary injection and result in a long-lasting improvement of the urban social and cultural environment. The research issue of how to achieve this has being explored in several cultural capitals of Europe (e.g. Venice, Salzburg, Rotterdam, Bruges).

The Tourist Historic City of Bruges: An Ideal Research Laboratory

Bruges is, in many ways, an interesting case study and has frequently been the object of tourism studies on carrying capacity and on heritage management (Jansen-Verbeke, 2003; Jansen-Verbeke & De Keyser, 2002; Russo, 2002; UNESCO Venice Office, 1999). The results of empirical studies in Bruges are representative for many historical cities where the pressure of tourism is increasing, where questions about carrying capacity are being asked and, above all, where policies for a sustainable development need to be set in motion. Comparisons with, for instance, Venice, Salzburg and many other heritage cities could contribute strongly to a better understanding of the dynamics of tourism in the urban system. Previous studies in Bruges offer a useful reference framework (Jansen-Verbeke, 1998b). Empirical research has focused on the tourist activities, tourism policy and tourism impacts on the local setting of a small-scale city which also had the ambition of hosting a mega-event in 2002, as one of the Cultural Capitals of Europe.

Spatial dynamics

Spatial analyses – at different time intervals between 1990 and 2002 – of the location pattern of the main tourist attractions (historical buildings, museums, sightseeing routes) is the input for the study of changing tourist space use. The location of these magnets structures the tourist city.

A concentration model was introduced in the 1990s as a planning tool for managing the hardware of this tourist historic city. The effectiveness of such a planning instrument to manage the physical impact of tourist activities has been evaluated (Jansen-Verbeke & De Keyser, 2002). In fact the spatial clustering of tourism supporting facilities (secondary elements of the local tourist product) increasingly characterizes this city. This dimension of mutagenesis was analyzed using spatial analysis methods on the location patterns of souvenir shops, restaurants and cafes, sidewalk cafés, hotels, parking spaces and street markets. In addition, the patterns of tourists' use of space (city walks, horse and carriage routes, sightseeing tours by mini-coach, canal tours) were mapped over an interval of 10 years.

This exercise of fieldwork and of focusing on the hardware has enabled researchers to delineate the areas of tourism pressure and eventually to locate the critical areas where the perception of overcrowding has become problematic. The hypothesis of this research approach was that the stage of saturation, when tourism tends to unbalance the urban system, could be identified by parameters of land use and tourist space use.

Social dynamics

The priorities in resource management (often expressed as conservation) and the lack of spatial management in the urban space in general were strongly criticized (Russo, 2002). This criticism explains why the social carrying capacity is indeed determined by the physical impact of tourism.

The interesting part of the research results is that there is indeed a limit to the acceptance of the tourismification process, which becomes more manifest as tourism is booming. The fact that tourism has become part of the daily life and scenery, interfering with the quality of the urban environment and the costs of living, explains the sensitivity over tourism-related issues.

The social carrying capacity, in particular the acceptance of tourism by the local population, was investigated in surveys (in 1990 and 1999) conducted amongst opinion leaders and decision makers and in 2002 among the residents of this top tourist destination (current Ph.D. project by J. Bryon). In each of these surveys the link was made with the spatial patterns of tourismification and with the growing economic dependency.

The cumulation of daily problems, such as congested traffic, shortage of parking, crowded walking areas, an imbalanced range in the retail trade, rising prices, intrusion in the private domain and, above all, a general impression of overcrowding, inevitably leads to some antagonism of the local community toward tourism.

A longitudinal and integrated approach will allow for a better understanding of the dynamics of tourismification and, above all, the infiltration process of tourism into the economic, social and cultural aspects of the community.

The Cultural Capital of Europe event: Tourism in acceleration?

The decision of the city of Bruges to apply to host the mega-event, Cultural Capital of Europe, in 2002 has opened a new debate on the pros and cons of the initiative among policy makers and the local community and in particular on how the mega-event might accelerate the process of tourismification. It is an almost impossible mission to isolate the additional impulses of the event from the ongoing trends in the tourist destination. A key question is which parameters can be effective in measuring the acceleration effect of the event on, for instance, changed uses of buildings, reduction of the residential housing capacity, intrusion of hotels and tourist-oriented shops, expansion of the catering sector, rise of property values and demand for second homes by non-citizens. These issues are now on the political agenda.

In preparation for the event a policy plan was published, including the objectives and critical reflections on the interaction of culture and tourism (Caron, 1999). The possible synergism between culture and tourism is outlined in the tentative way, somewhat emphasizing tourism as an overruling force in the city. Clearly the policy plan includes reflections on the issue of sustainable tourism, albeit with the formulation of rather vague objectives such as:

* reducing the erosion of culture by tourism;
* optimizing the cultural experience of visitors; and
* improving the long-term economic benefits for the tourism sector.

The situation in Bruges points out the need for a strong and coherent policy inspired by views on sustainability. However, this implies an understanding of the complex interaction between the tourist activities and the urban setting with its cultural resources and the impact of a cultural event. This means defining the goals in terms of conservation of cultural resources and finding a compromise between the short-term requests of the tourism industry and the long-term objectives of cultural heritage conservation. The only possible option in order to move towards sustainability lies in an integrated planning approach, referring to the cultural heritage and its environmental setting, the physical infrastructure and the tourist facilities in combination with a resource and visitor management policy.

Bruges, as many other cities, suffers the duality of a social task as a residential city and an economic task as a tourism destination. The fear of becoming an open-air museum, with all the consequences of this, is manifest. Therefore, the priorities of the cultural organization team – Bruges 2002 – include the following:

* Focusing on "quality tourism" (as an antidote to cultural consumption by mass tourism?).
* No mass tourism but cultural tourism (are these market segments really exclusive?).
* Improving the quality of life in the inner city (such as accessibility and use of public spaces).
* Managing the process of tourismification, in particular in the tourist zone (the effectiveness of management tools need to be assessed).
* Safeguarding the authenticity of fabric (back to conservationism?).

In addition, the policy in the plan includes a list of traditional objectives such as image improvement, professionalism in hospitality, guided tours and tourist services, and opening the cultural resources and heritage sites for a wider public. These raised the question of to what extent the cultural event is seen as a marketing instrument and to what extent it is seen as a real opportunity to improve the quality of the tourist destination.

There is a certain expectation among decision makers and residents that new additions and improvements to the infrastructure, which are planned in the context of this event (e.g. a new concert hall), will have a long-term and tangible impact on the attraction of Bruges as a cultural destination.

A new élan in the cultural sector, deserving diversification and expansion of the cultural agenda, could create greater momentum for a wider spectrum of tourist opportunities, if the city can manage to maintain this high level of activity and develop cultural resources into tourist attractions in a sustainable way.

As a rule, the organization of such a mega-event brings together different stakeholders and decision makers on a temporary basis, with specific targets to be met. The event as such is a real incentive for closer collaboration and can eventually become a lever for an integrated destination management model. The question remains to what extent this will generate a continued greater involvement of the local community in the management decisions concerning the future of their home town. As argued above, a multidimensional evaluation of the mutagenecity of an event implies a study of the changes in the hardware, the software and the orgware. The latter also refers to the degree of professionalization in the organization of tourism, and the new partnership between culture and tourism and between the distinct policy sectors (including culture, tourism, spatial management and conservation).

An internal evaluation report has been made for the local authorities; obviously an economic assessment of the return in investment serves the purpose of the organizers. Apparently and unfortunately, the question of the long-term impact of this one-off event which intrigues many tourism researchers had no high priority on the political agenda. When the show is over, and all the debts are paid, the key question will still be what has this cultural event contributed, in terms of added value, to a city which has, in every respect, reached the saturation stage in the tourist area life cycle?

Handicaps and Perspectives for Future Research

Empirical data that can demonstrate the hybrid impact of tourism and of cultural events in particular on the urban system in general are scarce (Fayos-Sola, 1998; Montanari, 2002). This handicap can be explained in two ways: a general lack of data on the one hand and a limited understanding of the mutagenecity of events on the other. Many answers to the question of events' impact could be met by developing a monitoring system and by widely communicating the results. To date, many descriptive case studies on cultural events have failed to refer to global trends, or to venture into a discussion of long-term impact assessment, or to share the lessons from comparable examples.

The threat of oversupply and severe competition in the target market of cultural tourism has become very realistic but often underestimated by event organizers. The competitive advantages of many an event need to be seriously questioned. There may be a loss of authenticity, a strong inclination among decision makers and organizers to imitate successful formulas in product development and marketing and in standardization of products, imitation of themes and an absence of local roots or anchors.

Creativity is not the only answer – research-based understanding of the mutagenecity of events is far more crucial in view of the need for successful policies for a sustainable cultural tourism destination.

References

Ashworth, G.J. and Tunbridge, J.E. (2002) *The Historic Tourist City: Retrospect and Prospect of Managing the Heritage City*. Oxford: Pergamon.

Bryon, J. (2002) The challenge of measuring tourist-resident impact. In M. Jansen-Verbeke and R. De Keyser (eds) *Tourism Studies in Bruges* (pp. 42–51). Bruges: WES.

Bryon, J. (in progress) Measuring tourist-resident impact. PhD project, KU, Leuven.

Caron, B. (1999) *Culturele hoofdstad van Europa: Brugge*. Bruges 2002.

Faulkner, A. and Tideswell, C. (1997) A framework for monitoring community impacts of tourism. *Journal of Sustainable Tourism* 1, 3–28.

Fayos-Sola, E. (1998) The impact of mega events. *Annals of Tourism Research* 25 (1), 241–245.

Getz, D. (1998) Event tourism and the authenticity dilemma. In W. Theobald (ed.) *Global Tourism: The Next Decade* (2nd edn) (pp. 409–427). Oxford: Butterworth Heinemann.

Jansen-Verbeke, M. (1997) Urban tourism: Managing resources and visitors. In S. Wahah and J. Pigram (eds) *Tourism Development and Growth: The Challenge of Sustainability* (pp. 237–256). London and New York: Routledge.

Jansen-Verbeke, M. (1998a) Tourismification of historical cities. *Annals of Tourism Research* 25 (3), 739–742.

Jansen-Verbeke, M. (1998b) Le tourisme culturel dans les villes historiques: Révitalisation urbaine et capacité de charge: Le cas de Bruges. In G. Cazes and F. Poitier (eds) *Le Tourisme et la Ville: Expériences Européennes* (pp. 81–97). France: L'Harmattan.

Jansen-Verbeke, M. (2003) Parameter für die Touristifizierung von städtische Riesezielen. In R. Bachleitner and H.J. Kagelmann (eds) *Kultur/Städte/Tourismus* (pp. 35–45). Munich and Vienna: Profil Verlag.

Jansen-Verbeke, M. and De Keyser, R. (2002) *Tourism Studies in Bruges*. Brugge: WES.

Jansen-Verbeke, M. and Lievois, E. (1999) Analyzing heritage resources for urban tourism in European cities. In D.G. Pearce and R.W. Butler (eds) *Contemporary Issues in Tourism Development: Analysis and Applications* (pp. 81–107). London: Routledge.

Jurowski, C., Uysal, M. and Williams, D. (1997) A path analytical approach to community tourism attitudes. *Journal of Travel Research* 36 (2), 3–11.

Lindberg, K. and Johnson, R.L. (1997) Modelling residents' attitudes towards tourism. *Annals of Tourism Research* 24 (2), 402–424.

Pearce, P.L. (1998) The relationships between residents and tourists: The research literature and management directions. In W.F. Theobald (ed.) *Global Tourism: The Next Decade* (2nd edn) (pp. 129–149). Oxford: Butterworth-Heinemann.

Montanari, A. (2002) Tourism and mega-events: The restructuring of urban areas and the dream of a global city. Paper presented at the conference, The Historic Tourist City, Bruges.

Porter, M.E. (2000) Locations, clusters and company strategy. In G.L. Clark, M. Feldman and M. Gertler (eds) *Oxford Handbook of Economic Geography* (pp. 253–274). Oxford: Oxford University Press.

Russo, A.P. (2002) The vicious circle of tourism development in heritage cities. *Annals of Tourism Research* 29 (1), 165–182.

UNESCO Venice Office (1999) *Sustainable Tourism Development for the Heritage City of Bruges: A Stakeholders Analysis of Tourism Policy*. Venice: UNESCO.

Wall, G. (1997) Rethinking impacts of tourism. In C. Cooper and S. Wanhill (eds) *Tourism Development: Environmental and Community Issues*. New York: Wiley.

WTO (1993) *Sustainable Tourism Development: Guide for Local Planners*. Madrid: WTO.

Chapter 13

Tourism and Terrorism: The "New War"

VALENE S. SMITH

September 11, 2001 (9/11) has been described as a "watershed" in world history (Zakaria, 2001: 308) as the first attack on the American mainland by a foreign adversary since the War of 1812. For the terrorists whose activities precipitated the "new war", the destruction of the two World Trade Center towers was a psychological success, bruising the image of Wall Street and the world stock market. The near-simultaneous terrorist strikes – including the US military core, the Pentagon, in Washington DC – publicly illustrated the vulnerability of America's defense system. The use of four passenger-laden airplanes as human bombs enabled the entire world to see, *live*, on television and to understand the two prime strategies of terrorism: (1) to strike fear into a target population by a "high-intensity, low-volume" effort, and (2) in so doing, to effectively destabilize the targeted area.

This chapter examines the nature of terrorism, its development since World War II, and the economic and psychological "costs" that have precipitated the "new war". In contrast to traditional warfare, which generated the world's largest known genre of tourist attractions and destinations (Lloyd, 1998; Smith, 1996), the covert nature of terrorism and the "new war" suggests that increased civilian casualties, refugees, and threats of bioterrorism may leave few tourist markers.

The Costs of Terrorism

The death toll on 9/11 neared 3000 and shocked the world. The economic blow has had far-reaching global effects, giving substance to the statement that "when the USA catches cold, the world economy has pneumonia". To date (as of March 2003) that has not yet happened, but the "new war" with Iraq is yet to be fought and finished.

The Milkin Institute (Navarro & Spencer, 2001) assessed the immediate costs to the USA, including: (1) the physical damage to US property as at least US$10 billion; (2) lost economic output in the immediate further aftermath (including diminished airline and hotel revenues and reduced consumer spending) at US$47 billion; and (3) the costs for "terrorist tax" (security) as up to US$41 billion. These outright reconstruction and security costs are up-front, but to them must be added the government bailouts, lost tax revenues, the foregone (and taxable) life earnings of deceased victims, and fluctuations in the stock market as well as the value of the US dollar. The estimated total price tag approaches US$2 trillion.

For the transportation and tourism industries, which by September 2001 were already shaken by a deepening USA recession, the impact was immediate and serious. In February 2002, Hilton Hotels reported its net income for the fourth quarter (October–December 2001) had dropped 94% despite aggressive cost-cutting, with the lowest occupancy rates in San Francisco, Washington DC, and Hawaii (Binckley, 2002: B11). Similarly, the casino and hotel industry in Las Vegas was severely depressed. United Airlines discontinued its round-the-world service, with mid-point connections in India, and domestic carriers in the US reported sharp decreases in passenger load. The Milkin study predicted for the year 2002 a loss of 1.6 million urban jobs, of which 760,000 would occur in travel and tourism. To try to offset terrorist fears, the Travel Industry of America (TIA) produced and aired widely on television an infomercial that included words and music from the air carriers, hotels, and cruise lines, and featured an appearance by President G.W. Bush. The message: it's patriotic to travel; it creates and supports jobs. Similarly, in an unprecedented act, the World Travel and Tourism Council (WTTC) placed full-page ads in trade journals to reassure travel suppliers that "we are with you" in efforts to stimulate tourism.

The fear factor established on 9/11 continued to spread in conjunction with the further weakening of the world economy, including the stock markets of Europe and Asia. To cut costs, many businesses deleted travel budgets and substituted teleconferencing. By March 2003, increased costs for aviation fuel, labor, and security threatened survival of the three major US air carriers – American, Delta, and United. Passengers on most carriers earn Frequent Flyer miles when enrolled in programs that generate free tickets and/or class upgrades; these programs are popular with business travelers who pay higher fares for onboard service and for late bookings. In 2002 46% of all US air travelers were members of a Frequent Flyer program, up from 44% in 1999. The participant level jumps to 68% for travelers who make three or more trips per year (NFO Plog Research, cited in McDonald, 2003), and helps to maintain customer loyalty in a competitive industry.

Another fear and business factor is hostage insurance, especially for executives traveling in troubled Latin America, the Philippines, and Indonesia. Airport security and baggage check are costly but necessary precautions.

The fear factor spread to the hotel and restaurant industry. The Frequent Flyer business travelers were among their most profitable guests. However, these same individuals were also gaining more skills with on-line bookings with their preferred carrier where special "internet fares" are available, and also with the use of consolidators such as Orbitz, Priceline, and Expedia for air and hotel reservations. For some, "surfing" for vacation bargains became a new form of vicarious or virtual tourism, from which they individually benefited financially but with reduced cash flow to the carriers.

And, lest we forget mercantilism as a solace to fear, the malls were challenged "to protect shoppers, and soothe nerves" (Zimmerman, 2001a: B1). Subsequently, because of the "wall of people" (tourists) who were flocking to Ground Zero (destroyed site of the World Trade Center), interfering with the clean-up and gawking at residents in nearby buildings, the New York Mayor's Office of Emergency Services established a plan to convert "tourists into shoppers". The Viewing Platform was opened to holders of mandatory tickets, obtainable free but only at a store in a lower Manhattan shopping district, where one could dine and also buy from a wide selection of souvenirs (Petersen, 2002: 2).

The initial financial loss to the US economy must have delighted the attackers, but the economy proved more resilient than anticipated. By September 2002, the Milkin Institute (DeVol, 2002) improved its 2002 predictions by 5% thanks to stronger than anticipated consumer confidence, low interests rates for home and auto loans, and tax cuts.

The global economic loss of tourism revenues is incalculable, but the impacts were evident worldwide: two national European airlines (Sabena and Swissair) declared bankruptcy, and literally thousands of US travel agencies went out of business. The lost tourist jobs were critical to many international destinations, including Kenya and Tanzania, where it was suddenly remembered that the same terrorist group, al Qaeda, had attacked the American embassies in their capital cities on August 7, 1998. The author visited both countries in May 2002 and found that some safari lodges were entirely without guests, and the driver-guides lounged by empty vehicles, planning to return to their countryside villages when the operators gave them formal termination. Meanwhile, al Qaeda was reportedly recruiting new members. Cash payments plus food, shelter, and activity appealed to homeless and unemployed youths who loitered on street corners. They saw it as a road to status in preference to the squalor of the slums, devoid of potable water and sanitation.

The spontaneous search for terrorist cells changed the political climate: Western nations friendly to the USA tightened their surveillance on potential criminals and spent heavily to heighten security at their borders and airports. Somalia and the Philippines, two countries which potentially harbored allied terrorist groups, hastily solicited US military aid to rout terrorists, lest their nations also fall victim to an Afghan-type bombing.

Levels of Warfare

The immediate US military response to the 9/11 attack – termed the "new war" by the media channels – probably caught the sponsoring group, al Qaeda, by surprise. Americans are sometimes caricatured as "overfed, overpaid, and oversexed", and might be presumed soft targets. Margaret Mead is noted for the 1965 study, *And Keep your Powder Dry*, in which she detailed the fighting spirit of the American public when aroused by a somewhat similar "sneak attack" at Pearl Harbor on December 7, 1942. The relation of this new militarism to tourism raises several questions: whence comes this pan-national hatred of the United States and its citizens? Initially anti-American attitudes were directed toward government policies, but by March 2003 some terrorist groups offered cash rewards for "dead" Americans comparable to the rewards offered by the US Central Intelligence Agency (CIA) for the capture of al Qaeda leaders. This "new war" raises questions of importance to the future of tourism: in what ways does this "new war" differ from traditional (pre-1990) warfare? What types of tourism markers will it generate?

Traditional wars

Traditional wars were fought on battlefields or at sea, and often involved elaborate strategies taught in military academies. The nature of the battle depended on the lay of the land, supply lines, and available water for troops and cavalry, to name only a few of the many criteria. Communications were often slow and imperfect, originally by horns and bugles, or by carrier pigeon and smoke signals. American folklore cherishes the story of the patriotic silversmith, Paul Revere, who in 1775 raced on horseback to warn the local militia (warriors) of the pending arrival of the British troops by lighting candles in the steeple of Boston's Christ Church, "one if by land, two if by sea". The narrative poem, *The Midnight Ride of Paul Revere*, by the American poet Henry Wadsworth Longfellow is an example of the vast literature associated with war.

The pictorial knowledge of war came originally from sketches and paintings, then still photos and, during World War II, motion pictures flown by airmail from the respective areas. The scenes shown in motion picture theaters were often 2–3 days old. The first TV did not appear until 1950, and then was poor in quality and very expensive. During World War II the media was constrained, and the newsreels did not show details of the corpses at Omaha Beach in Normandy, nor the so-called "red beach" at Saipan, or other bloodied destinations. Instead, viewers saw the long lines of British soldiers awaiting evacuation from Dunkirk. The viewing public at that time had not yet been subjected to the violence of video games or horror movies, on-site violence as in the Somalia debacle of America's Blackhawk Down, and the violence of motion pictures such as *Schindler's List* and *Saving Private Ryan*.

The classic activity of war – two or more nations vying for possession or power – spans at least three millennia, and has scarred much of Europe and Asia. Boundary lines were redrafted as some nations were vanquished and disappeared, and new nations were created and undertook to establish their political role. Wars became the time markers of society and, in essence, the titles for chapters of history books. *Before the War* outlined the events that led to the hostilities. *During the War* described battles, strategies, generals, and heroic activities. *After the War* became the period of accommodation to new status and adjustments. Warfare has always been feared and left untold horrors occasioned by sieges, burned cities, scorched earth, and human torture. Despite this record of abominations, the pervasive nature of war and the centuries of history have yielded a tourist harvest of activities that constitute the largest identifiable body of tourist destinations, attractions, and graphic arts on this planet (Smith, 2001).

Local and regional insurgencies have disrupted national governments in a wide array of civil strife, and date at least to battles between the city-states of Athens and Sparta. Demands for revenge and restitution can leave deep emotional scars that last for centuries (Zimmermann, 2001b: 323–332). The US Civil War (1862–1865) was economic, as a test of regulations governing agriculture and manufacturing. This divisive altercation was also ethnic, involving the issue of black slavery. Demands for hegemony in Northern Ireland continually disrupt public safety and deter tourism to the area. The economic disruption caused by the Mugabe regime in Zimbabwe over land ownership has created widespread food shortages and, for some farm owners, a necessary choice between voluntary emigration or confrontation with murderous mobs.

Terrorism

Terrorism differs from other forms of civil strife in terms of actions and intent. The US Federal Bureau of Investigation (FBI) defines terrorism as the unlawful use of force and violence against people or property to intimidate or coerce a government, the civilian population, or other segments to further political or social objectives (http://www.fbi.gov). Anthropologist Turney-High (1981) defines soldiers as persons conscripted by a government, which they are legally bound to serve, and who may be disciplined or subject to court martial for unauthorized leaves or other infractions of duty. By contrast, terrorists are warriors who usually join a leader to whom they owe allegiance in support of a cause, are commonly unpaid, and are seldom governed by constitutional or legal precepts. This distinction was adopted by President G.W. Bush on November 13, 2001 as the US interpretation of the 1948 Geneva Convention, which identifies prisoners of war as soldiers who must meet four criteria:

(1) that of being commanded by a person responsible for his subordinates;
(2) that of having a fixed distinctive sign recognizable at a distance;
(3) that of carrying arms openly; and
(4) that of conducting their operations in accordance with the laws and customs of war.

Individuals involved in the 2002 Afghan war who have been transferred to Guantanamo Base in Cuba are either soldiers or warriors. Members of the Taliban are considered to be members of the fighting force of Afghanistan and are therefore POWs; but the detainees from the other 28 countries are illegal combatants or warriors who claim allegiance to the ideology of al Qaeda – with its intense hatred of and avowed intent to kill Americans.

The paramilitary al Qaeda developed training camps and cells throughout the Moslem sphere of influence, and established connections for their operatives. The trail of the WTC hijackers, pieced together by intelligence sources, demonstrates the extent of their network. Funding was derived in part from the personal fortune of billionaire Osama bin Laden, from donations by sympathetic philanthropic organizations, from narcotic sales, and from a unique tourism souvenir. Tanzanite, a stone of minimum gemstone quality because of its fragility, is mined in a remote district in Tanzania. The evidence suggests that the al Qaeda cell responsible for the attack on the US Embassy in Zanzibar on August 7, 1998 became on-site buyers for tanzanite (Simpson & Block, 2002: B1) and smuggled it into international trade. A massive promotion popularizing the stone increased its value, and made it one of the most-sought purchases offered to American cruise passengers and tourists visiting the US Virgin Islands. Americans account for 80% of the global market (Block, 2002: A18). JC Penney (a national department store chain) featured tanzanite in their pre-Christmas 2001 low-budget jewelry. When the presumed al Qaeda tanzanite link became known, leading US jewelers removed the stone from sale. Because of lost export tax revenues, the Tanzanian government subsequently instituted more supervision at the mines, and now requires employees to wear badges to exclude illegal miners and dealers.

The Seeds of Terrorism

Many Americans have only rudimentary knowledge of 20th-century history, as such high school history courses often terminate with the colorful figure of "Teddy" Roosevelt or the League of Nations. As a case in point, and not at all unusual, this author was asked to coordinate a current affairs panel comprised of outstanding twelfth-grade students from five local high schools. These students are members of the Y generation born about 1985–1986. Their parents (and possibly even their grandparents) were Baby Boomers, born post-World War II starting in 1945. In such cases, only their great-grandparents (if still living) had any personal knowledge of the events of that war. At the conference, a possible parallel was drawn between the genocide of Hitler's Holocaust and Saddam Hussein's weapons of mass destruction. At once, a hand flew up: "Who was Hitler?"

The Balfour Declaration

Americans in general have only a vague awareness that the nation of Israel was created to provide a homeland for Jewish refugees who fled Germany after World War II. Their limited knowledge probably stems from one of the Holocaust exhibits which travel from town to town across the USA. Most Americans do not understand that the Balfour

Declaration, which created Israel in 1947, was a *British* decision implemented by Winston Churchill. Nor do most realize that, in the process of relocating 250,000 Holocaust survivors, some 780,000 Palestinians were forced into United Nations Refugee Camps where most still live. The Mid-East crisis dates to that event and has smoldered into the terrorism that brought down the World Trade Center – it is a resource war over land and political hegemony.

Most Americans are unfamiliar with the Arabic proverb, "the friend of my enemy is *my* enemy" and its implication in relation to the US economic aid liberally given to Israel but not to the stateless Palestinians. Most Americans are equally unfamiliar with the basic tenets of the Moslem religion. This indictment of American public schools is supported by the observations of European students who spend a year in the USA as exchange students and freely acknowledge that they "have a good time at the school parties" but, academically, it is a wasted year. This personal comment may seem out of context here, but the fundamental lack of knowledge is frequently perpetuated in the popularity contests labeled "talk shows" and "opinion polls", and may serve as the information base for some voters.

Contested Kashmir

Even more remote from public knowledge is the political conflict between India and Pakistan involving a small Himalayan valley, Kashmir. Multiple local skirmishes and potentially nuclear war are often portrayed by US media channels as a conflict between militant Moslems and peaceful Hindus. Again, the political decision was *British* and also in 1947, during the partition of India into two religious states, Hindu India and Islamic Pakistan. By proclamation, each area was to be acceded to the respective new nation according to their religious majority. In 1947 the state of Kashmir had an 80% majority of Moslems, but the ruling Maharajah was a Hindu whose ancestor five generations back had purchased the land from India. Lord Mountbatten, serving as the final British Governor-General of India in 1947, intended that Kashmir should become part of Pakistan. But, when Indian troops appeared on the border at the request of the Maharajah, the unarmed Moslem residents rioted. Mountbatten, to obtain a temporary peace, *provisionally* acceded the land to India with the promise of a duly monitored United Nations election to follow, but 56 years later the election has not been held, Meanwhile, India has encouraged Hindu migration into the valley in order to secure the intrinsically valuable tourist trade (when peace prevails).

A further geopolitical factor complicates the possession of Kashmir. Pakistan depends on the Indus River as its primary source of culinary and irrigation water. The five tributary streams which coalesce in the Punjab (literally, "five rivers"), all rise in India or Indian-held Kashmir. The Pakistanis fear that India could hold them hostage for water by diverting any one or all five of the streams. Clearly, the fighting along the divided border known as the Line of Control (LOC) is a resource war over land, water, and political hegemony.

Religious fundamentalism

The mission here is not to debate the nature of religion or even the term fundamentalism, but rather to understand the 2001 terrorist role of religious fundamentalism. Barber (2002: xii), coined the terms *Jihad* (not referring to Islam) as "the forces of disintegrated tribalism . . . and the complaints of those mired in poverty and despair as the consequence of unregulated global markets and a capitalism run wild because it has been uprooted from the humanizing constraints of the democratic nation-state". His *McWorld* (not restricted to the USA) represents the forces of integrative modernization and aggressive economic and cultural globalization. According to Barber, "The struggle of Jihad against McWorld is not a clash of civilizations but a dialectical expression of tensions built into a single global civilization as it emerges against a backdrop of traditional ethnic and religious divisions" (Barber, 2000: xvi). "The issue is no longer the Utopian longing for global democracy against the siren call of consumerism or the passionate war cries of Jihad; it is the securing of safety. Following September 11, global governance has become a sober mandate of political realism" (Barber, 2000: xxiii).

Juergensmeyer, writing in *Terror in the Mind of God: The Global Rise of Religious Violence* (2001: xii) notes that:

activists such as bin Laden might be regarded as guerrilla antiglobalists. Even ethnonationalist struggles, such as in Kashmir, have arisen in part because of an erosion of confidence in Western-style politics and politicians. The era of globalization and postmodernity creates a context in which authority is undercut and local forces have been unleashed, in saying this, I do not mean to imply that only globalization causes religious violence. But it may be one reason why so many instances of religious violence in such diverse places around the world is occurring at the present time.

Ethnographers may choose to see religious terrorism as a human outburst of fear and rage in the face of helplessness occasioned by a breakdown in social, economic, and political norms. Generations of acquired knowledge have provided mankind with the information to solve most day-to-day problems irrespective of the level of technology. For some, it is associated with the food quest and its production; for others, it is the manufacturing process or the service sector. Most societal members have learned the prescriptive behavior for gender, age, and status relations. Most cultures have extensive knowledge to cope with disabilities associated with minor accidents and illness, and they possess routinely accepted answers in cosmology.

This acquired knowledge is geographic and ethnic but, in the processes of de-territorialization and re-territorialization associated with globalization, that information can be quickly modified and reapplied (Short & Kim, 1999). Humans are not coded robots but cognitive beings whose survival has been and still is dependent upon sensitivity to observed cultural standards. Physical disasters beyond human control – droughts, earthquakes, and floods – are dismissed as "Acts of God", unless science establishes that they can be attributed to global warming or a widening hole in the ozone layer. Many circumstances involving luck (or lack of it), disappointments, and failures are dismissed as "God's will", or in the Islamic faith are ascribed to the *jinns*. Good luck is often a "blessing" or "Heaven sent".

Anthropologists see humans operating in societies, amidst networks of family (both nuclear and extended), in expanded units – family clans and tribes – or in associative units including the "church family". Larger and perhaps remote are the prescriptive encompassing forces of government that may have a familial nomenclature, as Mother Russia, *das Vaterland*, or America's Uncle Sam. Embraced by this network, most individuals ease through life using established patterns of acquired knowledge. But when all those socially secure institutions have disappeared, or been rendered useless, mankind has lost control and must turn to god(s) or death, or both. The ethnographic literature is replete with instances of messianic movements including the Ghost Dance of the American Plains Indians, the revival cults in Papua New Guinea, and the Doomsday cults awaiting an Armageddon.

Zakaria (2001: 316) notes that:

radical Islam grew on the backs of failed states that have not improved the lots of their people. It festers in societies where contact with the West has produced more chaos than growth and more uncertainty than wealth and although radical Islam may not have many adherents in the West, more than a billion people around the world are potentially receptive to this message.

D'Amore and Anunza (1986) cite a study by Risks International, Inc. of the profile of the "typical terrorist" as a young single male (between 20 and 23 years of age), from a middle- or upper-class urban family, who averaged 2.5 years of college and affiliated on their university campus to a Marxist ideology. Liever (2001) reports a similar experience, specifically among young Pakistanis who feared the degradation of poverty that forced their sisters (and potentially their daughters) into prostitution. They sought escape from poverty either through smuggling heroin or the religious simplicity and austerity in the jihadist version of Islam.

The "new war"

The "new war" was announced to the public by leading television channels almost immediately after the attack on the World Trade Center. The President and the Pentagon clearly established their intent to engage in a new form of militarism – namely to deploy troops and to bomb a foreign nation which had previously been an ally and to which they had provided arms and support. This superpower commitment was being undertaken to hunt down and destroy a band of international warriors.

The global terrorist network, al Qaeda, had quietly developed its cadre of militants while US intelligence failed to link the individual incidents to a common source. Jenkins (2001: 4–5) calls attention to some 10,000 incidents of international terrorism that have occurred since 1968, only 14 of which caused 100 or more fatalities. The worst included:

> 325 killed in the 1985 crash of an Air India flight; more than 300 killed in 1993 by car bombs in Bombay; 270 killed in the 1988 crash of Pan American 103; 241 killed in 1983 by a truck bomb in Beirut; 171 killed in the crash of a UTA flight in 1989; 158 killed by a truck bomb in Oklahoma City in 1995; 115 killed in the 1987 sabotage of a Korean airliner.

The evidence points to a span of terrorist tactics from local small-scale separatist activities to increasingly large-scale indiscriminate violence based on a religious mandate from God to kill one's own foes. "Those convinced they have [this] mandate have fewer moral qualms about mass murder and care less about death in God's name because it brings rewards in the hereafter (Jenkins, 2001: 5).

Significantly, the profiles of the hijackers who participated in the September 11 attacks differ from the Risks International profile cited above. Older, better educated, and more sophisticated, at least six of the 19 perpetrators knew they were on a suicide mission. According to Jenkins (2001: 8):

> Not all were members of a single bin Laden organization but the contacts among them enabled operations to draw on multiple resources. Analysts estimate the number of activists in the bin Laden network to be several thousand. ... This is sufficient to permit specialization: scientific, military, aviation, or, in another form, the willingness to commit suicide. With several thousand volunteers, 5 to 20 willing to die can be found.

The hallmarks of the "new war" are speed and penetration. Global Positional Systems (GPSs) and cellphones are both wireless and instantaneous, provided there is sufficient bandwidth available to operate all the needed electronics simultaneously. It has "been said" that the US military faces possible shortages even for the operation of their drone aircraft. The implied ambiguity in the previous sentence is deliberate, for it reflects the fact that the entire world is constantly on view, through one TV or radio channel or another, with the viewer's attention directed to some detail by an announcer, an analyst, a talk show, or even an "expert". Undocumented information passes through the sound waves in a continuous stream. Sources are often unnamed, and there is little or no recourse to written data, even if one had the time to interrupt the ongoing verbalization (and possibly miss another tidbit of news). The War Museum at Ypres (Belgium) mounted an extraordinary exhibit in March 2002 to illustrate the power, even control, of the media in their selectivity and reporting of war and military affairs.

Strong parallels exist between terrorism and the "new war". Supersonic jets flying at greater than the speed of sound (Mach 1) are upon a target before their presence can be heard, and their strikes can be just as frightening and deadly as the airplanes that plowed into the World Trade Center or the little boat that slid next to the USS Cole and released a bomb. Penetration combined with speed is the most dangerous of the hallmarks. This author, an instrument-rated pilot and avid reader of high-tech aviation novels, sat transfixed one night during the Gulf War, as she watched TV and the camera sighted down the missile and the cross-hairs pinpointed its course straight to the target. This is deadly force, and the virtual tourism of the "new war". Penetration now carries explosives as deep as 30 stories below ground, while tiny camera-equipped drone birds flutter into a room to spy. Miniature drone fish patrol coastal installations and act as sensors for ships.

The "New War" and Tourism

The dust had barely settled on Kuwait in 1991 before the first tourists arrived, but the numbers were not large, and they were generally related to individuals who had served there. War zones following the "new war" will leave behind rubble and bodies. The effect of war on civilian casualties has "climbed from 5 percent in 1900 to 15 percent during World War I, to 65 percent by the end of World War II, and to more than ninety percent in the wars of the 1990's" (Machalm, 1996: 2). These statistics foreshadow problems in postwar reconstruction.

Although the Somali war is presumably over, the country is still rated an unsafe destination. If or when Afghanistan is stabilized with a functioning central government, it is doubtful that many Americans will seek it as a destination. Unlike neighboring Iran, which boasts beautiful mosaic-tiled mosques and the ruins of ancient Persepolis, barren Afghanistan possessed only one prime attraction, which the Taliban destroyed – the great Buddhist statues at Bamian. Every tourist area has a focal point or center. If the visitor must travel long distances through wasteland to reach the "center", then the "pull" to travel must outweigh the distance and/or inconvenience.

To visit Afghanistan for the sake of "time and place" in relation to the military and their families who served there will undoubtedly attract a limited number of visitors. But not all war tourists are deeply concerned about site authenticity or family participation. Thailand is a very popular international destination and Bangkok has a rich tourist hinterland. A motion picture and a song, *The Bridge on the River Kwai*, has captured an audience which joins veritable pilgrimage buses to knowingly visit a non-existent bridge in a fictional story.

The Tourist Markers

Until the "new war" engagement ends it is difficult to assess needs and procedures, but a series of questions arise in relation to the tourism markers that this war will create.

Because this "new war" may involve chemical, nuclear, and biological strains, how will both civilians and military be affected? In the week of January 6, 2003, the US military indicated that it planned to cremate *in situ* the contaminated bodies as a matter of public safety. With apparent public protest, the idea was immediately withdrawn. If, however, health risks mandated this procedure, how would ashes be distributed and the names of the deceased recorded? Do sufficient resources exist to undertake DNA identification of all such bodies, civilian as well as military?

If, by contrast, the decision is made to consecrate the land and bury the dead, will a new Iraq government be willing to dedicate a suitable tract and designate it as "US soil" and permit American military personnel to staff the site, with a US flag flying above it? France accorded this honor to the US troops who died in the French liberation, but did not do so for the Germans. German military cemeteries exist in France, but they are attended by volunteers who come periodically from Germany to clean, garden, and maintain. Battlefields and cemeteries do attract thanatourists in some numbers (Seaton, 1999: 27–50), but who will undertake (and presumably win) this conflict? Will they be welcomed as US forces were in 1945 in France as heroes? Or will they be portrayed as in the infamous War Museum in Ho Chi Minh City, which still exhibits photos that scorn the Americans being airlifted to safety from the roof of the US Embassy? Who will build this museum, and what will it exhibit? What other types of ceremonial structures are appropriate for a "new war" in which airplanes are drones, and computers the pilots? Are we to honor Artificial Intelligence (AI)?

As Jenkins (2001: 9) above has noted, there are a billion adherents to the Moslem faith, and, for some at least, Osama bin Laden and Saddam Hussein are heroes. Has multiculturalism advanced to the stage that they, too, may be honored with mausoleums, statues, and annual memorial celebrations that will become tourism markers? Or will the giant statues of Saddam be thrown, broken, into some park as are those of Stalin in Moscow?

These questions totally ignore the refugees who, before the commencement of this war, already numbered some 39 million, 80% of whom are women and children (Human Rights Watch, 2003) who must be fed and housed – becoming a still greater financial burden. Further, they cannot and do not contribute to the costs of construction and maintenance of war memorials and commemorative events.

Conclusion

The "new war" – in a best-case scenario – raises more questions than can be answered. In a worst-case scenario, the potential exists for massive depopulation and increased lawlessness and areas of the world could degenerate into a 21st-century equivalent of medieval Europe's Dark

Ages. By whatever political yardstick one uses, President G.W. Bush may have correctly assessed this point in time as a "moment of truth" (March 17, 2003).

References

Anonymous (2002) Geneva Conviction *Wall Street Journal*, February 11, A22.

Barber, B. (1995) *Jihad vs McWorld: Terrorism's Challenge to Democracy*. New York: Ballantine Books.

Binckley, C. (2002) Travel downturn takes heavy toll on results of Hilton, Park Place. *Wall Street Journal*, January 30, B11.

Block, R. (2002) Tanzania plans to tighten control over trade exports of rare gems. *Wall Street Journal*, February 11, 2003, A18.

D'Amore, L. and Anuza, T. (1986) International terrorism: Implications and challenge for global tourism. *Business Quarterly* (Fall). School of Business Administration, University of Western Ontario.

Gordon, B.M. (1998) Tourism and war: Paris in World War II. *Annals of Tourism Research* 25 (3): 6–16.

Jenkins, B. (2001) The organization man. In J. Hoge (ed.) *How Did This Happen: Terrorism and The New War* (pp. 1–14). New York: Council on Foreign Relations Press.

Juergensmeyer, M. (2000) *Terror in the Mind of God: The Global Rise of Religious Violence*. Berkeley, CA: University of California Press.

Lloyd, D. (1998) *Battlefield Tours: Pilgrimage and Commemoration of the Great War in Britain, Australia, and Canada – 1919–1939*. Oxford: Oxford University Press.

Machal, G. (1996) *Impact of Armed Conflict on Children*. Geneva: UNICEF. (Reprinted at http://www.unicef.org/graca/pattems.html.)

Mead, M. (1965) *And Keep your Powder Dry*. New York: Morrow.

Mylroie, L. (2001) *War Against America: Saddam Hussein and the World Trade Center Attacks*. New York: Regan Books.

Navarro, P. and Spencer, A. (2001). September 11, 2001: Assessing the costs of terrorism. *The Milken Institute Review* 4, 16–31.

Seaton, A.N. (1999) War and thanatourism: Waterloo 1815–1914. *Annals of Tourism Research* 26 (1).

Short, J. and Kim, Y. (1999) *Globalization and the City*. New York: Longmans.

Simon, G. and Block, R. (2002) Diary offers more on Tanzanite, Al Qaeda Link. *Wall Street Journal*, January 24, B1 and B4.

Smith, V. (1996) War and its tourist attractions. In A. Pizam and Y. Mansfeld (eds) *Tourism, Crime and International Security Issues* (pp. 247–264). New York: John Wiley & Sons.

Smith, V. (2001) Hostility and hospitality: War and tourism. In V. Smith and M. Brent (eds) *Hosts and Guests Revisited: Tourism Issues of the 21st Century* (pp. 367–379). Elmsford, NY: Cognizant Communications Corp.

Trofimov, Y. (2001) Brandishing weapons and aid, Hezbollah tests U.S. Resolve. *Wall Street Journal*, December 17, A1.

Turney-High, H. (1981). *The Military: The Theory of Land Warfare as Behavioral Science*. West Hanover, MA: The Christopher Publishing House.

Zakaria, F. (2001) The return of history. In J. Hoge and G. Rosse (eds) *How Did This Happen: Terrorism and the New War* (pp. 307–317). New York: Public Affairs.

Zimmermann, A. (2001a) Malls' challenge: Protect shoppers, soothe nerves. *Wall Street Journal*, October 18, B1.

Zimmermann, F. (2001b) European Union cross-border cooperation: A new tourism dimension. In V. Smith and M. Brent (eds) *Hosts and Guests Revisited: Tourism Issue of the 21st Century* (pp. 323–332). Elmsford, NY: Cognizant Communications Corp.

Part 5: Conclusion

Chapter 14

Tourism Development: Vulnerability and Resilience

JULIO ARAMBERRI AND RICHARD BUTLER

A Funky Feeling

For the first time in a history that is only quite recent – not much more than 50 years – mass tourism and the industry that caters to it are feeling their vulnerability. The feeling, which affects the industry worldwide, is not only disturbing but also unexpected and new. There have obviously been other uneasy periods of stagnation or some downturns, but they did not have the global reach of the present one. The economic crisis of the late 1990s in Southeast Asia, to take one recent example, was mainly a regional financial crisis that, among other things, forced a sudden drop of international tourist investment in the local economies as well as a dip in domestic demand for travel and tourism (T&T). However, the devaluation of most currencies in the area was followed by an increase in foreign tourist demand that allowed the local industry to bounce back in a short period of time. The year 2000 saw the recovery of Southeast Asian destinations, broke a new record in foreign arrivals and foreign receipts for the global industry, and once again it seemed that in the long term nothing could affect a booming business. *The Economist* said so in a nutshell in summarizing the year 2002 and before the war in Iraq:

> For wealthy westerners, travel is now an addiction. The past 18 months show that neither economic nor security threats can get them to kick the habit for anything but a very short period – especially if there are bargains to be had. Once Saddam is sorted, it will be time to pack a suitcase and be off again. Almost anywhere. (*The Economist*, 2003)

Accordingly, the T&T industry has until lately been eagerly optimistic in viewing its future. All the long-term forecasts published by WTO and

WTTC strengthened this view. A few years ago WTO (2003) saw international tourist arrivals reaching a threefold increase by 2020 as shown in Table 14.1. In total, international arrivals should exceed 1.56 billion (twice the number for 2002) in 2020.

WTO (2003) also estimated that long-term (up to 2020) annual T&T growth worldwide would be around 5%, with some regions exceeding this average. East Asia and the Pacific (EAP) were predicted to surpass 7%, while Africa, the Middle East and South Asia would go over 6% (see Figure 14.1).

For the long term, WTTC (2003a) also showed a confident disposition. The T&T global economy should nearly double within the next 10 years,

Table 14.1 WTO Tourism 2020 Vision: Forecast of inbound tourism, region by world; international tourist arrivals by tourist-receiving region (millions)

	Base year	Forecasts		Average annual growth rate (%)	Market share	
	1995	*2010*	*2020*	*1995–2020*	*1995*	*2020*
World	565.4	1006.4	1561.1	4.1	100	100
Africa	20.2	47.0	77.3	5.5	3.6	5.0
Americas	108.9	190.4	282.3	3.9	19.3	18.1
East Asia and the Pacific	81.4	195.2	397.2	6.5	14.4	25.4
Europe	338.4	527.3	717.0	3.0	59.8	45.9
Middle East	12.4	35.9	68.5	7.1	2.2	4.4
South Asia	4.2	10.6	18.8	6.2	0.7	1.2
Intraregional (a)	464.1	790.9	1183.3	3.8	82.1	75.8
Long-haul (b)	101.3	215.5	377.9	5.4	17.9	24.2

Source: World Tourism Organization (WTO), 2003
Notes:
(a) Intraregional includes arrivals where country of origin is not specified
(b) Long-haul is defined as everything except intraregional travel
Actual data as in WTO database, July 2000

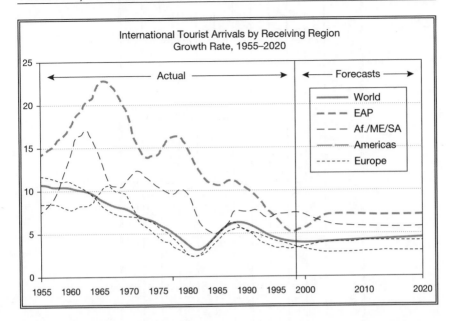

Figure 14.1 International tourist arrivals by receiving region: Growth rate, 1955–2020

going from US$3.53 trillion in 2003 to US$6.46 trillion in 2013. The average annual growth foreseen by WTTC would be around 3.9% for the whole period (See Table 14.2).

However, since 2001 a feeling of uncertainty has descended on the industry and doubts are being expressed that the earlier prevailing optimism might be warranted. T&T is not a world insulated from disturbing facts happening in the global arena, and there has been an excess of the latter over the last three years. The current year, 2003, started with a flurry of really discomfiting news. The outbreak of SARS in the spring; the political instability in parts of the Arab world followed by the war in Iraq during the same period; and, above all, the lingering threat of local and global terrorist actions all cast a pall on those sanguine assumptions. The mood of helplessness has been compounded by the fact that none of those events was caused by developments in T&T, and though they have all taken an impressive toll on it, the T&T system cannot do much to prevent them on its own. Therefore, it is thought that any new similar situations, which will surely happen again in the future, might create a snowball effect to make increasing numbers of people abstain

Table 14.2 World estimates and forecasts

World	US$ bn	2003 (% of total)	Growth[1]	US$ bn	2013 (% of total)	Growth[2]
Personal travel and tourism	2,135.9	9.9	2.2	3,862.3	10.8	3.7
Business travel	488.8	–	0.6	871.7	–	3.7
Government expenditures	224.1	3.9	2.8	378.2	4.1	3.0
Capital investment	686.0	9.6	2.8	1,308.6	10.1	4.3
Visitor exports	530.9	5.9	3.0	1,332.1	6.0	7.1
Other exports	479.0	5.3	8.9	1,187.0	5.4	7.2
T&T demand	4,544.2	–	2.9	8,939.7	–	4.6
T&T industry GDP	1,280.4	3.7	1.1	2,279.2	3.8	3.6
T&T economy GDP	3,526.9	10.2	2.0	6,461.4	10.8	3.9
T&T industry employment	67,441.1	2.6	0.1	83,893.6	2.8	2.2
T&T economy employment	194,562.0	7.6	1.5	247,205.0	8.4	2.4

Notes:

(1) 2003 real growth adjusted for inflation (%)

(2) 2004–2013 annual and real growth adjusted for inflation (%): '000s of jobs

from leaving their homes in pursuit of unfamiliar landscapes and experiences. The feeling that the industry is vulnerable has reached many sectors and is especially felt in those destinations that were hit hard by one or more of those events. Are we in for a significant downturn or, at least, a lackluster recovery that will fall short of the expectations formulated for the long run? In our opinion, the answer should be a clear no, though perhaps not so resounding as would have been proffered a few years ago.

It is about time that the T&T industry swallowed a portion of humble pie and shed some of its outlandish expectations of unending growth; it was wrong to assume that expansion would grow unabated in spite of short-term business cycles and long-term Kondratieff eras. On the other hand, it would be equally misguided to presume that the T&T industry lacks resilience. In fact, as soon as there is a lull in the occurrence of bad news, it tends to bounce back quickly. The year 2002, one of relative calm amid a maelstrom of political and social disasters, became an unexpectedly good year for the industry as a whole and, with a total of 715 million international arrivals, surpassed the previous record of 2000. This may be taken to represent pent-up latent demand, temporarily put on hold because of the events of 2001.

In the following pages, we will argue that there is nothing surprising about this state of affairs. On one hand, there is the long-term demographic boom that has affected some regions of the world, and has been followed by significant economic growth in China, East and Southeast Asia and, to some extent, India, involving just under half the present population of the planet. Boosted by rising disposable income, millions of people in this part of the world are increasing the demand for both domestic and international travel, adding to that already existing in the developed countries. This trend is not likely to decline for many years to come. On the other, and this should be stressed given its cumulative effects, the industry has become more nimble in its response to the unexpected. Among other things, improved economic forecasting, better understanding of the ripple or indirect effects of T&T on the rest of the economy, and increased mastery of marketing, advertising and PR techniques have all been instrumental in lessening the impact of the recent chain of potentially damaging events. In this way, T&T providers (from the big European and American tour operators to the local suppliers of travel-related services) have become aware that risk reduction, crisis management and creativity in the face of the unexpected are skills that can be learned and planned for.

No Monkey Business

In this section we will try to quantify the impact of some recent challenges to the development of T&T. The data we use are mostly estimates and cannot be taken as the final measure of inflicted damage. We have selected some of the most recent destructive events that have affected T&T in 2003, namely SARS, the war in Iraq and global terrorism linked to some Islamic organizations (the effects of the outbreak of foot-and-mouth disease in 2001 on tourism in the UK is discussed elsewhere in this volume; see Chapter 10 by Butler and Airey).

SARS

Severe Acute Respiratory Syndrome (SARS) was first reported in the western press around February 2003. Among patients the illness created a variety of flu-like symptoms including fever, pain in the joints, breathing difficulties, nausea and diarrhea. The virus was extremely contagious and spread easily, and without proper treatment would cause the patient's death. In the first stages of the outbreak doctors and the World Health Organization were unable to find a way to contain the illness. The virus, which apparently originated in southern provinces of China, traveled fast in all directions. Many patients carried it with them to distant destinations via air travel and other means of transportation. Although the total number of actual deaths was limited, the deadly consequences of the infection and the initial inability to even detect the spread of the virus, repeatedly stressed by the mass media, contributed to the creation of a general state of anxiety that quickly led many people to avoid travel to any of the localities and countries infected and even to abstain from consuming foods and other products manufactured by them or grown in non-infected areas but cooked in Asian restaurants. A survey conducted in the US at the time found that:

> [s]ixteen percent of Americans are avoiding people who they think may have recently traveled to Asia, while 10 percent are staying away from all public events, and 14 percent are shunning Asian restaurants and stores. [. . .] Seventeen percent of Americans who have traveled outside the United States in the past year have avoided international air travel because of severe acute respiratory syndrome since they learned of the outbreak, according to the nationally representative survey by the Harvard School of Public Health. (Stein, 2003)

SARS caused severe and acute damage to the tourism industry of the countries to which it spread (see Table 14.3) and had a number of still

Table 14.3 Economic impact of SARS: selected *TSA* categories

Country	Visitor exports (%)	T&T demand (%)	T&T industry GDP (%)	Jobs (%)	Jobs (000s)
China (PRC)	–55.2	–13.4	–24.5	–20.0	–2800.0
Hong Kong	–46.5	–10.4	–41.1	–37.7	–27.3
Singapore	–45.2	–13.4	–43.0	40.9	–17.5
Vietnam	–41.0	–4.9	–14.5	–11.9	–61.7
World	–2.5	–0.6	–1.0	–4.3	–2900.0

Source: Authors' elaboration on WTTC, 2003

undetermined consequences for domestic and international T&T. WTTC (2003b) has estimated that the global economic impact of SARS made the global T&T industry GDP (the value added directly by this economic branch) lose 1% of the growth forecast for 2003 and the global T&T demand (value added directly and indirectly by tourism activities) decreased by 0.6% during the same period. Jobs expected to be created by the industry globally during 2003 would be reduced by nearly three million. China and Southeast Asia felt the main brunt and their T&T economies will suffer a severe blow, with reductions in visitor exports (what WTO calls International Tourism Receipts) varying between 41% (Vietnam) and 55% (China) over the previous estimate for 2003. Their T&T industry GDP and T&T demand would be equally seriously affected. The decrease was also contagious for other countries in the area (Thailand, the Philippines, Indonesia, Malaysia), even though they were never affected directly by the epidemic outbreak. It is perhaps reflective of media coverage and somewhat biased perceptions, particularly of the American tourist market, that the effects of the SARS outbreaks in Canada did not have as severe an effect as they did in Asian destinations (which may also reflect the desire by western governments not to "offend" a longstanding ally, see below).

The war in Iraq

Using its TSA (Tourism Satellite Accounts) methodology, WTTC also circulated estimates for the cost of an eventual war in Iraq before the hostilities broke. It made two different forecasts. One was for the case of a so-called base scenario and the other for that of a protracted war. The base scenario assumed, among others, the following events: Iraqi attacks on oil facilities in the region with limited damage but political and economic effects; an Iraqi attack on Israel with widespread lethal effects; limited Israel intervention in the war; rising political unrest in the region; and low-level civil tensions and clashes in Iraq after the military conflict was over.

Under those conditions, it was estimated that T&T demand would be –2.7% over that of the year 2002, with a total of US$120 billion less than anticipated, while T&T industry GDP would decrease by 2.4% or US$31.1 billion. Visitor exports or international receipts would decline by 3%, in total US$50 billion, and there would be a fall of about 3.15 million in jobs (WTTC, 2003b). If there was a protracted war with a quick esca-lation in the parties involved in the conflict or in the type of lethal weapons used, plus a prolonged disruption in the world supply of oil, the economic consequences for the T&T industry were expected to rise exponentially with permanent damage being inflicted.

As we know now, the real war wound up with even less economic damage than the base scenario. However, short of a better calculation, if we take WTTC's basic forecast, and compound it with the effects of SARS on the global scene, we are talking of very steep losses in economic T&T activity and jobs. The reduction in T&T demand could have reached the US$150 billion mark and the job losses might number in the region of six million.

Islamic terrorism

Before September 11 the connection between tourism and terrorism had been little discussed among academics (Chew, 1987; Pizam & Mansfield, 1996; Poirier, 1997; Richter & Waugh, 1986; Ryan, 1993). The few contributions on the subject dealt with localized events in some areas of Western Europe (Northern Ireland, Basque Country, Corsica), where disputes over national rights had fostered the emergence of terrorist movements (Buckley & Klemm, 1993; Tremblay, 1989); or with actual war, as in the former Yugoslavia (Sönmez, 1998; Weber, 1998).

The brutal eruption of Islamic terrorism and the declaration of a Jihad against the new crusaders who were said to be ready to defile Islamic holy sites and trample Islamic culture came as a surprise in many western quarters. Both the global scope and the spectacular actions of this new kind of terrorism were unexpected, even though there had been some attacks on tourists in Egypt (Aziz, 1995) and a previous number of other similar actions. The attack on September 11, 2001, was not an act of direct aggression against the tourist industry, but the latter would be, after those who lost their lives and their families, the main casualty of the attacks (Lepp & Gibson, 2003). In the wake of September 11, Islamic terrorists aimed their aggressions against primarily tourist targets. The bombing of the Sari Club in the Balinese resort of Kuta Beach on October 12, 2002 killed nearly 200 people, most of them vacationers. On November 28, 2002 three terrorists committed suicide and killed 12 other people, mostly Israeli tourists, at the Paradise Resort in Mombasa, Kenya. Both opportunistic reasons, such as the assured media interest, and ideological excuses, such as the Jihad against alleged idle parasites or Zionist aggressors, seem to be at the base of such actions. In this way, the tourist industry has become fair game for global terrorism the world over.

The real effects of those crimes on international politics and relations among cultures will be discussed for a long time. The brunt born by the tourism industry, on the other hand, has already started to be reckoned with (Blake & Sinclair, 2003; Goodrich, 2002). Following the September 11 attacks, the T&T industry experienced big losses and faced newly imposed expenditures as a result of increased security measures, particularly in the US, and to a lesser extent the world over. Among the first, civil aviation was grounded in the US between September 11 and September 13. The number of US air travelers, both domestic and international, plummeted between September and November 2001 and had not recovered from its August 2001 mark 12 months later. Travel in general was also significantly reduced in the US, causing also severe losses in the accommodation sector. Other T&T-related businesses, such as car rentals, cruises, food and construction, were not exempt from the sudden downturn. If counterbalancing measures taken by the US government to offset those impacts (the Air Transportation Safety and System Stabilization Act, or ATSSSA, and the Aviation and Transportation Security Act, or ATSA) are taken into account, it was not the air travel industry, but hotels that suffered most (see Table 14.4).

These immediate losses were later accompanied by newly mandated expenses, some of them to be borne directly by either the T&T industry or the consumers, that increased the amount of the collective bill. Stringent demands on the security at airports and in aircraft have been followed by increased security at seaports, bus and train stations. Hotels, theme parks, museums and other collective venues had to step up their security arrangements. All in all, the combined September 11 cost in the US as per Goodrich's estimate may have reached US$105 billion. Numbers for the US T&T are not provided, but the author concludes that:

Table 14.4 Fall in constant-dollar factor employment ($bn change from base)

Industry	Effects of September 11, without ATSSSA and ATSA policy responses	Effects of September 11, including ATSSSA and ATSA policy responses
Hotels	–7.3	–5.9
Air transportation	–11.0	–5.0
Eating and drinking places	–1.9	–1.2
Food and kindred products	–1.2	–0.9
Arrangement of passenger transportation	–1.5	–0.7
Construction	–1.1	–0.6
Other accommodation establishments	–0.7	–0.6
Fitness, sport and recreation clubs	–0.7	–0.6
Drugs and cleaning preparations	–0.4	–0.3
Theatres and entertainers	–0.3	–0.2

Source: Blake and Sinclair, 2003

[t]here have been over 100,000 layoffs in the airline industry; decline in the value of airline stocks; layoffs in the hotel industry; decline in sales revenue of many support firms, such as food companies, cleaning services and airline mechanics; and cancellations of travel and vacation plans to countries outside of the USA. (Goodrich, 2002: 579)

in addition to the costs of the additional security programs going into many hundreds of millions of dollars.

Blake and Sinclair (2003: table 1) speak of a September 11-linked total loss in T&T of US$50.7 billion and 559,000 jobs (203,000 alone in the air travel industry and 174,000 in the accommodation business). If one considers (Blake & Sinclair, 2003: table 2) the crisis management measures taken by the US government (ATSSSA and ATSA plus some budgetary adjustments), losses have been limited to US$37.47 billion and 335,000 jobs (93,000 in the air industry and 141,000 in accommodation).

There are no similar estimates for the world T&T economy. The ones we have are still sketchy and need greater refinement. WTO, for instance, concluded that:

> international air traffic from Europe has registered a bigger decrease than domestic tourism in 2001; particularly air traffic to North Atlantic area [sic] (–10.4%), Middle East (–6.9%) and North Africa (–7.1%). Revenues passenger-kms of all services of commercial airlines from the U.S. were reduced by 6.8 per cent according to the latest data of Air Transport Association of America (ATA) in 2001; Transatlantic (–9%) and Pacific (–8%) destinations were the most affected areas. (WTO, 2002)

This is still too general a figure to give us a correct view of what has happened as a consequence of September 11.

At the micro-economic end of the spectrum, observations are also limited, although they provide a reasonable idea of the pervasive nature of T&T. The collapse in travel to Bali that followed the massacre in Kuta Beach meant economic disaster for many local Balinese. The rule of thumb there was that there are 25 jobs per hotel room, including receptionists, cooks, gardeners, money-changers, guides, dancers for night-time entertainment and even lifeguards for protection at the beach. With occupancy rates plummeting after the bombing, most of those people were immediately unemployed. At the time, the World Bank estimated that half of the 1.7 million employed might be out of work if the immediate big slump in arrivals continued. Many local service people (from cab drivers to translators) and craftsmen (from eggshell painters to restaurateurs) were driven out of business (Perlez, 2002).

Those figures and impressions reveal something the T&T industry has been stressing for quite a few years – its key role in the world economy. If the vulnerability of the industry increases, the whole world economy will feel a heavy drag on its development. Furthermore, it will be the weakest links in the economic chain – the destinations in developing countries – that may suffer the biggest losses. Thanks to T&T, people in Bali, for instance, had relatively high living standards compared to the norm in that region – a situation that will be difficult to maintain (Perlez, 2002). If the executors of those terrorist acts had in mind, as they say, the liberation and betterment of the downtrodden, they are obviously fighting for it in the least efficient way.

Conclusions

The events of the past three years have demonstrated, more clearly than anyone would want, the vulnerability of tourism to external factors. Few of the events discussed above have had anything to do with T&T directly but they have had profound effects upon the industry and potential tourists' attitudes toward travel. Because tourism and leisure travel are voluntary activities and because there are many alternative destinations to choose from, travelers on leisure journeys have great flexibility in terms of time and location of visits. As much leisure travel also involves families, parents are likely to be particularly sensitive of traveling to possibly dangerous locations with children. The threat or perceived threat of danger or lack of security is often sufficient to deter people from traveling at all, as was seen in the US after September 11. Despite the fact that all planes involved in the events were heading to domestic internal US destinations, one effect of the Twin Towers disaster was to curtail travel overseas by US residents to a greater degree than travel within the US, although logic would have suggested the opposite strategy was safer. It appears to have been the perception of flying as a US citizen abroad that was the deciding factor and a perhaps misplaced faith, on the basis of previous events, in US airline and airport security arrangements.

One of the results of the crises of the early 2000s has been the revelation of the particular vulnerability of the US tourist market to such disasters and the effects of a downturn in US travel on global statistics. The world media is heavily dominated by US events, and prognostications in the immediate aftermath of September 11 of significant falls in global travel for the next year by WTO and WTTC, based heavily on US data, proved incorrect and overestimated. Comments made at a major international conference in Australia in November 2001 suggested that events such as the failure of ANSETT Airlines had a greater effect on T&T to Australia than the events of September 11, and it was argued at the same meeting that the effects of the foot-and-mouth outbreak in the UK would have a greater effect on tourism to that destination than the Twin Towers disaster. Other tourist markets have proved more resilient to such events than the US market, possibly because of an unfortunate greater familiarity with terrorism and its effects at first hand.

Most of the attention so far has been paid to the direct and more immediate effects of such events upon T&T and to date no research has been published on the indirect effects of these occurrences and their results on T&T, such as increased time and inconvenience involved in travel because of added security arrangements. It would be remarkable if at least some non-US travelers did not choose to avoid traveling via the US by air because of what seems to many to be excessive changes in procedures as a result of what might be overzealous security and subsequent disruptions and delays to travel.

Irrespective of the effects of such measures and the added inconvenience and costs associated with them, tourism is unlikely to decline overall, certainly not when domestic tourism is considered, as the US market in the immediate aftermath of September 11 demonstrated. People place great importance on their holidays and are not likely to relinquish them easily. The more likely effect of terrorist events and other disasters is to see specific destinations or regions suffer a decline in tourism with travel moving to other locations. Many years of Basque independence-related terrorist activities do not appear to have deterred Europeans from visiting Spain, despite a declared intention to target tourist facilities and destinations in 2001. Such apparent indifference to "regular" occurrences of terrorism in what are perceived to be "friendly" and "civilized" countries is demonstrated by the refusal of the UK government to issue a formal warning to or restriction on UK visitors to Spain, in contrast to the immediate issuance of a travel warning with respect to Sri Lanka after the Tamil Tigers attacked Colombo airport in August 2001, despite the fact that no tourists were injured in that action and the Tigers had never indicated their intent to attack tourist targets as ETA in Spain had done the same month. As in so many aspects of tourism and travel, perception is a key factor and probably much more influential in determining people's actions than fact. As long as this remains reality, tourism is likely to remain vulnerable to the threat or possibility of danger in innumerable forms for a long time to come.

This situation does perhaps provide an element of added attraction to destinations which are perceived safe (Butler & Capper, forthcoming), but, given the propensity of a lunatic fringe to challenge anything official, it would be rather risking fate or the attention-seeking desire of an aggrieved group or individual for a destination to promote itself as being safe and secure from terrorism or other dangers. The situation is analogous to airlines which rarely publically discuss the issue of air safety, and traditionally have never competed in advertising on the grounds of one airline or aircraft being safer than another. To do so would advertise the fact that there is an element of risk in flying – a fact which airlines and probably most passengers would prefer to be unstated. The outcry by other airlines which followed an advertisement by Virgin

Atlantic, when it introduced a four-engined Airbus, that implied four-engined planes were safer than two-engined ones is indicative of this sentiment.

It would not be surprising, however, to see destinations promote their security or imply that they are trouble-free destinations in order to compete with rivals suffering from problems, as did the Republic of Ireland at the time of the foot-and-mouth disease outbreak in the UK in 2001 (Butler & Airey, 2004). The unfortunate fact is that, in order to improve security from terrorist acts, personal freedoms and liberties often have to be curtailed – a fact which is of great benefit to the protagonists in political terms. There is no evidence as to whether the effects of visible security measures are viewed as positive by travelers, being seen as an indication that a destination is taking threats seriously, or are seen as negative because they indicate that the authorities are taking the risk of terrorism as real, thus making a destination seem unsafe. In some cases the decision to travel to a specific destination or not is taken out of the hands of the potential tourist. Following the terrorism at Luxor in Egypt in 1996 (Capper, 2003), a number of UK tourists wished to remain in Egypt, expressing the rational idea that, as all perpetrators of the atrocity had been caught or killed, Egypt was probably safer than it had been previously. The tour operators who had brought them could not allow them to stay in or to travel to Egypt (in the case of those who had bought packages beginning after the events) because of a UK Foreign Office advisory saying Egypt should not be visited. The effect of such an advisory was to invalidate the liability insurance held by the tour operators, which meant that they could not afford to risk taking visitors to Egypt or allowing them to stay there. The tourists themselves had no choice but to return to the UK or not to visit Egypt until the order was lifted. The role of political influence in the pronouncements of such advisories, if any, is unclear, but was raised as an issue in the case of Spain and Sri Lanka, noted above, in a letter to *The Times* newspaper in 2003 (Pellatt, 2003)). One would be naive to expect that tourism does not have a political dimension, and other researchers have argued effectively that tourism and politics cannot be divorced (Hall, 1994; Richter, 1989). The links between tourism and terrorism offer clear evidence of such a relationship, and as a truly global industry tourism is likely to have considerable appeal as a target to those wishing to gain international coverage for their concerns. Given the considerable economic significance of tourism to many economies and the vulnerability of the industry as discussed in this volume, one may conclude with concern that tourism is likely to become even more of a weapon in the arsenal of those who see violence as a legitimate solution to political problems. Its status as a vulnerable industry seems assured for the predictable future.

References

Aziz, H. (1995) Understanding attacks on tourists in Egypt. *Tourism Management* 16 (2), 91–95.

Blake, A. and Sinclair, M.T. (2003) Tourism management crisis: US response to September 11. *Annals of Tourism Research* 30 (4), 813–832.

Buckley, P. and Klemm, M. (1993) The decline of tourism in Northern Ireland: The causes. *Tourism Management* 14(3), 184–194.

Butler, R.W. and Airey, D. (2004) The foot and mouth outbreak of 2001: Impacts on and implications for tourism in the United Kingdom. In Julio Aramberri and Richard Butler (eds) *Tourism Development: Issues for a Vulnerable Industry*. London: Channel View (forthcoming).

Butler, R.W. and Capper, D. (forthcoming) Awareness and effects of terrorist events on tourism destination choice. *Tourism Review*.

Capper, D. (2003) The effects of terrorism on the decision-making process of tourists. Unpublished PhD thesis, University of Surrey, Guildford.

Chew, J. (1987) Transport and tourism in the year 2000. *Tourism Management* 8 (2), 83–85.

The Economist (2003) Find bargain, will travel, January 23.

Goodrich, J.N. (2002) September 11, 2001 attack on America: A record of the immediate impacts and reactions in the USA travel and tourism industry. *Tourism Management* 23 (4), 573–580.

Hall, C.M. (1994) *Tourism and Politics: Policy, Power and Place*. Chichester: John Wiley.

Lepp, A. and Gibson, H. (2003) Tourist roles, perceived risk and international tourism. *Annals of Tourism Research* 30 (3), 606–624.

Pellatt, M. (2003) Letter to the editor, *The Times*, May 26.

Perlez, J. (2002) Bali's broken economy: As fragile as an eggshell. *The New York Times*, December 2.

Pizam, A. and Mansfield, Y. (1996) *Tourism, Crime and International Security Issues*. Chichester: Wiley.

Poirier, R. (1997) Political risk analysis and tourism. *Annals of Tourism Research* 24 (3), 675–686.

Richter, L.K. (1989) *The Politics of Tourism in Asia*. Honolulu: University of Hawaii Press.

Richter, L.K. and Waugh, W.L. Jr. (1986) Terrorism and tourism as logical companions. *Tourism Management* 7 (4), 230–238.

Ryan, C. (1993) Crime, violence, terrorism and tourism: An accidental or intrinsic relationship? *Tourism Management* 14 (3), 173–183.

Sönmez, S.F. (1998) Tourism, terrorism, and political instability. *Annals of Tourism Research* 25 (2), 416–456.

Stein, R. (2003) Americans changing habits because of SARS: Poll finds. *The Washington Post*, March 7.

Tremblay, P. (1989) Pooling international tourism in Western Europe. *Annals of Tourism Research* 16 (4), 477–491.

Weber, S. (1998) War, terrorism, and tourism. *Annals of Tourism Research* 25 (3), 760–763.

World Tourism Organization (WTO) (2002) *The Impact of the September 11th Attacks on Tourism: The Light at the End of the Tunnel.* At http://www.world-tourism. org/market_research/recovery/itb0302/ExcerptITBendtunnel_en%20final.pdf. Accessed July 2003.

World Tourism Organization (WTO) (2003) *Tourism 2020 Vision.* At http:// www.world-tourism.org/market_research/facts/menu.html. Accessed July 2003.

World Travel and Tourism Council (WTTC) (2003a) *Tourism Satellite Accounts 2003: Executive Summary.* At http://wttc.org/measure/PDF/Executive% 20summary.pdf. Accessed July 2003.

World Travel and Tourism Council (WTTC) (2003b) *Media and Ministers Briefing: Third Global Travel and Tourism Summit.* WTTC's TSA Research and Special Report on SARS. At http://www.wttc.org/measure/PDF/SARS%Briefing.pdf. Accessed July 2003.